LANGUAGE POLICIES
Language Across the Curriculum in Some Secondary Schools

Edited by Mike Torbe

Ward Lock Educational

ISBN 0 7062 3978 4

First published 1980.

Set in 11 on 12 point Baskerville by Jubal Multiwrite Ltd, London SE13
and printed by Biddles Ltd, Guildford, Surrey
for Ward Lock Educational
116 Baker Street, W1M 2BB
A member of the Pentos Group

CONTENTS

FOREWORD

It is never easy for a local authority to decide where its priorities lie, and it is even harder, once a decision has been made, to abide by the decision. When it happens that an LEA not only publicly states its priorities but also holds firmly to them over a period of years, then one can be sure that the commitment is real. That is what happened in Coventry. Work on language had been going on before the Bullock Report was published, in 1975, but the publication of the Report led to a much more widespread interest, which we built on in two ways: firstly, by having the Report and its implications on the agenda at meetings of the secondary heads' group, and secondly by a decision to make work on language a fundamental priority for in-service work throughout the authority. Thus, there was a clear indication that the messages of the Report were seen to be important by the authority.

But we also made another, harder, decision: and that was to set about the work of innovation and dissemination in a particular way. I know that many of my colleagues in other authorities decided to approach the problem boldly, and to request statements from schools about their language policies; or to arrange courses for heads designed to inform them in their work in their schools. I respect those decisions, and perhaps we too could have done the same and had the success that others have had. But we tried something different. To use a term which Mike Torbe himself uses in this book, we went not for direct attack, but for the more subtle 'seepage'; we tried to find ways to let the ideas have a currency in our schools, to make them so familiar to everyone that even if a teacher was not completely certain about their detail, he or she did know that they were widespread, and that talk about them was common amongst colleagues. Many of our courses may have directly addressed themselves to language in its many forms — early reading in the Infant school, topic work in the Junior school, how to communicate with parents, and so on: but perhaps it was still more important that reading the course notices which Elm Bank, our teachers' centre, sends out weekly, even a teacher who never went near a course would recognize the importance the authority was placing on language work in all its aspects, and so be sensitized to thinking about it in his or her own classroom.

In addition, all the advisers and advisory teachers in Coventry were working hard, chipping away from all directions at the idea that 'language' belongs only to English teachers. You will see in this book the way our advisers have worked in their subject area to arouse first interest and then action on the part of teachers. Perhaps we have demonstrated in our own fashion the way the ideas spread best: first the appointment of one man to support and develop work on language, and then the interaction between that man and his colleagues, with give and take on both sides. Now we have a state we are very happy with, where what might in other areas be seen as the province of an English Adviser is here shared by the whole team of primary and secondary advisers.

Even this, though, is only part of the story: there are only hints in this book of the other massive commitment of Coventry to community education. Perhaps that is the next big step for the profession to take, to see the interaction between home and school curriculum and to explore it in ways that will make the communications between teachers, pupils and parents as meaningful as possible.

To quote an extract from this book 'the children are, after all, the reason why the whole thing's there at all: schools and teachers exist for the benefit of pupils'.

Finally, I'm happy to have the opportunity of paying public tribute to the energy, hard work, commitment and vision of our schools and teachers: this book is a fitting testimony to the quality of the work they produce daily as a matter of course as they go about their professional business.

Robert Aitken Director of Education

PREFACE

This book is unusual. It may even be unique. Every word of the main text was written by practising classroom teachers who have had no previous experience of writing for a public of any kind. They were writing not for you, the reader of this book, but for their colleagues in their own or in neighbouring schools who were involved, as they were, in work on language across the curriculum; and their purpose in writing was to introduce to their colleagues ideas, information and discoveries about their own school and pupils.

It is an unusual book in other ways, too. Many of the separate pieces were originally circulated round a staffroom or a staff meeting, typed and duplicated on sheets of paper: the idea of them appearing in a neat printed book would have seemed extraordinary to the first readers and indeed the first writers. (See Appendix 2: 'Form and function' p. 284). That form gives the pieces a permanence that was never imagined by the original writers, and it does actually change the effect they will have on the reader, too. It is important for you, the reader, to remember that what you will read appeared in several different places, in many different forms, over a period of three years, that each piece was quite detached from all the others, and that the appearance of coherence, neatness and unanimity is something artificial, created by the editor, and by being brought together in a book.

At the same time, though, there is a kind of coherence of a different kind, if you think of 'coherence' as not simply the arrangement of the book, and the way that it matches the actual sequence of events, but as the way ideas spread throughout the authority. The first packs appeared piecemeal, but through the documents ran recurring ideas and emphases that were the evidence of something coherent emerging through the contact between schools.

The original readers of the pieces read them differently from the way you will read them: your purposes and what you hope to gain from the book are utterly unlike theirs. You are not part of the real-time experiences in which each separate piece was produced, as the original readers and writers were; you are

1

reflecting at a distance, on the experiences of others, of which this book seems to be a report. But it is not a report: it is a series of moments out of other people's professional lives, and thus as different as possible from conventional writing about education. There are few hard and fast conclusions: much of it is tentative, a sort of explorer's report about new territory. The writers were never distanced enough from what they were writing about to be dispassionate, nor were they ever far from what they had written or who they had written it for: they were as involved in the aftermath, and the responses of colleagues for whom it had been written, as they had been involved in the group discussions which in most cases produced the writing itself. There is, though, something odd about the act of writing that does create a distancing effect, so that even within a school there is a sense in which a teacher becomes separate from what he or she has written. There is a curious distance between writer and reader, even if one is writing for a colleague who is sitting in the same staffroom at the precise moment the writing is going on. Writers in schools often receive little response to their writing, and this does not necessarily denote a lack of interest.

The publication of any of the pieces had its effect in the school or the authority, sometimes immediate and far-reaching, sometimes a gentle, barely visible ripple. None of these effects and consequences will be visible to the reader of the book; but we want to try and recreate the process of living through a particular series of events and experiences in one group of schools working towards the creation of conditions in which a language policy could begin to take root and grow. We hope that by seeing the kind of things that happened in Coventry schools, other teachers will have the chance of learning from our experiences in ways that might be useful.

INTRODUCTION

What you will read in this book represents only part of what a language policy in its fullness is. Inevitably, you will see here nothing of the long discussions, informal and formal, that go on between colleagues; nothing of the meetings between teachers from different schools which are so important; nothing of the long, slow process by which individual teachers try out new ideas and grope towards different ways of teaching, and, above all, nothing of the particular classroom meetings between teacher and children which trigger off interest, and which are always the reference points in working groups. All of these are left unrecorded. What you will see is merely the public face of the work — the written pieces published within schools to introduce, explain, or spread particular ideas.

The pieces were originally collected together from schools and distributed to all the secondary schools in the LEA, as a result of a meeting between those people who were trying to begin work. One thing discussed at that meeting was how useful it would be to see what other schools were doing, and the first Language across the Curriculum pack was simply intended as a way of sharing ideas with each other. The documents were not written for the pack. They were originally for specific internal use in the individual schools, and were brought together only because they were asked for. They did not, therefore, ever set out to present a particular image of one school to others, or to be anything more than working papers. Most of the work of groups in the various schools had been much less public.

A year later, several more schools had become involved, some of them as a direct result of reading pack I. So pack II was bigger, and contained more varied materials. Again, though, all the papers collected were originally produced as working documents for a group or their staff colleagues, and none was specially written for the pack. And, of course, not all the schools who were actually working on language across the curriculum contributed something, because the groups in some schools did not happen to have produced documents. That leaves a crucial gap in this book: the private writing and talks

3

are often the seedbed from which the whole thing grows. A teacher may collect a file of scribbled notes, and jottings of meetings, notices, memos; things that might appear like ephemera but which can be more influential than the 'public' writing. Documents do form a large part of most schools' work: but there is no real reason why they should.

> A language policy is not merely a document, though a document may form part of the total approach . . . It is more a statement of intent than a book of rules.[1]

Definitions of what a 'language and learning policy' is in detail are bound to run into difficulties. This is not to say that a language policy cannot be defined: that would be absurd, and would lead anyone to have serious doubts about something that could exist, but not be defined. The problem comes in defining 'in detail'; that is, in enumerating the specific items of behaviour and content that go to make up a language policy. These, very properly, vary from school to school, and from group to group, depending on the particular interests, problems and approaches found in that place. But they vary within the broad outline defined by the basic stance and general beliefs that underpin theories about language and learning. I do not intend to describe these theories here, because it is one of the things that the teachers themselves do, especially in Section 1, **Starting points**. But there are some characteristics of the theories that do need to be made explicit, because they lie, as unspoken assumptions, behind most of the other pieces in the book.

Firstly, there is the shock of discovering that there is a big difference between what is commonly thought to occur in classrooms, and what actually occurs. Section 2 reports two such discoveries, about the complexity of reading materials, and about the amount of useful talk one pupil engages in during one day. The consequence of this shock of discovery is the realization that if the reality of these apparently simple things is different from what we expected, then perhaps we need to be equally cautious in talking about 'good lessons' and successful learning by pupils. Thus, the examination of one's own practice, that is evidenced by Section 5, is perhaps an inevitable consequence of paying attention to what really happens.

Secondly, once this paying attention to what really happens

4

begins, then it becomes apparent that pupils' problems in learning may be of the teacher's making, rather than the pupils'. The way the teacher speaks and questions; the kinds of worksheet and textbooks presented; the kinds of task and assignment set by the teacher; the kind of working relationship in the classroom between pupils, and between pupils and teacher: these may all cause difficulties for the learner. The result of this is to make us begin to be more conscious of our own behaviour in the classroom, and more self-critical.

Thirdly, once we begin to explore our own teaching, and to ask questions about its effectiveness, then we also begin to look for ways of exploring *learning*: and this leads to the teacher who tries to become more sensitive and aware of the effects of his or her practice: so there is careful reading of pupils' work, close observation of *how* pupils read, write, talk and so on. With a certain inevitability, then, we reach the idea that pupils have important things to say about their own learning. Sometimes, they can say it very explicitly, as in 'The pupils' view of the school' (Section 4). Sometimes what they say is partly explicit, partly implicit, as in the pupils' comments recorded in 'Is there room for reading?' in Section 3.

Fourthly, once pupils have been consulted in this way, they become partners in a process, rather than passive receivers of information. This is not to say that the teacher becomes unimportant or that the teacher's knowledge is not to be passed on: it means that the teacher tries to make explicit to the pupils what is going on (you will see an example of this in 'Medway's method' in Section 4), and also that pupils' opinions are listened to, respected and where appropriate acted upon. It is certainly true that by consulting pupils, a staff may discover things it could not have known about in any other way. The 'Homework survey' of Section 7 illustrates this well. It is also true that a teacher can learn things from pupils which enable him or her to change basic classroom procedures, and open up entirely new ways of teaching, as 'Making choices' in Section 5 demonstrates.

Fifthly, what we are concerned with above all in education is the pupils' learning. 'We teach and teach, and they learn and learn: if they didn't we wouldn't.'[2] Our job as professionals is to make that learning as effective as possible, so that our pupils gradually and steadily acquire control over information, knowledge and events, and over themselves as learners so that they become people who know why they're doing what they're doing, and how they themselves will best be able to do it. At the heart of a language policy is the conviction that it is through the pupil's use of talking, writing, reading and listening, and through his active engagement with ideas and information, that many kinds of school learning can occur, and that, as the Bullock Report put it, 'a child can learn by talking and writing as certainly as he can by listening and reading', (*A Language for Life*, 4.10). Thus we need to pay attention to language *explicitly*, and not simply accept it as the necessary but unimportant way in which information is transmitted. We need to ask, as these teachers have, what *kinds* of talk? of writing? of reading? in what situations? what works *best*?

Sixthly, and most importantly, when we have asked these questions, and begun to collect information, what do we do about it all? The problem with most educational research has been not just that it has most often been done by people other than teachers, but that most of it has been content to describe and quantify, or to prescribe practice so radically different from what is current that there has been considerable resistance to it. In these pages you see examples of a kind of action-research which tries simultaneously to discover what is going on and what can be done to improve it. Unlike conventional educational research, the teachers have used themselves as the subject, and have had the courage and humility to expose their own weaknesses and vulnerabilities.

Language Policies in Action will not answer all the questions about language across the curriculum that the reader may want to ask. What it does is to demonstrate how theoretical ideas were given practical shape by a particular group of schools and teachers in one part of the country. What answers there are, will be inconclusive, largely because they are caught in mid-process. All the schools represented have moved some distance from where they were, in one direction or another. Staff have moved, new staff have come, new preoccupations have caught the attention of some teachers, while others, previously uninterested, are now deeply immersed in thinking about language. Schools, like any institutions, are not static places, fixed forever in one set of attitudes: they grow, shrink and change direction constantly. The pieces published in this collection do not give you the full flavour of this organic growth, but they may give you insights into the way schools consider the nature of their curriculum work.

Section 1 Starting points shows you three different preliminary addresses to colleagues.

Section 2 First steps contains two surveys, typical yet unique, in which groups set out to map the existing situation.

Section 3 Spreading the word has four items all originally published in pamphlet form in the schools, which raise questions about the problem of communicating with colleagues.

Section 4 Consulting the pupils gives two examples of exactly that.

Section 5 Examining practice is the closest any of the items gets to being recognizable, formal educational research, in the descriptions of teachers exploring their own teaching.

Section 6 Language and the subjects contains the reports of what happened when two groups of subject specialists spent some time considering language across the curriculum and its relation to their subject.

Section 7 Putting it together contains only one piece, an example of the full movement from theory through survey to changing practice for a whole staff.

Section 8 In its context tries to put the work into the context of Coventry as an authority, and the way it operates. It also tries to explore some of the less obvious questions about school organization and its effects upon the search for a language policy.

Appendix 1 contains a book list, which also looks at the question of how much theory is wanted: *Appendix* 2 discusses briefly some of the different forms and functions of printed materials.

Notes
1. *Language across the Curriculum: Guidelines for Schools,* NATE. Ward Lock Educational 1976.
2. J.N. Britton, 'Talking to Learn', in *Language, the Learner and the School* Penguin 1971.

SECTION 1
STARTING POINTS

There are as many different ways of starting work as there are schools. Not all schools have chosen to begin with a public written statement, and it's important to see that what is illustrated in this section is only one among many ways of beginning. Almost by definition, beginning with a written statement means that the first step is a formal one, and this may not be the best thing for a school. Equally, the same thing applies if the first introduction is at a full staff meeting.

> The full staff meeting can be a successful beginning, it seems, when the staff is already accustomed to that way of introducing new ideas. In other words, the way language across the curriculum is introduced depends on *how new ideas are normally introduced to the staff.*[1]

More will be said in Section 8 about meetings and their effects. For the present, though, it's interesting to note that the first two pieces from two different schools are very similar in origin, though not in form or content. Both were written, at a head's request, by heads of English, to be presented to a meeting of other heads of department and house heads. Both were talked to by the head of English at the meeting. But what happened afterwards, as you will see, was very different.

The first paper uses a quite common idea, that of asking questions. These questions are probing ones, and worth both asking and answering, though even here, there are some loaded questions, where one suspects the asker knew what answer he wanted. For instance, the answer to question 3b — 'could there be a greater variety?' — is obviously meant to be 'yes'. That can very easily lead a reader to feel he is being both manipulated and patronized, even if nothing was further from the writer's mind. Indeed, the apparent simplicity of the question as a device for making points has created difficulties for many writers of documents who find that their questions generate considerable hostility and opposition among readers, because

8

they feel (sometimes rightly), that the asker is in fact sa,
obliquely 'You don't do or know this, and I think you oug.
to'. It is also, as any teacher knows, easier to ask questions
about something one knows, than to answer them about something unfamiliar or complex.

The piece that follows, then, was presented in the form you
see, to the consultative committee of the school, the policy-
making body composed of heads of department and house
heads. Interestingly, the head of department based his paper
on one he'd had from John Caperon, head of English at Ban-
bury School. This is the first example of many you will see in
this book of ideas being shared, and of the way they seep from
person to person and place to place.

Note
1 *Language across the Curriculum: Guidelines for Schools*, NATE (Ward
   Lock Educational 1976). There are other relevant comments in the
   section on 'Possible Pitfalls'.

1 Some questions arising out of the Bullock Report (1975)

> Every school should have an organized policy for languages across the curriculum establishing every teacher's involvement in language and reading development throughout the years of schooling. Bullock Report, *A Language for Life* 4.

Much of the secondary curriculum depends upon the pupil's ability to handle language in various forms. The Bullock Report's insistence on the need of a school language policy, therefore, seems realistic: all teachers are teachers of English, to the extent that they use the language in the classroom, and expect certain uses of language, reading, writing, talking from their pupils. The following paper is intended to outline some of the questions we shall have to consider if we are to develop a language policy for the whole school.

1 Language and learning

Recent work has emphasized the importance of language in the learning process — 'We know now how language can be crucial to learning and how the knowledge, information and experience which the child meets in the school need to be gone over in his or her own language if they are to be understood'. (Medway: *'From Talking to Writing'*.) It seems that if information is to be really grasped, the pupil needs to have the opportunity of reworking it, articulating it for herself. (Traditional 'howlers' show the absence of this — the pupil has simply mistranslated information superficially, without grasp.) The leading question here would be:

(a) How do we, in our particular subjects, allow for the importance of language in learning?
(b) Do our lessons provide sufficient opportunity for pupils to rework — in talk or writing — the information we wish to convey?

2 Talk

The Bullock Report comments that 'neglect of pupil talk as a valuable means of learning stands out sharply' (p. 189), and goes on to say that exploratory talk flourishes best in small groups in a well organized and well controlled classroom.

We might ask:

(a) What small group discussion would be appropriate in our various subjects?
(b) At a practical level, how much talking, and of what kind, do we allow in our lessons?
(c) Are we prepared to evaluate pupils' talk as well as their writing?

3 Writing

During the school week, the pupil has to perform a wide variety of writing tasks — essays, notes, reports and so on. Recent Schools Council research indicated that the single most important use of this writing is to *test* — the teacher, as reader, is an examiner. Again the chief *mode* of writing is the 'transactional' — in which the subject matter, not the writer, is of chief interest.

Several questions suggest themselves:

(a) Why, in our subjects, do we ask people to write?
(b) What *kinds* of task do we test? Could there be a greater variety?
(c) Do we teach sufficiently the kinds of writing we require?
(d) Who do we consider responsible for the development of the pupils' writing skills?

4 Reading

Considerable demands are made upon pupils' reading abilities every day — instructions, worksheets and textbooks require careful and accurate, sometimes quite sophisticated, comprehension. Different subject areas may make different demands — in terms of their own special 'languages' and ways of thought.

Again, we might ask several questions:

(a) What special reading demands does our particular subject make?
(b) Is the reading material that is offered to pupils sufficiently clear to them? (Textbooks, perhaps, pose a particular difficulty.)
(c) Is reading taught in our particular subject? What help do we give in comprehension?

11

(d)   Who do we consider responsible for developing the pupils' reading skills?

5 The 'language environment'

Each classroom offers a different 'language environment' and the pupils, we hope, soon learn how they should behave, linguistically, in our different classes — what is expected and appropriate. The teacher's own use of language is, of course, important; the way he uses words will be crucial to his effectiveness in the classroom and his approach, for instance, to *questioning*, will determine the kind of involvement pupils are allowed.

Questions in this area might be:

(a)   What rules or expectations do we create about language in our classroom?
(b)   How much are our own usages of language adapted to different teaching situations?
(c)   What use do we make of questioning? Are we asking predominantly 'open' or 'closed' questions, and why?
(d)   What encouragement is there for pupils to question, interrupt, and sidetrack in a lesson?
(e)   To what extent do we accept, or attempt to modify, our pupils' own use of language?

6 Responsibilities

Many language skills are expected in school — and the responsibility for developing them is often assumed to be that of the English department. In fact, the time a pupil spends using language *outside* the English classroom outweighs the 2½ hours or so she is under the guidance of an English teacher each week. What does this suggest about responsibilities?

There are numerous related questions:

(a)   Who, in particular, should be concerned about technical matters of handwriting (particularly in lower school)?
(b)   Should *all* writing in *all* subjects be corrected by teachers?
(c)   Who should teach spelling?
(d)   Who should be involved in general skills like note-taking and summary?
(e)   Who should be concerned to develop and extend a pupil's vocabulary?

(f)   Who should be involved with developing comprehension?

It might be useful if departments could consider some of the issues here. The Bullock Report is not merely an edict from on high: it draws our attention to the area — language competence — where our pupils' ability to succeed in school is determined. Some consideration of this report may enable us to help our pupils more effectively.

What happened next is important. The head asked the head of English to present the same paper to a full staff meeting. The head of English felt strongly that this was not a good idea because of the way the document might be received, and also because of his own feelings about how best to develop work on language and learning, and so instead, after consultations between himself, the head, the curriculum deputy and myself, a very different pattern of activity was begun, with small group work. You will see more of this school's work later.

The second paper was also presented by a head of English to the other heads of department of his school, the Academic Board. His paper is different: it presents more of the background theory, and reads more like a personal statement than the first one. It is also much longer, and this raises a question we shall also return to later: how much reading can teachers actually do and what do they choose to read?

2 Guidelines for discussion

A language policy is an evolving and collaborative enterprise, the value of which is the discussion and involvement of teachers and not in the written formulation which may be one of the end products.

Bernstein suggests that where a school is organized on traditional subject lines the boundaries around subjects are likely to be jealously guarded against any incursions, because any breach represents a threat to the power and autonomy of subject teachers, especially the head of department. This can obviously be a barrier to any across-the-curriculum approach. Furthermore, in schools organized in this way, a teacher who is not an important member of the hierarchy may have no means of influencing discussions or policy making. Does all this suggest (a) a dialogue between heads of departments (b) departmental discussions (c) interested volunteers to discuss ways and means? Whatever the ways in it is clear that 'authority' sanctions, approves, encourages and initiates/'demands' a sympathetic exploration of language across the curriculum.

If it is to mean anything, a language policy requires an understanding of the relationship between learning and language. Perhaps it could be slanted towards a learning policy. Whatever it is, it will require from many teachers a radical change of emphasis in their relationships with their pupils, based on their altered awareness of what learning is. For example, they may have to recognize that just telling children something and then assessing their efforts to reproduce it is not necessarily helpful in enabling children to make sense of things for themselves. Knowledge has to be seen as something which every learner has to make for himself by constructing a relationship between new information and what he already knows. This can *only* be done through the learner's own language in talk or writing in a context which affords him the security to make mistakes and above all a sense of purpose in making the attempt. The teacher, from perhaps being an assessor, must now become a responsive partner in a collaborative enterprise.

So with the weight of authority behind the exploration, there could be an entry via the heads of departments perhaps with the head of English initiating a discussion and then organizing an informal staff meeting for interested members of staff. The emphasis perhaps needs to be placed on a learning policy for the school. This would naturally lead to the major discussion of the use of language which would necessarily entail lengthy discussion of methodology and organization. Tactically it may be better to appoint a neutral chairman, say the head of mathematics.

There are inherent dangers, however, in any initial approaching of staff on these issues. One of the common yet mistaken decisions about a language policy is that all teachers should make a point of correcting all punctuation and spelling errors in written work. Such a belief is really concentrating on surface issues at the expense of fundamental learning issues. A more detailed approach and awareness of the purpose of using language should erase the superficial obsession with spelling and punctuation. A common marking scheme is important but it is not in any way a language policy. For instance, an English teacher would not necessarily regard the misspelling of 'effervescence' as worthy of severe marking down in a child's work with a line like: 'the effervessense of sparkeling dew drops'.

How could a teacher of English interested in the generation of language and with the philosophy of by 'indirections find directions out', cross out in red both effervescent and sparkling? The comment would more likely be one of encouragement and excitement at such a description. In a different subject context and if there were a common marking policy of 'mark everything' in sight, such a spirited use of the word would be condemned and perhaps lead to indifference on the pupil's part. In one subject a misspelt word could be viewed as a lack of knowledge but in another viewed as a deliberate searching for effective language and as a sign of a child's development.

Bullock's request for every school to have a language policy across the curriculum establishing every teacher's involvement is difficult because staff are not usually accustomed to making policy decisions which affect individual classroom procedures. As I suggested earlier, it is particularly difficult in schools organized on the basis of autonomous subject departments. The ethos of this system can encourage the view of 'you mind your own business and I'll mind mine'. It makes it improper for one specialist to suggest what another specialist should do in his or her lessons. Emphasis then has again to be placed on the fact that language is the common teaching tool not dictated by a specific subject content.

Perhaps one of the largest emotive areas is the way in which the staff as a whole regard the English department and especially the head of English. Many staff see language as the sole province of the English department. If English teachers did their jobs properly, other teachers could concentrate on teaching their subjects. But this obviously does not work as subject specialists regard the written work their pupils do in history, geography or science as *their* responsibility. Teachers regard the Bullock Report as a report on English teaching — thinking, perhaps, that there is little in it to concern them. What therefore needs to be stressed is that language cannot be developed as an end. It needs to be learnt on the job, so the best way of developing it is to see it as a means of learning rather than an end in itself.

So teachers who are aware of the importance of the Bullock Report have to ask themselves:

Why do we need a language policy?
How do we get a language policy?

We can answer the first and discuss the second. But facts are needed. Perhaps a survey could be made throughout the school on the use of language. The impetus has to come from within the school.

The theory
Children must be encouraged to write within contexts which are meaningful to them and more closely linked to their educational development than the kind of writing often found in schools, sometimes in the form of exercises, note-taking (rather than note-making) or just copying from board or book. As teachers we are interested, not in the development of children as writers, but in writing as a means of development — cognitive, affective and social. That writing may be such a means is due to the nature of its two faces: on the one hand it looks to other people and seeks to transfer something to them by way of informing, advising, persuading and sharing; on the other, it can also organize more clearly for the writer himself whatever perceptions he has about the world he lives in and his own relation to it. Using this second face he is able to select and hold for further inspection aspects of his own experience which can be scanned for particular features. This process of personal selection, contemplation and differentiation is very important

16

because it changes the writer, he is a different person when he has done it, because now he has articulated a feeling or a thought or an attitude more clearly, or seen how a bit of his experience fits into the pattern which he is gradually building up for himself; in other words, he is more conscious than he was. It is these processes which can go on in writing which can make it so powerful in an educational sense. But in encouraging all this to happen we must also take into account the other face of the writer which seeks an *audience* outside himself, because most voluntary writing is *motivated by this sense of communication.*

Audience

The notion of audience has powerful implications for school writing because children in school write mostly for the teacher. But what makes for differences between the pieces of writing is not who the reader is but how the writer *sees* his reader. Children see their teachers in different ways. Research has shown that the single most important use for writing appears to be as a means of testing or monitoring knowledge and performance. The writing is seen not as *part* of the learning process but as something which happens *after* the learning. The 'examiner' audience situation inhibits thinking and speculation. The child needs what he writes to be read with interest and sympathy rather than to be judged as a performer of a task.

Functions of writing

Three functions of writing which can be distinguished in language are expressive, transactional and poetic.

Expressive

Here it is taken for granted that the writer himself is of interest to the reader; he feels free to jump from facts to speculations to personal anecdote to emotional outburst and none of it will be 'used against him'. It is all part of being a person *vis à vis* another person. It is a means by which the new is tentatively explored, thoughts half-uttered, attitudes expressed, the rest being left to be picked up by a listener or reader who is willing to take the unexpressed on trust. This writing is very much like speech written down, reflecting the ebb and flow of the writer's thoughts and feelings. Expressive writing sharpens a child's ability to use language in any subject where the mode of writing is usually transactional, but expressive writing with all its richness and vitality is the only possible soil from which in the early stages a child's writing can grow into the transactional.

Transactional

Here the writer means what he says and his writing can be challenged for its truthfulness to public knowledge and logicality. It does not derive its validity from a particular person. It is typical of the language of science, technology, arguing and theorizing — and, of course, the language most used in school writing. Many teachers expect this language technique far too soon. You can only objectify your writing in statements if you understand the statements you are trying to convey and if *personal involvement* has been motivated through *oral* discussion. Of 2,000 pieces of writing analysed by the Schools Council Project on *The Development of Writing Abilities*, 80 per cent was of a formal nature especially in geography, history and above all science. The Project has emphasized that the philosophy 'I do therefore I understand' has got out of hand. Emphasis has not been placed on understanding. Opportunity *has not* been given for written speculation which encourages personal response.

Poetic

The poetic is the synthesis of the two in that it is an end in itself where a child has the vocabulary to use words to their fullest effect and an awareness of shaping a piece of writing to influence, control and involve the reader. This is the sort of language use aimed for in the senior school.

Writing, like talk, organizes our picture of reality and communicates it to someone else. The moral, if we want writing to be a means of thinking and active organizing, is to make sure as teachers that the writer has a genuine need to communicate and is not just performing an exercise. Writing is an inseparable blend of giving an account and expressing a response. But if we discourage the personal element in it we risk making writing an alien instrument instead of a natural extension of the child's *own* mental processes. The expressive form is vital if children are going to reach the transactional and not just mimic the transactional style of arid textbooks and as teachers we must, if we are concerned with improving a child's understanding and our own understanding of how a child learns, put him into situations which are so constructed that he feels a genuine need to operate in a particular way.

'You write it down just to show the teacher that you've done it, but it doesn't bring out any more knowledge in you, it's just a way of giving homework and marks . . .'

Perhaps there are many children who see writing in this light. Again we must return to the purpose of writing and genuine communication. A child's early writing in secondary school is necessarily expressive because he has not yet come to differentiate his purposes nor appreciate the differing needs of differing audiences. But the mixture of thinking and feeling, subjective and objective, personal and public, which is found in children's writing is characteristic of our mental processes too and this is so *at all stages* and not only when we are young. This would suggest that the expressive ought to continue to be an important vehicle for assimilating new ideas met in school, even after the child has learned to use the transactional and the poetic. In that case, the need will probably persist for an audience which is seen as sympathetic and non-evaluative and for an audience in whose presence the child feels he can, as it were, talk to himself – think aloud. For example, you write in the transactional for publication but all the thinking and feeling and motivation is done in the *expressive* through *discussing* and *personal involvement.*

Many children never come to be at home in the transactional. Too often they perform a sort of empty mimicry of the style of the adult academic writing they have met in textbooks and elsewhere without the transactional ever becoming the natural means for setting out information and ideas for specific purposes. It would be better to devise situations in which informative writing has a genuine informative feedback, so that someone is going to use the information, discuss it and evaluate it. Children are commonly asked to write down information for a teacher who, they are well aware, knows it better than they do. And what is the point if the information is already in a book? Such a practice leads only to a docile imitation of style and tone, producing so much of the lifeless posturing in school writing.

Until children are actually operating writing in different

modes they can't see the differences; all they will see will be the different surface features such as the convention of not using 'I' in science reports. In practice there is no reason why the first person should not be used, particularly in the early years of learning, since the separation of the doer from what he does is a sophisticated mental activity and may, for younger children prevent assimilation of new knowledge and *reflection* on it. In the two main writing areas used in schools — the real and the imaginary — teachers of all subjects could help pupils more by discussing with them what a particular piece of writing is for and who it is for — the teacher? the writer? the class? And is the writing to show what the pupil knows or to explore ideas for the pupil or to share his ideas with someone else? This is not to say that the child should ever be told to write an expressive or transactional piece of writing as it would shift his attention from what he wants to say on to how he is to say it. The attention on *how* should be focused on what went on before the writing began, for example the imaginary situation, oral discussion about it etc. Being able to envisage an audience and shape one's utterance to take account of that audience is part of growing up. Young children tend to see everything through a filter of their own viewpoint, so discussion of who is actually going to read what they write, or who they imagine will read it, may help children because it reminds them of the speaker—listener situation in speech which they have always known and where they have resources they can draw on.

So the need for expressive language remains the same wherever there are new experiences to be assimilated and the expressive is the continuing source from which specialized forms of language can grow.

A language policy requires a willingness on the part of subject specialists, in the sciences for instance, to allow for a gradual development of scientific purposes in language, rather than to impose a sudden switch. Then they will be less likely to meet writing that fumbles after the teacher's words and formulation and more likely to find something that speaks of personal effort to look at an object with the personal curiosity and detachment that may grow into a scientific attitude.

I suppose that all our efforts in a broad educational sense are to bring new territories into a living relationship with the old. If in English a child is alive to new possibilities in the familiar centres of experience, there is some chance of other teachers encouraging successful exploration in untracked areas of science, history, geography etc. If the encounter with new territory is a lively one — not a conducted tour dictated by the bus driver — there will be repercussions in the older areas. Each territory becomes old and familiar: it relates and connects in more and more complex ways with the primary centre of life. These are the concerns of English in its widest sense.

After that meeting, several of the other heads of department expressed interest. The head of English therefore arranged a working lunch, which he made quite open — anyone who was interested could come. He also invited me to come along to what turned out to be an extremely pleasant lunch of french bread, cheese and red wine. Not, I was assured, their usual lunch. The talk was informal, and afterwards, five heads of department, and some other teachers were interested enough to form a small working party.

One of the first questions they asked was, how shall we tell the rest of the staff what we're doing? This led to long discussions, not just about what was to be said, but about how it was to be presented. It was seen to be important that staff should be informed that something was happening; and that what was happening should be seen to be both important and relevant to all members of staff. Perhaps because of the particular personalities who made up the group, but perhaps also because they asked 'What would attract and interest me?' they produced this pamphlet.

Do you get annoyed when pupils yawn,
laugh, grunt, fidget,
when you're talking?

Do you get embarrased when no one answers questions in
class?

Do you ever suspect that pupil's don't understand all the words
you use?

– YES?

– READ ON . . .

3 Do you get annoyed . . . ?

Coundon Court is one of five schools in Coventry investigating ways of learning through language across all subjects. Your committee has done considerable background reading and the Bullock Report has been our constant companion.

So what are the facts and how do they affect you as a teacher using language?

The basic notion of language across the curriculum grew out of the work of the London Association for the Teaching of English. In looking, some ten years ago, at talk in English, they found that it was impossible to confine their study solely to the English lesson, so they invited colleagues from other subject areas to join them in their work. The major curriculum theory that grew out of this work is that the teacher must not consider how teaching works but how *learning* works: in other words, the central focus became the learner, not the teacher and they believed that using *language* is above all the way we learn. The Bullock Report stresses this aspect:

> It is a confusion of everyday thought that we tend to regard 'knowledge' as something that exists independently of someone who knows, 'What is known' must in fact be brought to life afresh within every 'knower' by his own efforts. To bring knowledge into being is a formulating process, and language is its ordinary means, whether in speaking or writing or the inner monologue of thought. Once it is understood that talking and writing are means to learning, those more obvious truths that we learn also from other people by listening and reading will take on a fuller meaning and fall into a proper perspective. Nothing has done more to confuse current educational debate than the simplistic notion that 'being told' is the polar opposite of 'finding out for oneself'.

In the Committee's view there are certain important inferences to be drawn from a study of the relationship between language and learning:

(i) all genuine learning involves discovery, and it is as ridiculous to suppose that teaching begins and ends with 'instruction' as it is to suppose that 'learning by discovery' means leaving children to their own resources;

(ii) language has an heuristic function; that is to say a child can learn by talking and writing as certainly as he can by listening and reading;

(iii) to exploit the process of discovery through language in all its uses is the surest means of enabling a child to master his mother tongue.

The report is here defining 'learning' as something which necessarily involves a 'formulating process'; in other words, memorization does not itself involve learning. Information remembered becomes active knowledge when it is *used* in some fashion. This is clearly a notion which cuts clean across any subject boundary: some questions were, it was found, fundamental, and needed answering by all teachers.

Talking and listening

If talking is a way of learning, and if group talk, with or without a teacher is the most important kind of talking, what changes in classroom organization have to be made to encourage it?

What kinds of furniture? Where should it be placed? What length of time — what about the conventional 'period'? Is that sufficient?

Some subjects have always encouraged children to talk — HE, PE, craft. Others have been encouraging children to talk, and then for several reasons, have requested very different formulations, for example science. Some have never, in general, encouraged free-flowing talk, but have left the control of classroom dialogue entirely with the teacher. If more casual kinds of talk are extended into modern language or history, for example, what will happen to the curriculum?

Writing

Which kinds of writing are most helpful for the writer? Which are least likely to help the learner?

The major sub-divisions within 'function' were into transactional, expressive and poetic writing. These three functions were conceived of as lying along a continuum, so a piece of writing may have been classified as lying, for instance, somewhere between the transactional and the expressive uses of language.

In the transactional category we find language in which the writer is engaged in a task, such as recording, reporting, classifying, persuading, hypothesizing, speculating, theorizing. In the poetic category his concentration is on making something, on constructing a whole and concentrating on making, in language, something which is the outcome of his personal vision and which his reader is expected to take as a whole, rather than merely the sum of its parts.

Expressive language is close to that of talk, often loosely structured and context-bound; it makes the assumption of a common interest between writer and reader — and an interest in the writer as a person as well as in his subject matter.

Expressive language was looked upon as a sort of matrix out of which the more specialized functions could grow. It is the language typically associated with young children, but it is also the language often used by adults when first grappling with new ideas — a language of the early stages of assimilation.

It seemed that expressive language had an important role to play in learning; that ideally, it would offer the opportunity to a pupil to make sense of ideas and information in his own terms; that it would also allow him to relate the new to his existing picture of 'how things are'; to relate his outside experience to that of the classroom — in total; allow him to undergo the processes which Piaget called 'assimilation' and 'accommodation'.

It may be that much of what expressive writing may have to offer is gained equally through the talk that should go on during a lesson, but the actual writings in the research survey gave a strong impression that assimilation was not complete; that the pupils had been asked *to write their thoughts on the subject before those thoughts were finalized* — and to write in someone else's language, using a textbook style which was foreign to their own thinking.

Even if assimilation were taking place to some extent through talk, writing has, by its very nature, a number of things to offer which talk could not have: time for reflection, freedom from interruption, the possibility of holding ideas together for long enough to see the links, to forge new understandings.

So, it appeared that expressive language had much to offer the learner, but nevertheless it was little used in schools. Only 5 per cent of the writings from all subjects fell into this category; even eleven-year-olds, just entering secondary schools, only used the expressive in 6 per cent of their school writing. In science lessons no evidence was found of expressive personal writing being used at all.

By far the greatest bulk of the writing in all subjects was

transactional — and of that the vast majority was to give information, either in the form of report or in generalization; and in science all the writing was transactional — again nearly all reporting or generalizing. The absence of speculation and hypothesis in the pupils' writing, even amongst sixth-formers, was noticeable. The strong impression was gained that the unbroken 'diet' of transactional writing had led the pupils to believe that their own thinking 'didn't count' — that what was required of them was the regurgitation of someone else's language. That could well explain the absence of speculation and hypothesis.

When the writings were examined for 'Sense of Audience', it was found, as would be expected, that most of the writers had a teacher audience firmly in mind. But, on examining these scripts more closely, it became clear that very often it was a particular sort of teacher that the writer was considering — a teacher seen in the role of examiner.

The following table shows the incidence of that particular audience:

Subject	Percentage of all scripts in 'teacher seen as examiner' category
English	18
history	69
geography	81
RE	22
science	87
all subjects	53

The overall impression of secondary school writing, then, was of its being used to convey information in a test situation — informing the already informed.

This writing is seen not as *part* of the learning process but as something which happens *after* the learning. The argument is that if a child wrote imaginatively and personally involving himself in a period of history, a discovery in science, a landscape in geography, Shylock's feeling after the trial, then the learning would take place during writing and reinforce the content of a 'factual' lesson rather than as one boy puts it:

I mean you write it down to show the teacher that you've

done it but it does not bring out any more knowledge in you. Well, just getting a piece of paper, saying oh I'll write this all down you know and just to show the teacher you've done it, and he just ticks it and you've done that bit of homework. He already knows it and so do I. I could learn it from a book.

Reading
What has interested those schools that have considered language in general, is not the 'skills' side of reading, but the question — what kinds of response to reading can be generated? What other ways of responding are there other than answering questions (in talk or writing), writing one's own version of the passage or writing the ideas and information for specific assignments?

A sense of audience
Two pieces of research into classroom language are also relevant. One considered classroom interaction in talk, and concluded by formulating the 'rule of two-thirds': two-thirds of the time in the classroom is talking and two-thirds of the talk (at least) is by the teacher. The other is potentially of great importance to education. The London Institute of Education's Writing Research Unit discovered that the single most influential element in the writing process is the *audience* the writer has in mind. They laid out the following categories of audience:

1 self
2 peer group
3 teacher (i) as examiner (ii) as trusted adult
4 wider, known audience (e.g. other classes in school; parents or friends)
5 wider unknown audience.

Of the categories, 3(i) accounted for 90 per cent of all school writing. It is, they discovered, the category least likely to encourage learning.

A whole-school language policy does not mean a discussion of who should teach spelling or handwriting. It means that each department takes upon itself the responsibility for the kinds of language that best help pupils to learn; and the schools that have done it, have discovered that generalizations can be made about language modes, so that science and English teachers, history and maths departments, find common ground in discussing the language processes of talk, listening, reading and writing.

The School Committee's view at the moment is that in all writing situations particularly, in any subject, real or imaginary, teachers could help their pupils by discussing with them what a particular piece of writing is for and who it is for — the teacher? the writer? the class? and is the piece of writing to show what the pupil knows or to explore ideas for himself or to share his ideas with everybody else?

Perhaps too much time is spent writing, and far greater emphasis should be placed on the other activities, such as listening, talking and reading, so that eventually, by these language motivations, the children write better because they write less.

I said that the public statement is only one among many ways of beginning. But that might then have been observed by the close concentration on documents in this section, so I need to say that there have been several other ways to start work. One school, after a period of discussion in a working party invited all the teachers who taught one second year class to meet regularly to discuss the class, particular pupils, particular problems and so on. Another school began with a well-organized survey, conducted partly by staff, partly by pupils, to discover the range of experiences offered to pupils. One school began with a voluntary Saturday conference to which they invited me, which was planned by the school and myself in conjunction, and which was attended by well over half the staff. A fourth school used meetings between the secondary school and its contributory primary schools as the forum for discussions about language. And so it goes. What works in one school may not work in another: or it may work in unexpected ways.

Note
1. Piaget J. (1951) *Play, Dreams and Imitation in Childhood.* Heinemann.

SECTION 2
FIRST STEPS

Once a group has begun to meet and talk, at the same time, in our experience, it begins to ask how it can begin to interest other teachers in the ideas of a language policy. It seems to be generally agreed, at least in Coventry, that lengthy expositions of theory are not helpful:

> *Staff will expect to be told, in writing, exactly what you are doing and what you have achieved. This is a big problem, because it's difficult to communicate enthusiasm and the fruits of valuable discussion to those who haven't been involved. What's more, because of the number of pieces of paper around in a staffroom, although staff receive such information, they may well not actually read it: so expect accusations of being kept in ignorance even if you write detailed reports. Your communications to staff should be about what the group is doing, and not theoretical justifications ... The committee should not dictate or prescribe to staff, but should present them with facts for consideration.* [1]

The survey, of one kind or another, is one way in which groups have tried to be practical, to bring ideas about language to the attention of colleagues, and also to show that there may be areas of the school's practice that need attention. A very popular first step has been the exercise of some kind of readability formula.

Readability formulae are ways of trying to assess the difficulties posed by particular stretches of text. The 'Fog index' has been the most popular formula, and is the one used in this example. The formulae have been popular and have often been used by schools as starting points in their work for language across the curriculum, perhaps because they seem to offer rapid returns. None of the formulae is fully satisfactory, as the first paper here tries to show, but those who use them do find, at least, that it draws their attention to the differences

29

in difficulty between various texts, whatever the cause of the difficulty is. There comes with that the recognition that it may not be simply the incompetent readers who struggle when first year pupils are faced with a science text suitable for a reader with a 'reading age' of 16+.

You see here, incidentally, an interesting use of published materials. The teacher's comments on readability are drawn from the Open University's Reading course PE261. This does suggest one way in which ideas from books might be used, by being discreetly introduced into home-produced documents.

Note
1. All the comments printed in italic throughout the book are from a paper called 'Guidance for working parties', put together by working parties in Coventry at a day conference. The idea was to make available to everyone a collection of what people had discovered in their work.

4 Readability

An investigation into the reading material given to a first-year class, has been carried out using the Fog index. An explanation of this can be found at the end of this report. The class chosen was E.1. Tests were carried out to determine the reading age and the reading experience of each boy in the class.

The subject areas chosen were: English (Group II)
science
history
geography
RK

The reading material given to E.1. over a five-week period, was analysed using the Fog index.

Summary of results

Science	Readability
week 1	11
	15
week 2	9.5
	15+
week 3	11–12
week 4	10–11
week 5	16+
	16+
	15

RK	
week 1	14+

History		
week 1		16
weeks 2, 3, 4, 5		3 books used
	Book 1	13–14
	Book 2	12–13
	Book 3	11–12 (for 2 very poor readers)
	Examination	12 yrs

Geography
week 1   12—13

English
>   Reading book   11.5
>   2 pieces poetry 15½
>   16 yrs

Points
1   All the printed material is from publishers, and even though much of it is designed for first-year pupils, the reading ages required are very often too high.
2   Some technical subjects (e.g. science) score badly due to the use of specific words, e.g. energy, distillation etc.
3   The LAC Committee offer to look at any material, for any year, in connection with readability. This we feel could be useful, especially in connection with specimen copies.

LAC WORKING PARTY

Readability
A readability measure indicates where a particular text lies on a scale of difficulty. Such measures are not perfect (as will be shown later) but they do provide a good idea of the level of difficulty of a text. They help in allocating texts into rough categories for a particular reader, e.g. *frustration level* (too difficult for a particular reader), *instruction level* (suitable for a particular reader with the teacher's help); *independent level* (suitable for a particular reader on his own).

How can we know which scores on a readability measure place a particular text in which level? For this, we need the second kind of measure, i.e. some global estimate of the pupil's reading ability. The problem facing us then is relating the first measure — that of the readability of the text — to the second measure — that of the reader's reading ability. There is, in fact, no very precise way of doing so, since the two scales are measures of different things. However, a teacher can soon develop a fairly good subjective judgment of how to match pupil and text if he or she has a good idea of the pupil's reading ability and, in addition, a readability index of some kind for a particular text.

As I mentioned earlier, readability measures are not perfect and can go badly wrong because whole texts are more complicated than the words and sentences they contain. They contain ideas, the relationship *between* words and sentences, and so on. For example look at the following two short passages, A and B, and ask yourself which is more difficult.

Passage A
Then Cinderella saw the beautiful and wonderful magician riding high over the battlements, carrying in his hand the miserable toy elephant which had disappeared on that beautiful night. Her Prince must be coming, she thought or else why had the wonderful magician flown back with her elephant which she loved.

Passage B
The self and death are twin concepts in his thoughts. Man must reach selfhood first and then reject it. Thus he prepares for death. In death then is his real self. Life is thus a fitting trial for the true life of death.

I'm sure you will agree that passage B is more difficult than passage A — because the ideas are more difficult. Yet, on a readability measure, A is more difficult. The reason is simple: A has fewer sentences and longer words.

Method of calculating Fog index
 (i) Take a number of samples from the text, each sample should contain 100 words.
 (ii) For each sample count the number of complete sentences, and the number of words in these sentences. Divide the number of words by the number of sentences. This will give the average *sentence length.*
(iii) Count the number of words of three or more syllables in the total sample. Divide by the number of 100 word samples. This gives the *percentage of long words* in the sample.
(iv) To obtain the Fog index add:
Average sentence length plus
Percentage of long words
Then multiply this total by 0.4

Example taken from the Coventry Evening Telegraph

Sample	complete sentences	words in complete sentences
1	3	54
2	4	79
	7	133

Average sentence length = $\dfrac{133}{7}$ = 19

Number of words of three syllables or more

Sample	words of three syllables
1	9
2	7
	16

Percentage of long words
$$\frac{16}{2} + 8\%$$

Average sentence length plus percentage of long words
$$19 + 8 = 27$$
$$: \; 27 \times 0.4 = 10.8$$

Fog index = 10.8

This index indicates the grade level equivalent of the reading material.

Age	6	7	8	9	10	11	12	13	14	15	16
Grade	1	2	3	4	5	6	7	8	9	10	11

So we know that the paper required a reading age of 15½ years or thereabouts.

Some interesting facts:
Using the Fog index it has been calculated that:
  (i)   the Highway Code needs a reading age of at least 13 years
 (ii)   an income tax form, 15 years
(iii)   instructions on what to do if you accidentally get splashed by bleach out of a proprietary bottle, 16 years
(iv)   a trade union application form and the supplementary

34

benefit form, a reading age of 17 years

(v) the average hire purchase agreement needs a reading age too high to be calculated!

Another school chose a quite different approach. Interested in ideas about talk, and having encountered the kind of ideas mentioned in 'Language, the Learner and the School', they decided that one of their group would spend a day tracking one pupil, and trying to assess how much he actually spoke during one day. The results were then published to the whole staff.

5 Survey of a boy's day

Report on an enquiry, conducted by Joyce Ellis, into the amount and variety of spoken language used by a first-year pupil during lesson time.

The enquiry was conducted on Wednesday 16 March as Wednesday is a day I do not teach. The boy observed had the following lessons: 1 double lesson, double PE; 4 single lessons (music, history, maths, English).

1 Time spent answering teacher's questions   13 secs
2 Time spent asking questions   9 secs
3 Time spent discussing classwork with neighbour or in a group   none
4 Time spent reading aloud from book or board, including singing   15 mins
5 Time spent offering explanations or comments to teacher   8 secs
6 Number of times volunteered answer but not asked   33/82

General observations

1 The boy was chosen at random by another member of the working party from a class I teach, as it was felt a known teacher in the classroom would be less likely to provide abnormal responses. Neither the teachers concerned, nor the boy himself, were aware of the identity of the individual under survey.
2 He made a more than average contribution to his lessons.
3 Approximately one-third of the class made significantly less verbal contribution than the boy throughout the day.
4 Although some bright children dominated the oral work, other equally bright children made virtually no verbalization throughout the day. Equally many of the least able said as little.
5 The opportunity to observe classes being taught by other members of staff is a valuable and rewarding experience which ought to become more commonplace in schools.

Several questions of considerable importance are raised by both these papers. To take the readability piece first: once one has discovered the range of complexity, *what does one do*

next? There are several lines of development open, of course —
to change the books; to use homemade worksheets instead
(carefully measured for readability, presumably); to begin
discussions in a department about textbooks and their use;
or, in a completely different direction, to complain to the
English and remedial departments and to the primary school
about their incompetent teaching of reading. But which action
is useful? What has actually been discovered, anyway?

It's probably fair to say that those schools who have begun
with surveys of readability have found that the major reward
has been a heightening of awareness among teachers about the
complexities of reading; but that what is wanted then are
answers to questions like, how do I teach my pupils to cope
with their reading? How do I teach them to use indexes and
chapter headings, to skim for information and so on? In other
words, the readability formulae can serve to bring to the
teachers' attention other matters, far more important than how
many three-syllabled words there are in a passage. For example,
the surveys can raise useful questions about the kinds of book
that ought to be available, and how they should be provided —
as small sets, as class sets, as class libraries, and so on. It is these
other matters which then need the attention. Thus, what is
happening in the school needs to be complemented and supported by a thoughtful in-service programme in the LEA as a
whole.[1]

The survey of the amount and variety of spoken language
poses different problems. Some of them are methodological:
it would be a legitimate question to ask how the timings were
collected and how the definitions were made. In an ideal
situation, other members of staff would want to replicate the
work to see how similar later findings were; and would also
check with existing research procedures and systems of cate-
gorization.[2] This is unlikely to happen, though, and perhaps
wouldn't be very helpful anyway. Rigorous research procedures may produce quantifiable data, but it's arguable that
that's not what teachers need. (Anyway, as one teacher remarked, 'I think teachers know in their bones that these things
are true, and they don't need "research" confirmation'.) More
important is the suggestion in this of the enormous abyss of
language between teacher and taught. If the boy talked for
thirty seconds of the day, and if he 'made a more than average
contribution to his lessons', who was doing all the talking?

But then the problems begin: for not all teachers would agree that this was necessarily a bad thing. The debate that grows out of such a finding may very sharply polarize opinion within the staff. And again, it leads towards the question, what does one do next? It is here that the basic theories of language and learning offer an answer. The theories suggest that learning is more likely to occur if pupils have the opportunity to talk over and explore ideas, to write things in their own way. They suggest that it's important to look for evidence that learning has occurred. They lead us, therefore, towards asking how we can discover whether learning has or has not occurred, and towards seeing that we may discover the answer to that by exploring the language life of the classroom. You will see in Section 5 what this next step involves.

Notes
1 See Section 8.
2 See booklist.

SECTION 3
SPREADING THE WORD

I have given this section a title that has deliberate overtones of missionary work, and evangelizing, because there is the very real danger that the fervour of adherents may become a little out of control.

Learning of this kind is new and sometimes difficult to put into words for other people, so colleagues can be left feeling disappointed at the 'obviousness' of what a group says when it tries to explain itself.

Indeed, it can be so difficult that one consequence is that the group gives up trying to communicate and folds in on itself, becoming closed and inward-looking:

You need the strength of the group around you for support: but beware of becoming too inward-looking. It's no good being happy in your closed group and then complaining because nobody else is interested ... keep colleagues in touch with what you're doing in formal and informal ways.

When this closing-in happens, we have discovered that there is often the temptation to talk in missionary terms — spreading the word among the heathen. Above all, this must be resisted: the cooperative endeavour that is at the heart of work for a language policy can never be sustained alongside the arrogance of supposing that a small group has seen the light but that most of the staff remain in benighted ignorance. It is crucial then, that if staff are to be told things, they should be kept informed in ways that are helpful. This section demonstrates formal ways of informing colleagues — the use of published pamphlets, written by the staff. They speak very successfully for themselves, and show a variety of different concerns: teachers describing their day-to-day practice; mulling over the implications of their experiences; examining their pupils' work; reviewing the literature and so on.

Three of them are from the same school, and show one important job a concerned teacher can have — the editing of such publications. In this case the head of English has seen it as his job to do the arduous work of organizing and seeing through the publications. You can judge for yourself the quality.

The effects of such publications are intangible and undefinable. They are not exhortatory or aggressive: who knows what residue of thought they will leave behind in the head of the reader in the staffroom?

What we can say is that we have found that a publication causes more *apparent* stir in a different school from the one it was produced in; and that this is, for us, an argument for sustaining and extending the relationships between schools.

6 The place of talk

This paper is one of the ways in which the Committee on the Bullock Report thought interest in the Report could be kept alive and active in this school. We knew at the time of this suggestion that some people would get more from their own discussions within their own departments than they would from this; but, as teachers, we know the value of a variety of approaches! Besides, this could help those discussions to get started or to take new directions.

All the people who were asked to write for this did so most willingly and expertly, and are now exempt from further service — unless they feel like it again.

The paper will come out every term until there are no readers left. There could be supplements from time to time. I make some suggestions about the next issue at the end, but the shape of things to come really depends upon what staff decide and write.

The use of oral work in sixth-form teaching
Dorothy Morgan

We have in our sixth form three main groups of pupils: those who have few, if any, O levels or satisfactory CSEs, either because of very limited ability, or because they have wasted time and made little progress during the previous five years; those who have a few qualifications and now need time and encouragement to develop more mature attitudes and obtain more paper qualifications at O or A level or both; and those who are now well capable of tackling work of a serious and advanced nature.

For each of these groups, oral participation will have its place, so let us consider them separately.

1(a) *Pupils of very limited academic ability*
The purpose of these pupils must be to obtain examination results which have previously eluded them. The aim of the teacher must first of all be to 'feed' these pupils the necessary information and encourage them to learn and apply this. There must, for much of the time, be a strong sense of discipline, but as the weeks go by and the pupils acquire more positive knowledge, it becomes possible to

discuss the subject more generally and to encourage the pupils to express views and argue particular points. Care must be taken that the need for basic knowledge is not superseded.

1(b) *Pupils who have ability but have not used it*

These pupils probably regret lost opportunities and are eager to redeem the situation. They, too, must first and foremost concentrate upon improved written work, but discussion and argument will help towards maturity of outlook. Many of them return to school very disappointed in themselves, and the smaller sixth form groups enable teachers to encourage them to make the best of their abilities. Earlier 'misfits' and nuisances, when treated as near-adults, often 'blossom' when allowed to express their views in a small, rather informal group.

2 *Pupils needing time to mature*

There is often a large number of such pupils in the sixth form. As they are now able to drop some subjects and concentrate more on subjects which they like, and to tackle new subjects, they become more relaxed. The small groups, often taught informally round a table in a small room, are more friendly and intimate than in a classroom, and the majority of pupils soon enjoy discussion and argument about the subjects studied. Such activities increase the pupils' confidence and general understanding, and written work inevitably improves. It is, however, essential that pupils must always absorb the basic knowledge necessary for examination results and, also, that the less vociferous pupils do not become despondent.

3 *Pupils on A level courses*

Oral participation is clearly of the utmost importance. The very nature of A levels means that the pupils must now take responsibility for their progress, whereas previously this rested mainly with their teachers. In early months in the sixth form, the pupils must acquire a great deal of knowledge of their particular subjects, but after a fairly short time their own views and researches assume some importance and serious discussions will often take place. The teacher's role often appears rather passive during these discussions but, of course, he is really directing the debate and also imparting useful, relevant information and correcting any wildly inaccurate tenets. There is no doubt whatsoever that it is from such discussion that pupils learn a great deal, though they are probably unaware of the fact, because it is from the interchange, acceptance and rejection of views that a mature understanding of the various subjects is reached. For this group, also, it is important that the scene should not be dominated by a few pupils but that all should be encouraged and persuaded to express their ideas.

So far I have written about the importance of discussion in subject lessons, but, of course, the lesson is only a part of sixth-form life. Nearly all pupils have study periods when they are encouraged to do some of their academic work and also to find some time for informal 'chat' where, without the presence of authority, many fierce and grave debates take place. In this way, sixth-formers educate themselves, increase their verbal powers, and change from schoolchildren to adults.

In general studies, which occupy three periods per week, there is ample opportunity for our pupils to express their views. We encourage frank and open discussion on many topics, and our pupils feel free to express their own ideas and to argue with each other and with the members of staff without fear of recrimination. Sometimes a controversial topic is introduced by pupils, sometimes by staff, sometimes by a visiting speaker, but it is seldom that Tuesday morning passes without some heated exchanges! Sometimes, however, it is necessary to ask one or two members (perhaps privately) to refrain from entering a discussion, in order to allow some of the more reticent pupils to express their views. It is essential that the scene should not always be dominated by the same pupils.

I firmly believe that the aim of our sixth form is two-fold. We must try to send our pupils from the school with the best academic qualifications of which they are capable, and this must be our priority. At the same time, we want our pupils to develop into mature young people, able to exchange views and discuss a wide range of subjects with people from many different backgrounds and in many different occupations.

Finally, I would like to state that these are my own personal views, which are, of course, open to attack, though only, I hope, verbally!

Talk in the classroom
Adrian Griffiths

When I was a lad at school, no one spoke unless he was spoken to by the teacher, and the only noise that could be heard in the classroom was the sound of pen-nibs scratching down notes in exercise books — or, at least, that's how I think it was. After university, this impression was reinforced by the college tutor who visited on teaching practice; he would compliment you on maintaining a 'quiet and hard-working atmosphere' in your classroom. It is not my intention in this article to swing violently to the opposite viewpoint over the question of 'talk in the classroom', but to set down some thoughts, possibly very obvious ones, which have occurred to me over the last year.

I realize that some of these points may relate to certain departments more than others because of the very nature of the work in which particular departments are involved. In addition, with the pressure of syllabuses in the upper school, most of these comments are probably more applicable to the lower school, although it is often a very real difficulty for leavers who choose to go on to higher education when they are confronted with their first tutorial without the ability to organize their thoughts and ideas in a fluent and coherent way. The same undoubtedly applies in other spheres of work. In higher education, exchanges of ideas and opinions in a relatively informal way are recognized as being of value, and despite the fact that the average classroom does not accurately mirror the average tutorial situation, it would seem that this sort of activity is not beyond the realms of possibility. It really represents a middle stand between 'everyday chatter' and the more formalized presentation of views in a debating situation.

There is little to say on the question of organized talk such as debating, which is often teacher-led, as its value in getting children to adopt a standpoint and to organize their ideas on a particular topic is generally recognized. My concern is more with the ongoing chat during a lesson which is child-centred and in which the teacher is seldom involved to any extent. One of the major problems which I have found is trying to distinguish between idle chatter and work-talk, and in this respect thirty children have a distinct advantage over one teacher. It is often very simple to pick out idle chatter by the manner in which the individual or group is behaving; but what I would describe as 'borderline' chatter is more difficult to detect. For adults, it is easy to concentrate discussion on the particular topic in hand, but for children, from my own experience, there is invariably a very close intermixing of the two types of chatter. There have been many occasions when I have tackled groups about what appeared to be idle chatter to find that, in fact, they were discussing the work, and were very indignant at the interruption. A case in point occurred recently with a group of first-year boys working on the topic of jobs in Coventry. They were asked to write about the typical day which one of their parents has at work, and as the noise level in the room grew, I spotted a group who appeared to be having a very lively chat. I became suspicious when I heard 'Manchester City', and went to find out what was happening, assuming that one of the more important topics, football, was being discussed. They were, in fact, talking about football, but this had apparently arisen in the context of the leisure pursuits which one boy's father enjoyed as his means of relaxation. I sat down with the group, who carried on chatting, and despite what seemed like a chain of digressions the conversation eventually got back to jobs, and came to a stop. A lot of different points of view, about types and relative merits of jobs, as well as football, had been ex-changed by children who, under different circumstances, might reasonably have spent some considerable time doodling and day-dreaming, interspersed with writing, to produce a piece of work which I am certain would not have been up to the same standard as regards content.

I am by no means advocating that lessons should be conducted along the lines of a 'mass chat', but I am convinced that it is necessary to accept a certain amount of idle chatter as 'the lesser evil for the greater good'. I do not see how children can develop an acceptable standard of oral and written work if they are unable to exchange views and ideas freely amongst them-selves or with me, instead of pounding away at their books in 'splendid isolation'. We know that reading habits have to be developed, that in many homes television is the common substitute for conversation, and that out-of-lesson-time chat is likely to include everything but academic work for the majority. Where else are children likely to get the opportunity?

There have been occasions when, during the marking of books, I have become aware of a peculiar similarity between two or three essays which, at first sight, I have put down to copying with the occasional words changed. Often this has been the correct assumption, but in one case involving two very conscientious second-year boys it came as a result of a discussion held at home about the topic, and the pooling of ideas to produce a first-class cooperative effort. Having always had the idea of one piece of work to one child firmly imprinted, I found this difficult to accept, but logically, I suppose, it was at least an indication that they were sufficiently interested, even to consider swapping views, and I am certain that they both gained far more from the exercise as a result.

Talk is a very difficult medium of work to assess and quantify, unless you issue tape-recorders to each group to check up on what has actually been achieved. I still feel the need to make sure that something is put down on paper during a lesson, either in the form of a piece of writing or a drawing, in order to have something visible and concrete. Talk is difficult to mark. The great danger with this, of course, is that children listen, read, and write, but when the topic is completed and you begin to scratch below the surface, you might find that real understanding is not there, despite the paragraphs of writing and the neatly labelled diagrams. I have sometimes found that a relatively informal chat with individuals or groups provides the means of explaining points more clearly, and it gets over, to some extent, the problem of children who are not able to ask questions in front of the whole class. They are also more able in this kind of situation to take explanation from their peers without showing obvious signs of resentment.

Asking questions
Dennis Whitfield

Most lessons in science begin with some form of question and answer session, perhaps to do with a practical lesson that has gone before, or perhaps to do with a practical to come. Questioning has a vital part to play in stimulating the pupil; and the Bullock Report suggests that when we ask questions we should try to generate answers which involve more than one word. There are, however, many occasions when there does not seem to be any alternative to a question that only requires a one-word answer, and perhaps a guess at that (so what is wrong with guessing?). Nevertheless, an awareness in the teacher that the participation of the pupil in the lesson, and the learning that goes on in the lesson, will depend at least partly upon the skill of the teacher in asking questions could lead to a more efficient learning situation. Individual thought by the pupil is one way in which the learning process continues, and is part of the process by which the pupil is eventually going to 'make the idea his own'.

Many lessons do not have this relatively formal system of question and answer sessions as part of their structure, but when we do find ourselves in a situation that requires this approach, are we making the best possible use of the question?

A lesson on surface tension: fourth-year physics
Introduction: various demonstrations of the way water behaves in thin films in narrow tubes.

Questions asked	Answers
1 What can cause these effects?	'Some sort of a force'
2 Why does the thread take up this curved shape?	The same sort of answer as above (no progress!)
3 Why is the thread a circle or part of a circle?	No answers
4 When the thin film breaks on this wire frame, what happens to the liquid?	At first no answer; then, after a repeat demonstration of the effect, several people were ready to answer, 'It goes in a spray of drops'.
5 What shape are these drops?	Again no answer at first; then, after the disintegration of the surface into drops had been watched again, and a dripping tap watched, the answer came, 'round'.
6 So why does a free liquid form into drops?	No answer
7 Does the drop have a surface?	'Yes'
8 Supposing the forces we have mentioned acted in the same way in the drop as they did in the surface, would this produce round drops?	'Yes'

The point of the demonstration here is to present visual evidence which, it is hoped, is so compelling and obvious that it must produce some insight, which, with questions and further thought, can lead to a fuller understanding. For example, the breaking up of a soap bubble, familiar to us all, can be explained in terms of a pulling effect in the liquid itself which tends to make the liquid contract into the most economical shape.

When the question and answer session seizes up, as it frequently does, one alternative is that of question restructuring, but the impetus of the topic and the interest seem to wane very rapidly. It seems that there is a need for the understanding to be quick and for the progress to be fairly rapid. Frequently the explanation has to be related by the teacher.

It seems to be fairly easy to ask leading questions that try to stimulate an answer containing more than one word, but, as an idea progresses, or as the train of the thought becomes bogged down in difficulty, the questions tend to become, almost in desperation, those that require a one-word answer and, perhaps, a guess.

Perhaps a less formal approach, an entirely different experimental approach, would have achieved more active participation. For example, small group work to begin with, followed by a discussion to bring together the experimental ideas.

Talk, the teacher, and the class
Bryn Hughes

It's very frustrating when you teach two completely different subjects — you're forever trying to achieve with one what comes so easily with the other. The basic difference is that in French/European studies there is a certain body of factual knowledge which is to be communicated in lesson time, while in careers this factual knowledge gets absorbed mainly outside the classroom.

To get the facts straight, I'm basically a careers teacher these days. In this role I don't give kids the answers so much as help them see/realize the questions which they ought to be asking. (Can this really be what Education is all about?) Many but not all careers lessons, are open-ended — I start them but there's no telling where they will end. In nearly all my French lessons

I feel I must have some point on the horizon to aim at — as much for my benefit/satisfaction as theirs.

Comparisons between third-year middle band third set and any fourth-year group (4T included) are bound to be invidious, but compare them I must.

The fourth-year will, in general, talk about anything connected with Life After School and Training (LAST) because it is real to them, it's what they see in their sights, it's what this whole business of being in school is all about. (Of course, they have to be helped to see that LAST is more than just the job they will do.) Because of this, everything is relevant to *them*; not because I decide it ought to be, but because *they* decide it. They'll talk for ever about their dreams, hopes and ambitions, about sex roles, about what they would want from an employee of theirs, about 'good' jobs and jobs they wouldn't be seen dead doing, about being 'grown-up', about the personal qualities needed to fit into a working environment, about the reasons people have for working — in fact, anything to do with their future lives. When they've worked out what they want in terms of money, responsibility, status etc. then we can help sort out on an individual basis how best to achieve these things in ways acceptable to them, such as money via hard work or theft.

The third-year group find it difficult to see the relevance of what they are doing, and few are able to relate it to themselves; for example, how do they think it would affect them if the wage-earner in their family had to work abroad and leave the family here? Talking is not work as far as they are concerned and they are happiest and most easily controllable when going over a map outline or doing a comprehension-type worksheet — neither of which requires any original thought. When I stick at it and insist [*sic*] on an answer, I get, 'Me mum would probably find another feller'. This answer is fine and could lead to discussion of this particular problem and other similar ones, but by now the class, having reacted with a guffaw, find it impossible to calm down sufficiently to contemplate any of the many ramifications of this statement.

A further difficulty is the size of this class. On a bad day all thirty-five are there. They are too physically close to each other even if they were in groups. To ask them to talk within their groups and perhaps record their conclusions would require a level of maturity and motivation which they do not possess and

I cannot provide. I am sure that there are classes in the third year where the teacher could group them and things would get discussed and conclusions (perhaps differing) would be reached. Some of my third-year group could not tolerate disagreement from another member of the class. Disagreements are solved by thumping — a natural reaction which has to be discouraged.

Almost every topic manages to inspire some anti-immigrant statement (which, of course, cannot go unanswered!). Food . . . and immigrants; transport . . . and immigrants; work . . . and immigrants; houses . . . and immigrants. A mock election provided another platform. They were at their most fluent on the subject of immigration. It's a topic which obviously means a great deal to the third- and fourth-year sets. Their ideas are not original to them; they are half-digested, partly understood and completely believed. Reason carries no weight — a quick appeal to the emotions wins every time. I find myself reverting to type and 'playing teacher' — the big authoritarian thing with the whole class. This is never necessary in the fourth year. Perhaps, occasionally with individuals, but not with a whole class. There is one class where a persistent disrupter is verbally set upon by the rest of the class. They *want* to continue with the topic under discussion. He is the archetype of male chauvinist piggery, and, on the occasion in mind, the whole group except him were wholeheartedly contributing to a discussion on how parents treat male and female offspring differently, perhaps influencing the way those children treat their offspring. This one lad's irrelevant (to the rest of us) comments were unwelcome, and the group turned on him.

Kids are supposed to dislike lessons where they don't do anything. Many have said that they enjoy careers lessons because they're interesting. I'd love to know what the magic ingredient is — I'd give the third-year group a double dose. Perhaps they have no opinions to talk about because they've never been asked for them, or, if they have, their opinions have been ridiculed. Should we start asking for opinions earlier? Are we as teachers constitutionally incapable of accepting any interpretation of facts which isn't the one we first thought of? What's so marvellous about facts anyway? It was a fact once that the sun went around the earth!

Obviously as a teacher I do not go out of my way to make difficulties for myself. It is far easier for me to adapt my behaviour to a class than to expect it to adapt to me, although

I think my behaviour is reasonably consistent with any one group. It would be interesting to discover whether others experience such feelings as:

(with my third-year group) better controlled non-participation than chaotic participation
(with my fourth-year group) apart from my opening a few doors to show them what's there, why shouldn't they make the lesson and decide which way it should go?

Fieldwork language and learning
Jeff Chatwin

Creating situations in the classroom in which spontaneous talking and real learning take place is often difficult for the teacher, with the many roles he or she must play. Understandably there are other situations which can be considered outside the classroom, which can provide the stimulus and motivation for learning, situations in which the development of language is an integral part. Fieldwork has always been an important aspect of geographical teaching, although until recent years its approach has been very traditional.

The very idea of a whistle-stop tour of hundreds of miles, in which pupils are expected to turn their full attention to the pedagogue delivering a twenty-minute monologue in between periods of travel on a coach, is still a reality and very frightening. However, changes in both the philosophy and methodology of the subject have meant radical changes to lower school syllabuses. Consequently, the dialogue, and the learning experiences, which can be developed in the field, offer whole new horizons, many of which are still relatively unexplored in the context of language.

Imagine the dialogue of question and answer sessions in the field, in which the teacher mainly directs the conversation, and leaves little for the imagination or development of the child's thoughts. Here is a transcript of a possible conversation:

Teacher	As we walked along the valley, what happened to the track which we have followed?
Peter	It was rocky.
Teacher	How did it change in the last quarter of a mile?

John	It became muddy and slippery.
Teacher	Can anyone suggest any reasons why it changed?
	Long silence
Teacher	(A long description of the quality of weathering and erosion of hard and soft rocks.)

It can be deduced from this type of approach that the pupils are being asked to contribute very little, yet absorb a whole new range of ideas and facts, which without actual involvement and discussion they cannot fully comprehend.

Much fieldwork in the past has been purely empirical in its approach, and required only the writing of a formal description of what has been observed on the 'day out'. Changes in the geographical framework do now require a much more scientific approach to the environment, which lends itself much more to an approach in which the child can use language and discussion in the understanding of ideas and hypotheses. Quantification for its own sake has to some extent now passed geography by, and the collecting and collating of material in the context of a real problem in the eyes of the children is very important. These types of situations of data collection provide ample opportunity for use of the child's own language and development of communicative skills. Very often a cassette recorder can provide an exact transcript of an interview made in the field, and can be used by the teacher for further analysis of the pupils' work.

Preparation work is important, especially where groups are expected to contact outside parties. Although most of the work I have done has been with older pupils, there is great validity in extending it to the lower age groups. At the thought of interviewing people in the street, some children, even older ones, become very shy, and find it difficult to explain adequately the purpose of their venture to the interviewee. For many children this is a very difficult, but a very worthwhile, exercise. The communicative skills involved in interviewing are fairly evident; but the developments from this approach in terms of discussion which can evolve about the problems that arose are limitless, and invaluable in leading towards a full understanding of the fieldwork research. Much of this is already being achieved in the subject without the teacher being fully aware of it happening! Yet it is perhaps the most important motivating influence in which the children are asked to participate. The experience is usually so meaningful to the pupils that discussion of the hypothesis being tested is usually embarked upon when they return to the classroom, without any incentives from the teacher. Very often, in experiencing field research in this way, the children gain an insight into the problems and possible solutions, which is more fully researched than the teacher's knowledge of the problem — and, literally, what more can one ask?

Having benefited from this experience on a number of occasions, and with a diverse range of ability groups, I can only take recourse to an extract of a conversation which is likely to take place once the interviewing groups meet up again in the classroom. The following extract is mainly concerned with the 'catchment area' of a shopping precinct:

Peter   Well I had three people from Bushberry Avenue which is only about a quarter of a mile away.

John   If I look at my results the majority of mine come from streets all within a quarter of a mile of the shops. How come most of yours come from a long way away?

Michael   That's because he did his survey next to the car park. I told you it wouldn't be right.

Stephen   Yeah, you should have chosen a place where all the people come from different places. It would have been much better next to the shops, or when they were coming out of the shops.

John   You won't be able to use those results, they're not right. You'll have to start all over again, and do the survey how we did in the middle of the shopping centre.

Peter   No I won't. I can draw up my results, and compare them with yours and see what differences there are and we could combine results, and then we would have even more figures . . . (and so on)

In this example, the children are not only learning about the problems of interviewing, by means of discussion of what actually happened to them in the shopping centre, but they are also analysing their individual results by discussion. As a result the children will understandably have a better idea of the problem or the hypothesis being analysed. They will arrive at a situation in which they are not passive learners, but active ones.

Out of the classroom
Kathy Klima

(Kathy has a group of 4T for the whole of Thursday morning.)
For my group, trips out of school are fairly frequent, and have proved of vital importance for many reasons:

> to become familiar with the surrounding environment
> to be able to manage skills out of school
> cultural interest
> to build up relationships between members of the group
> to build up relationships between pupil and teacher.

The members of the group seem to change considerably when going out of school. They consider it a great treat to leave the school premises, even if only to the woods. They find great pleasure in leading me to areas with which I am not familiar.

I find that during trips they really open up, and become far more friendly and more responsive. One of the group, who is normally rather lacking in confidence in the classroom, seemed to develop a sense of self-importance; during a walk to Willenhall, he was very keen to point out various places, such as the Chace hostel for homeless people.

David I know a couple of people in there, it's terrible, built before the war . . .

Archie About time it was pulled down . . .

After visiting Willenhall, we went to Cheylesmore. We discussed the differences between the two areas:

Susan Willenhall isn't beautiful, there's not much green, or many private houses. In Cheylesmore there's more green, and open space, private houses.

Back in the classroom they wrote about these areas:

In Willenhall they are flats and houses every where there is a train track going to London what runs right the way throw the middle. In the precicent they re shops, and above the shops they are flats. but at the terminus they is the Waggard youth Center and everybody goes there. They is three big fields and loads of places to play. In the shops there is a Dentist, Doctor, Washereta, CoOp, 2 Botcher shops A camera shop, A Libary and food shops, Willenhall has got litter all arround and it is untidy most the time the only time it is tidy is when people go round tidying it up.

Most of the houses are council houses
All the flowers add colour,
All the Doser are on the benches
And the 13 bus is always late
And the awfull smell of the Butchers Shop
And the pubs & clubs are always full of drunk men,
Streets are full Dosser cigerettes
And all fences have been crushed down.

As the town centre is crowded with people
    And the store are all open
They owners shout all day
    People queuing for buses
And the sound of cars blowing ther horne's at people
    And the occasinal boy being knocked over
And mother weeping for her boy
    And when night finally falls the sound of traffic gone . . .

Trips out of school are varied: they may be a walk to surrounding areas; they may be to the old, and new, cathedral. Many were interested in a display of the work of Oxfam, and asked numerous questions, and offered information. Nick had seen a film about Oxfam, and was keen to tell us about its work. Many were interested in a photography exhibition. The boys were particularly interested in wild life photography. They were keen to offer information.

Some enjoy the freedom of having twenty minutes to look around, and to investigate the old cathedral, and to browse around the cathedral shop. The art gallery is another place which attracts them. An exhibition of vintage cars stimulated great interest. The animal exhibition was again a topic of much excitement. David and Nick were very keen to talk about the fish:

David   We've got some of them in our pond.

Nick took much delight in describing many of the fish and their habits.

After getting to know the group better, I invited them back to my flat on two occasions. The first time they came back they were very shy and nervous and just sat still. After a while, they relaxed and started asking questions about the flat, volunteered to make coffee, wash up, tidy up the garden. They enjoyed looking around, selecting books, and music, games. Questions flowed: How many live here? How long have you lived here? Who lives upstairs? When did you last cut the grass? Who does the cooking?

Out of school my relationship with the group is far more relaxed. They behave well, and realize that if they misbehave they won't go out again. The group are far more familiar with Coventry than I am, so take pride in giving me information.

When I first had the group, during sessions in school, they were argumentative with each other, and hostile towards me; but since we have been going out quite regularly, they are far more open, but still feel more apprehensive towards me when in the classroom. The value of trips out of school is essential for groups such as 4T. It has become apparent that conversation generally flows more easily out of school, barriers are partially broken down. Some have developed a certain degree of self-confidence, friendship and genuine interest.

Talking to pupils: the organization of schools
David Kenningham

The wave of interest created by the Bullock Report should not obscure the fact that many of the problems associated with the role of language in learning have been recognized for a long time now, and many of the excellent suggestions in the report and elsewhere are not new. It is about fifteen years since the Nuffield Science Projects started to emerge. They contained clear guidance aimed to deter teachers from demanding a formal write-up from pupils immediately after they had come into contact with a new idea. Similarly, there have been countless discussions about the role of language in the classroom and the way in which children discuss things affects the way in which they learn. Nevertheless, the feeling is that progress has been very very slow, if not quite non-existent. Why is this?

I believe it is because almost no attention has been paid to the practical problems which face the teacher trying to implement many of the methods that we must face if we are going to move out of the educational 'stone age' — and make no mistake about it, that is exactly where we are.

The most important task that we face is to find better ways of arranging pupils and staff so that the former receive much more attention as individuals. This is true not only of the class-room situation but also of the pastoral arrangements within the house and tutor group. Almost all of us remember the few occasions at school when we received individual attention. I distinctly recall in the fourth year the arrival of the new English teacher, when, for the first time, my work was discussed properly with me. I don't ever remember learning anything from a remark written on my work, although I was encouraged if there were something complimentary, and certainly dis-couraged if I felt my work had not been looked at. In science, I clearly remember the day that the physics teacher came and spent time with me during a practical lesson and from that day I knew how to connect a voltmeter into a circuit. Five minutes spent by a teacher with a pupil is probably worth fifty minutes spent by the teacher on routine marking.

At present, for most of us, the giving of attention to indivi-duals or small groups is somewhat haphazard. I want to suggest that we deliberately plan to see pupils in this way on a regular and reasonably frequent basis. To do so we must:

  (i)   cut out the time wasted on non-productive effort — and we all have a long list of favourites under this heading
 (ii)   arrange the timetable so that staff can be used more flex-ibly in groups of varying size
(iii)   ensure that most subjects are not taught for such a limited time per week that regular reasonably frequent individual attention is virtually impossible, as it must be if a teacher sees a class of thirty for only seventy minutes a week
 (iv)   choose topics of sufficient length to ensure that every pupil gets attention either as an individual or at least as a member of a group during each topic.

Of these points probably the second is the most important. One hundred and twenty pupils might be split into five groups of twenty-four or four groups of thirty with one teacher spare who could either work with individuals or groups, or release the class teacher to do this. Numerous variations are possible. There is nothing at all new in this idea, but why is it so rarely tried? Possibly one of the failings of many team teaching situations is that the big effort goes into the lead lecture, but the equal effort which should go into organizing the individual and group work is not always made.

Whilst some pupils are being seen individually or in groups, some others must be able to follow a well-planned sequence of work which is not going to require much help. Referring again to the Nuffield Science Projects, it seems a great pity that this point was not recognized from the outset. All too often a wonderful set of experiments was devised which unfortunately required a superhuman effort to set up and get going for a full class, experiments of a more routine nature being despised. In fact, if only some of the pupils were doing the latter, the others might have got more out of the former. Indeed, working in or looking around science labs, I often get the feeling that if only about half of the pupils were doing practical work at any one time they might all make more progress in the long run.

Within the house organization, it should be possible to arrange for every pupil to have an individual discussion with tutor or househead at least once a term. One occasion might be to discuss a report, another might be to talk about a particular piece of work. Perhaps every pupil in a house should have to choose one piece of work per term to show to and discuss with his tutor. Clearly there are all sorts of other alternatives; what is important is to choose one that seems right for a particular pupil and teacher.

We all subscribe to the notion of treating pupils as individuals and to the value of giving them individual attention. We must now think hard about ways of enabling us to implement these ideals. As schools are organized at present it is not easy.

From Communication to Curriculum by **Douglas Barnes**
A review by Joan Worthy

This appealing little book, written by Douglas Barnes, can be read easily in one afternoon. The author is very much an authority in this field and has written many books. Currently, he is Senior Lecturer in Education at the University of Leeds Institute of Education.

Undoubtedly, language is the most subtle and pervasive of means by which we present our assumptions about role, subject matter, and about the people we talk to and with. And yet, as Douglas Barnes's fascinating survey of secondary-school class-rooms shows, teachers tend to talk too much and, rather surprisingly, pupils far too little (within the right situation!). Hence, children are often insensitive to the effects and significance of the language they use and expect. If we ask others to suggest why we use language, most will reply 'to communicate ideas', yet this is only a small part of the truth if we distinguish language for other people (communication) from language for self — hence, the functional duality of language. Barnes writes on page 19: 'Many adults report an audible inner monologue that comments, interprets and guides through much of their waking hours.' Thus, the importance of language lies in the fact that it enables knowledge and thought processes to become more readily available to introspection and revision. 'Language, however, is not the same as thought but it allows us to reflect upon our thoughts.' (page 20)

The purpose of this little book is to explore the relationship between communication and learning in school, for one of the fundamental intentions embedded in the concept of teaching is that of transforming the child's reality, of giving him new ways of understanding the world, and developing in him new kinds of awareness and skill. In order to do this, the teacher has to influence the child's thought. Conversion of knowledge into thought and its accommodation into existing thought is, however, an extremely complex process. Douglas Barnes devotes several pages of his book to the analysis of language within the context of lesson themes, and suggests that, quite contrary to teacher expectations, every pupil takes away from class a slightly different version of the lesson, for knowledge brought to the lesson holds relevance too. Thus, as Barnes writes on page 22, 'We shall not be able to understand what they learn without considering that they make sense of new knowledge by projecting it upon what they know already'. Classroom learning can best be seen as an interaction between the teacher's meanings and those of his pupils, so that what they take away is partly shared and partly unique to each of them. Barnes wrote that, 'It is misleading to see learning as the adding of new blocks of knowledge to an existing pile of blocks', for school knowledge, he reminds us in Chapter 3, 'is the knowledge which someone else presents to us. We partly grasp it, enough to answer the teacher's questions, to do exercises, or to answer examination questions, but it remains someone else's knowledge not ours, and if we never use this knowledge we probably forget it.' Thus, language becomes all important, for it is the chief means by which the objective world becomes represented in our consciousness as a subjective world, and through its use we construct our reality. In Chapter 3 of his book, Douglas Barnes tries to relate school knowledge to what he calls 'action knowledge', and makes a sensitive analysis of what counts as school knowledge. Furthermore, he discusses teaching styles and places them along a continuum from the transmission view to an interpretative style. We all fall somewhere along that continuum and only by reading Chapter 5 can we secure our position.

It is a lively book worth reading and well able to sensitize us all to new thoughts concerning language and the curriculum. Perhaps you will express some resistance to its many themes and regard it as a little idealistic. This is quite understandable, when we recall the writings of Blanche Geer who suggested that 'Teaching is an assault on the self, and resistance to it can be explained as an unwillingness to upset one's inner *status quo*'. Teaching and learning always become very much an elaborate process of negotiation, for to impose pedagogic desires upon an unwilling class inevitably affects the way language is being used by pupils and, thus, the kind of learning taking place. Therein lies the problem, for it becomes increasingly difficult to separate our consideration of language as a means of learning from consideration of language as a way of negotiating classroom relationships. Douglas Barnes, contrary to one's first impressions, is deeply conscious of these issues and, far from being stranded in idealism, is careful to emphasize on the one hand hypothetical and reflexive modes of thought, for they hold the secrets of responsibility and change, and on the other hand the teacher's arbitrary power over classroom knowledge, for, more importantly, it is this that can paralyse children's nascent sense of purpose.

(*From Communication to Curriculum* Penguin.)

Whitley Abbey staff paper
The next issue

A school is a place for talk, but the talk changes from class-room to classroom, from lesson to lesson, from person to person. There is a sense in which each new occasion is a new kind of talk.

It's interesting, in this paper, to notice the different kinds of talk mentioned by the writers, and to see something of the range of attitudes, situations and purposes that they reveal. There's a difference, too, in the ways words such as 'know-ledge', 'understanding', and 'learning' are used.

That's part of the difficulty of dealing with this topic. Another is that it is closely associated with just about every other issue that crops up in schools. How teachers talk to pupils, how pupils talk to teachers, how teachers talk with each other, how pupils talk to each other in classrooms, raise the question not just of how a classroom or a teaching staff is organized, but how a whole school is run.

But if we are agreed that there is a place for talk of all kinds in school, and, in particular, for the child's own voice in his learning, then we have to begin somewhere, or we stay in the Stone Age. I think we need to tackle two problems:

1 What is the place of talk in children's learning?
   Do children really learn by talking about things?
   How does it happen?
2 How do we organize our classes to encourage it to happen?

Using the tape-recorder could provide answers to both. I'd be glad to receive for the next issue accounts of how the tape-recorder is used by teachers, and accounts, too, of tapes, or transcripts of tapes, of children learning that have interested, surprised, or disappointed teachers. Some staff might want to tape each other or themselves teaching, or groups talking within their classes.

If a group discussed aspects of this paper, then that, too, could be taped. After all, what do we as adults learn by talking with each other? If teachers lose faith in their own talk with each other, which is quite easy in schools, how does this affect what goes on in the classroom?

61

7   The language of the classroom

As teachers we are all searching for ways of helping pupils to learn more successfully. The knowledge of the variety of such ways can be enhanced by an awareness of what other teachers are doing. Teachers of one department can greatly benefit through contact with teachers of other departments.

The Woodlands is a large and busy school and the difficulties of active interdepartmental communication are apparent. The heads of department have kindly contributed examples of lessons which show a variety of teaching methods and techniques being used throughout the school.

One of the aims of this pamphlet is to proliferate interdepartmental communications by helping staff to know where certain ideas are being tried and tested, should they wish to experiment themselves.

NEW ESTATE GAME   LESSON PLAN   3D Period 4
Friday
Room 16

Aims	1	To develop a basic understanding of planning problems.
	2	To allow for discussion about mechanical planning of a simplified estate on a town fringe.
Skills	1	Discussion of a problem on a group basis and as a class.
	2	Presentation of a plan of an estate together with the opportunity to present the reasons for it.
	3	Analysis of the result with the help of a questionnaire.
Attitudes	1	To develop a sympathetic understanding of the needs of people living on such an estate.
Materials required		Physical base model of estate and polystyrene buildings. Data + information sheets + cut-out materials. Base maps. Scissors, glue, spare envelopes. Colouring sticks (red, blue, brown, yellow)

OHP acetate.
Set of studies of a council estate in Coventry: photographs.

Plan of lesson (allowing 70 mins)

20—30 mins Use the model to discuss basic problems. Present problems in a systematic way and get as many pupils as possible to offer solutions. Get them to argue out their conclusions.

Deal with one aspect at a time, e.g. the position of factories or shops, or ten-storey block of flats. Build up the problem gradually. Relate to children's own experience, e.g. problems of bus routes, distances to shops, problems of noise from pubs, youth clubs etc. (Effect of this on planning.)

20 mins Issue base maps and building sheets. Children colour in blocks with the help of an OHP and cut them out. First attempts made to lay these out on the base map.

20 mins Children work in groups of four and discuss their ideas about the best planning layout for their estate. At the end all pieces go into spare envelope to take home.

5 mins Set homework to encourage children to play with the idea at home and discuss it with parents, brothers and sisters.

What really happened!
H. Wyatt

The Friday circus rolls again! Two tons of resource materials to have to be moved from York to Canterbury (different houses at the school) — a minor problem in a force 8 gale and pouring rain. (Abandon the lot and give them a test — nice and peaceful on a Friday afternoon.) I can't do that! I promised them we would use the Estate game this week, and they may be in an ugly mood after having Roger Greaves last period. Shall I drop in and ask him to dampen their outpouring of enthusiasm?

We've made it — overhead projector set up, model laid out, desks rearranged, resource sheets and information sheets distributed, scissors for cutting out scrounged from Dave Hicklin and glue from Harry Bott. If I've forgotten anything we will have to go without!

All wet and steaming nicely we have negotiated Canterbury stairs. What a block — like Stalag 5 with all the bodies after the tranquillity of York. The Head must have an evil sense of humour making me play away from home, last period on a Friday, with a third form!

We're off! Would they like to live on an estate? Place the ten-storey flats, locate the shopping centre, place the school in the best position. Problems? Problems? Problems? They really are interested — the ideas flow — everyone wants to have a say (at once!) The mind works overtime. Les Moore really has some good ideas — why can't he put them on paper? Geoff Jones isn't involved — get him involved.

'Where would you put the flats, Geoff?'

Half-asleep so I repeat the question. Don't give up with him, or he'll be a problem next year for somebody. Involve Mike Smith and Dave Bowyer in talking. They have ideas but they are too nervous to express them. Twenty minutes gone. We really are producing some good oral work — it was worth braving the rain, a test would have been so much duller. Everyone has had a say and they obviously do care about the area in which they live. We might have sparked a town planner, or stopped one of them writing on walls in future. Who knows?

Now for the difficult bit! Cut out and colour the pieces to go on the estate plan. Paper and scissors everywhere. I really have got it carefully planned, it just seems like chaos. Karl Bainbridge has finished first as usual — collect all the spare pieces — spend a bit of time talking to him about some of the more intricate problems. Tim O'Brien and Dave Barnacle join the group without invitation. They have a better grasp of the problem than me, so I feed on the ideas. Watch Geoff to see that he is cutting out and not cutting hair with scissors. Finished. Well done Geoff! collect scissors for me — means he has something responsible to do.

Only ten minutes left. We sort out the problems for home-work. They will plan their estates individually and hand them in next week. (They did the best piece of work this year — many had spent hours on it and a few even got their families involved — which was as I intended. Homework can be fun — they all agree — they have to, don't they?)

Get the desks back, tidy up — after all it's not my room.

3.30! Geoff stays behind and says can he do it now, he hasn't got any glue at home. My week is complete — he stays until 4.15. He chats and I look at my watch — four boys to get to cricket nets at Edgebaston by five. Get home at seven and take the girls to guides. Watch the under sixteens get to the last eight in England on Saturday morning — twenty staff still hard at it on Saturday morning, and another group getting ready for the Coventry table tennis competition in the afternoon.

Roll on Sunday — only the car to clean etc.

I'll be glad when it's Monday — but I'm glad I didn't give 3D that test.

Craft — designing a spanner

I wonder what goes on in the craft department? The following pages show a small part of a much fuller scheme . . . again the lesson is aimed at a third-year mixed-ability class. The project is assessed continuously and objectives are marked at the end. The full project is designed to last eight weeks.

PROJECT OBJECTIVES (What you have to do)
After completing this project, you will hand to your teacher for marking.
1 A sketch, done on the squared paper provided, of a spanner, designed to fit five different sizes of cycle nuts.
2 A fully dimensioned drawing, of the spanner also done on the squared paper provided.
3 A completed planning sheet.
4 The designed spanner, made from your own drawing to the instructions on your planning sheet.
5 A completed test sheet.
For this project you will work in groups of four, one of whom will be the group leader and you will finish the project inside eight school periods by following the instructions given to you in this guide.

NOW meet **MR C. SPANNER** (C for CYCLE) (*Called MR C. SPANNER for short*)

MR C. Spanner is going to guide you through this project.
With any luck!

WHAT ARE YOU TO DESIGN?
You are to design a *Spanner.*
   It must be able to TIGHTEN UP the **FIVE** cycle nuts shown here:

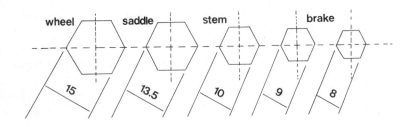

ALSO
   The spanner must fit into a *rectangular box* that is 125 mm long by 55 mm wide, and 20 mm deep.

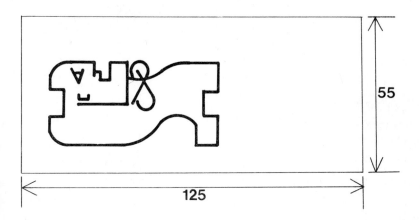

This is Mr C. Spanner pretending to be a **box** spanner.

OBJECTIVE 1

DESIGNING THE SPANNER

1. *What* do we *mean* by *DESIGN*?

In Engineering, design means:

PUTTING ON TO PAPER everything necessary to make an object, do the following:

It must

(a) *LOOK RIGHT*

(b) *WORK WELL*

(c) *BE EASILY MADE*

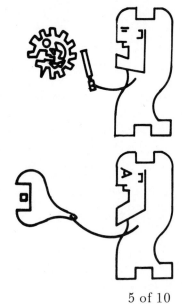

(d) *DO WHAT IT IS SUPPOSED TO*

HOW DO YOU DESIGN THE SPANNER?

Follow this GUIDE: (2 sheets)

1.1 Draw on to a piece of the squared paper provided, a *rough outline* of your spanner. *REMEMBER* the conditions on sheet 3.

1.2 *DISCUSS* this outline with other members of your group, changing it between you, until your group has *one common shape.*

1.3 Allow your group leader to guide the discussion, as he has a number of points about the shape that you must consider.

LOOK RIGHT

1.4 Make sure the shape is *strong enough.*
1.5 Choose a suitable material. (Your group leader has a list.)
1.6 Decide on the final condition of your material. (Are you going to leave it as it is or harden it or case harden it or what?)

1.7 Can it be easily made?
Discuss how you will make it.
1.8 Could you make it more easily by altering the shape slightly?

EASILY MADE

FINALLY and this is most IMPORTANT
1.9 Does it do what it is supposed to?

IF NOT then think again.

If, as a group, you are now satisfied with your design, then you are ready for the next step. KEEP your rough sketches for marking, at the end of the project.

HISTORY – Anglo-Saxon justice
Roger Pearce

First-year mixed-ability class
Aim (a) Explore the concept of law-making, the organization of a village community.
(b) Introduce information on Saxon justice.

Organization
1 Group work 6 groups of 5–6 boys.
2 Blackboard Do we need laws and rules?
How should we decide on laws and their details?
Does a village need a leader?
How is this leader to be chosen?
As a group put the following crimes in order of importance:

horse-stealing, witchcraft, murder, cutting down a tree, crop trampling, gossiping, untidy farming, laziness.

As a group of villagers, how would you react to the following news, and what would you do?

(a) Rumours of Viking attack on nearby village

(b) An outbreak of plague

(c) A missionary wants to stay in your village

(d) A group of villagers want to leave the village

3 Allow 20—30 minutes on this (a lot less if it isn't working!)

4 Each group elects a spokesman to report back.

5 For last 30 minutes, introduce two information sheets on Saxon justice: 'The were-guild', 'Trial by ordeal'.

NOTES

1 Rough paper to be provided if requested

2 Groups were unselected

3 No 5 above could become a written activity, depending on previous part of lesson. I used it as an open-ended chance for the village to discuss the Saxons' answers to the problems they had faced earlier in the discussion.

4 At some stage of the discussion it is necessary to give the pupils specific roles (this stimulates the silent majority).

(a) Your village contains 5 different types of person. Choose one. Would it affect your opinions and what you have said so far? e.g.: an eccentric, uncooperative highly individual type, always keen to try something new; comes from outside village, has a weird (non-local) accent. Or — a plodder, always does as he is told, usually follows the crowd, not very bright.

Geography department lesson plan
M.C. Sheffield

Aim

To establish that there are conflicting viewpoints when building urban motorways, using Coventry as an example.

Lesson structure

1 Introduction by the teacher, telling pupils what a Public Enquiry is, why they are used and the procedure adopted during an enquiry.

They are also informed that it is proposed to build an urban motorway through Coventry and that an Enquiry has been called for to put forward the issues involved (5 mins).

2 The class is divided into five groups to represent interested

parties at the Enquiry. These are:

(a) Coventry City Council who are proposing the building of the motorway on the grounds that it would ease traffic congestion in the rush hour and possibly attract new offices/industry to the city.

(b) Chapelfields Residents' Association who oppose the motorway on the grounds that some of their members will lose their homes and others will be inconvenienced by pollution (noise, fumes etc.)

(c) British Leyland Management who argue that the motorway will ease the movement of components between their factories in Coventry and would help their employees travelling to work.

(d) Hearsall Common allotment holders accept they will gain compensation for the loss of their smallholdings but are doubtful that this is sufficient compensation for the loss of a leisure activity. Economically they are able to produce vegetables at well below the increasing shop prices. There is no substitute for fresh vegetables either. Allotments elsewhere in the city are too far away and waiting lists for them too long.

(e) Covrad management are concerned at the loss of part of their factory for the motorway and argue that this will affect production and cause more unemployment in Coventry.

Each group appoints a leader and then discusses the case which they are to put to the Enquiry. During this time, the teacher moves between the groups to encourage and help if required (15 mins).

3 The desks have already been arranged before the lesson into a large square and the various parties are now seated round it. A boy from each group, in turn, puts forward their case. He has been told to represent as accurately as possible the person he is speaking for, e.g. a suave British Leyland Director, or an angry Chapelfields resident.

Some boys do this extremely well. In cases where the boy is struggling, the Chairman (teacher) may abandon his impartial role to make observations about the speaker's case in order to stir up feelings at the Enquiry and maintain the impetus.

After each boy has spoken, there is an opportunity to cross-examine that group. Often boys become very involved at this stage if they oppose the speaker (35 mins).

4 After all groups have spoken, the Chairman sums up and stresses that an issue such as the building of a motorway is bound to create conflicting viewpoints. He may at this point pass judgment on whether the proposal to build the motorway is allowed or not (5 mins).

Homework

Put the case for or against the building of the motorway for three of the five groups.

I have found that this role-playing exercise goes down extremely well with third-year pupils. It allows boys who are not very good at writing to make a meaningful contribution.

I have been surprised by some of the passions aroused by the exercise, especially by boys who live in the Chapelfields area. Sometimes the involvement is such that it is impossible to complete the exercise in one lesson.

English project work – water
P. Markley

'How heavy is a whale shark, Miss?'

This is just one example of the snippets of information you are required to have at your fingertips if you are foolish enough to tackle a project on 'Water'.

This enquiry is followed swiftly by Andrew Uttley wanting a diagram of the internal organs of a crocodile which sends the pair of us diving frantically among the various encyclopaedias and coming up with a lurid picture of an alligator's mouth and the dental arrangement inside a crocodile's mouth — which seems to satisfy him for a moment (strange boy!). My attention is side-tracked to helping find a suitable rhyme for 'menacing' when suddenly a book is thrust under my nose and Alun Thomas chirps up, 'Here, Miss, look at this, it says this crab is 11 feet wide! That's as wide as this room, isn't it?'

'Don't be daft, you can't get crabs as big as that!' scoffs Simon Venters.

'Well,' I say, trying to keep the peace as all eyes turn towards Alun who is proudly displaying the picture, 'well, work it out, I'm 5ft 5ins, the crab would be the same size as two of me.'

'Ugh!' gasps Ian Sutton, 'One of you's bad enough, Miss,

let alone two.'

Ian's name goes down in my little black book with the threat that any more out of him, and he would be used in Dave Gibson's shark baiting research. Dave has been very quiet trying to discover what sharks like to eat, and as he tackles 'man-killers' his face has taken on an unusual enthusiasm.

Yes, project work does seem like organized chaos and there is a strong need for the teacher to try and anticipate and be prepared for most needs — resources must be available within the classroom or hesitation can soon lead to discipline problems or loss of vital sparks of enthusiasm. The aim of this particular project is to encourage use of books and experimenting with different materials to produce a mass of work the boy can be proud of; to have them experiment with as many different forms of writing as possible. When planning the project, therefore, I had to have very set ideas about what I wanted the boys to try; I had to know what I wanted to avoid, and to anticipate materials needed.

This particular third-year class had never tackled project work of this sort before — guidance as to method and approach must be very clear and made as routine as possible. We began by discussing the possible trends of interest arising from the main concept, water. The boys were given a fortnight to hunt for relevant information and to decide what aspect they would like to study. When I gathered in the chosen topics, I was surprised to find the areas of research fell into eight main categories: sea creatures, sea legends, sharks, canals, sea vessels, sea birds, pond-life, and water sports.

Having seen folders that my second year had made for a fire project, the class asked if they could do the same for water. (I had thought them too old!) It was made quite clear to the boys I would not accept copied information; we discussed ways round this and the routine was established that all work must be preceded by a plan, a plan which asked questions to which they would find the answers by searching through a number of books.

There is a natural tendency with this sort of project for writing to become almost totally factual. To encourage boys to attempt different forms of writing, I keep file cards on each boy, showing work completed, the category of writing, e.g. imaginary, narrative, descriptive, personal etc. and also the quality of his work is noted. By this means I can point out very clearly to the pupil what areas he has not tackled and also control the quality of his work.

I produced guide-sheets for each of the eight categories, showing ideas that would help them to experiment with different forms of writing. These were only used if the pupil was searching for ideas. Each sheet has basically the same layout, except for the canal and shark sheets, i.e.

factual writing	descriptive or poetic writing
use of fiction	preparing a talk
using historical knowledge	reviews
collecting anthologies	imaginative, personal writing

The different forms of writing are designed to cater for a far wider audience than that of the teacher.

The shark and canal sheets are different because these subjects were chosen by boys of low ability on the whole. Therefore, the assignments were easier, less involved. One boy who chose canals as a topic is so low in ability that I found it handy to make him a research file of his own, a file containing very directed plans for work and easy reading. The boy has not been stigmatized in any way; his file is just part of a mass of materials available to the boys throughout the lesson.

The boys usually bring in their own books but there are plenty available in the classrooms from the school library, English department and my own resources. I also have a good list of books I can recommend to the boys.

Tapes are available on request from me. These contain a lecture on survival in shark-infested waters, water noises, records connected with water, nature programmes on sea-shore life etc. With the loan of the listening station from the English department, it is no problem to wire a boy in without disturbing the rest of the group.

For imaginative writing there are vocabulary cards to help a pupil plan his work. There are also poetry cards attractively presented to be a starting point for anthologies or personal poetry. There are also pictures to stimulate imagination. A tray of materials for model-making is always set, containing paints, brushes, paste, plain paper, plasticine, water and scissors, as models often motivate good instructive writing, and drawing helps the imagination and relieves the monotony.

I've listed only some of the things that go towards building a project, but, for all the preparation, when all's said and done, it is the enthusiasm of the boys that makes the project. Without it the work would be mechanical and empty.

French department – one period of French with a mixed-ability third-year group
H. G. Jones

The *Language unit* on which this group had been working for the previous two periods involved phrases and vocabulary to do with travel and transport in France. In order that the linguistically less able should be able to contribute to and derive benefit from the work, background study – an integral part of the course – had also been done on rail transport in France.

The lesson
This period has been singled out in that it stays in the memory as one in which all pupils seemed to have worked to their maximum in the mixed-ability situation.

First twenty minutes
Devoted to a guided/structured discussion on travel and transport in general in France. Certain of the questions demanded factual answers; time was also provided for any boy to ask his own questions or put forward his own observations. It would be blatantly untrue to state that each boy did avail himself of the opportunity to make such observations. It was noted that towards the end of the twenty minute period, some boys were restless.

The class divided itself into three groups; these were formed partly under the direction of the teacher, partly because boys decided upon the group which they would join. The latter did not always coincide with the teacher's (unspoken) ideas.

Group A
This consisted mainly of the most able – although one or two whom the teacher would have graded C/D did go to the group. The work consisted of the translation, done as a piece of group working, of a French passage on 'an outing'. The less able were obviously helped by the more able.

Group B
This consisted mainly of the 'C' boys. They had decided to work from work cards on certain structures to do with travel. The cards provided them with pattern-practice structures.

Group C
This consisted mainly and at first, of the least able; however, two or three boys from Group B did later join this one. The boys in this group were first 'plugged into' a listening set. The tape — from BBC productions — was an account, well illustrated with sound effects, of rail travel in France.

The three groups, with permitted transfers, continued in this way until five or ten minutes before the ending of the period.

None of the three groups was left to work alone. The teacher moved between the three groups discussing with them the work/material in hand. It was possible to spend ten minutes talking and listening to each small group.

The last five minutes or so of this lesson, totally unprepared in this way by the teacher, consisted of members of each of the three groups commenting to the others on what he/they had done.

Conclusion
1 It was a period during which things had luckily gone well.
2 It was necessary from time to time to ask certain boys in Groups A and B to lower their voices. In the case of Group C it was a question of keeping an eye on the listening sets.
3 The lesson most certainly had a novelty value.
4 For the teacher concerned the lesson was rewarding but very tiring.

Enquiry studies
M. K. Twiselton

Each boy chooses what he wishes to study from his own enthusiasm and interests. He is then given help to plan his sequence of study. This plan is written on a 'Planning Card'. Having obtained resources to help him study, he is then ready to proceed.

The following is the usual sequence of one session of enquiry studies

1 Registration.
2 (Every session there are six places available for any boys who wish to work in silence.) Boys volunteer to work in the 'quiet room' and this is recorded in the register (in order to achieve fairness over a period of weeks). No practical work is done in the 'quiet room'.
3 Issuing of material from ES resources as requested by individuals from the previous session's resources checklist. These resources have been placed in the room before the session begins.
4 Giving out of individual work from form folders. Boys go to 'quiet room'. Practical work given out from store-room.
5 Boys get equipment and materials from cupboard etc. as necessary.
6 Work proceeds on a completely individual basis except where boys choose to work together. Assistance is given only where requested — no direction or assistance should be 'intruded' by the adult. As the great majority of any group is at work without needing assistance, then those requesting help receive full attention. Throughout the session, every boy is seen, every activity is seen even where no interruption of any sort is made. Methods of working, communication and movement are completely free, providing no one is unnecessarily distracted from what he is attempting to do.

Boys use the ES centre upon request. The index system of the resource sets limits upon the numbers of people able to use it at any one time. (Without 'volunteer Mum' — maximum 3; with 'volunteer mum' — maximum 6.) All resources brought into the workroom are entered on the resources checklist (date, boy's name, resource number).
7 Usual time allowed for 'packing up' at end of session, 10—15 minutes.
8 All equipment returned to correct place by boys. Resources replaced on shelves by 'volunteer Mum'; (if no VM present, resources are replaced after the group has been dismissed).
The resources checklist is then used to record what resources are required by individuals for work in next session. Individual effort is recorded in markbook (see Assessment), session ends. Practical work is returned to storeroom, after the group has been dismissed.

Assessment
In enquiry studies, 'mistakes' are seen to be a very useful (and

often enjoyable), certainly inevitable part of all study—learning activities. Boys are allowed (encouraged) to do as much rough work as they wish before starting on the finished article. All rough work can be seen and checked for measurement, colour, spelling, proportion, accuracy, punctuation, etc. before the finished article is started. Thus, all individual work can be seen at all stages, and most assistance is requested during the rough or working-out stage. All corrections are made on the rough work. Every boy is encouraged to achieve his own best possible individual standard when producing the finished article.

No teacher's marks (red ballpoint symbols or such!) ever appear on finished work. Such work is entirely the product and possession of the student.

No assessment mark of any sort is given for standard of work. The work and its production have been part of a process of mutual interest and enthusiasm and all comments and observations have been made face to face.

The boys do know that the factor under continual assessment in enquiry studies is their individual effort (viz. how hard they are trying to get it as good as they can) with no comparisons made between one boy and another. This requires a knowledge of each individual child. All 'commendations' are awarded primarily for very good, consistent effort. This usually covers a period of 12—16 weeks.

Any finished work which a boy requests should be displayed in the room, is placed on display. No work is ever chosen by 'teacher' — no work is ever rejected by 'teacher'.

The most important 'assessment' during the whole year of enquiry studies is related to the development of the individual. The important thing is not 'pieces of work' but the effect of the whole experience upon the child. Some of the more obvious aspects of development under close observation are: independence, cooperation, confidence, skills, initiative, loss of fears, self-realization.

History – Hadrians wall
G. Sollis

Preparation
1 Lessons spent on finding out about the building of the wall,

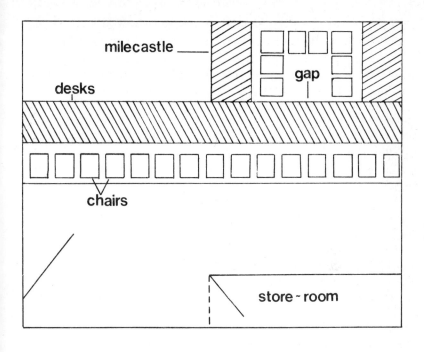

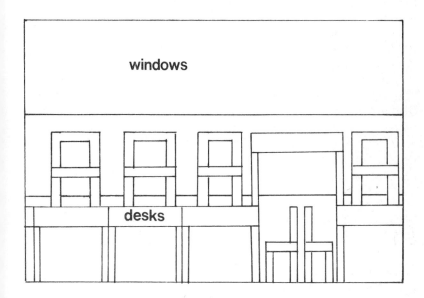

and how it operated. What life must have been like for individual soldier on duty.

The room

Procedure
Get the class sitting down in the best possible arrangement —
they are difficult to settle because of the unusual arrangement
of the room. This difficulty reappeared through the lesson.
   Listen to tape about a raid on the wall. The children have the
script to follow.
   Divide the class into Romans and Picts, and enact the general
story of the raid, but improvising dialogue.

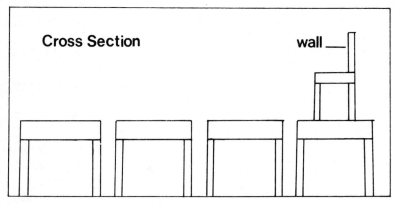

Homework
Tell the story of what happened as a survivor on either side.

Comments
Space for actions a problem. Roman soldiers not disciplined
enough.
   Perhaps we could have created a story rather than listening
to one, although it was a very good story.

Physics — fourth-year mixed ability

Uses of the bimetal strip

Aim
To help the boys understand the vital part played by a bimetal

strip in various instruments, especially the electric thermostat.

Background
During the previous lesson the boys had seen how a bimetal strip works, and had experience of a simple series circuit, but they received no instruction on the electric thermostat circuit — they were simply given a 'problem solving' exercise.

The problem
To make an electric circuit, incorporating a bimetal strip, which would switch on when it was cold and off when it became hot.

Resources
Apparatus that I thought would be necessary was counted out and put into trays at the side of the lab before the lesson.
Transparencies and real electric thermostats were supplied to show the practical application of their simple circuits.
Books were on the shelves, in their usual position, where boys could find any other information they required.

What happened
The boys were grouped around the master's bench — it's not easy to fill a large lab with one's voice. The heading 'Uses of the bimetal strip' is already on the blackboard. I explained the problem that needed solving, and showed them the apparatus available to be used in the way they wanted. (I had not realized how many uses crocodile clips could serve in addition to the one I used them for!)

The final circuit that they designed was to be drawn in their books, together with any comments that they thought would be of use when they came to revise. This was then to be compared with the practical arrangement shown in their textbooks and the real ones in the lab, noting any similarities with their own circuit.

Using diagrams where appropriate they were asked to write about other uses of the bimetal strips which I had listed on the board, and to add to these if they could.

To tackle the experimental part, the boys worked in their usual practical groups of two or three. Before sending them back to their own benches I suggested they spend a little time in deciding on a likely practical circuit, before setting one up.

They returned to their places, and set to work. I circulated to see how they were progressing and offered advice if asked. The transcript of the tape-recording of this part of the lesson illustrates how the boys tackled problem-solving.

Transcript

T   What I'd like you to do is to draw the circuit that you're going to use, so that you know what you're going to do; then we'll see if we can set one up to work — OK? I'd like you to decide what your circuit's going to be like, how are you going to use the main part of your circuit? What's the main part of a thermostat circuit?

P   The — er — bimetal strip

T   Right, the bimetal strip, so I want you to decide how you're going to use that in the electric circuit that you've got there. All right?

TIME LAPSE

T   Any progress?

P   No!

P1   Now let me think about this — look, when it's heat, er, hot, it comes back and knocks that.

P2   It don't knock it off does it?

P1   Oh, it's gotta be touching that little rivet.

P2   No, it ain't like that!

P1   It is! That's the way it works . . . when it's heat, hot it —

P2   (Very enthusiastically) Get another lead, get another lead, get another lead — ah — get another croc clip — another couple crocodile clips. We gotta have it set like this, right, when it cools — voila!

P1   No it don't you're wrong, this has got to be touching there you realize this has to be connected so if we get another one —

P2   That ain't right is it?

T   How are you going then? Right so that's the circuit you're going to use.

P2   Yeah, but it ⎰don't light up

P1   ⎱don't light up.

T   Let's see — why won't it light?

P2   Yeah, them two have got to be connected.

P1   There's a circuit there look.

P2   He hasn't connected them.

T   Well at the moment I think he has. Now I wonder why it's not alight? Because you've got a circuit there — what do you think could be wrong?

P2 The bulb is broke.

T Yes, it could be, I should test it with another one, it's quite possible you see. (goes away)

P1 Get another bulb — it was lighting a minute ago, though.

P2 It weren't.

P1 It was.

P2 Yeah, I know it was — mm — faulty connection.

T Still not working? Right, let's see —

P2 Ah.

P1 Aha.

P2 There we are!

P1 So well done Will, how did you do that?

P2 It was a faulty connection, *you* had a loose connection.

P1 I've got to find a way of fixing that . . .

8 Getting it taped

Introduction
This is the second in a series of papers written by members of staff in our school. In the first, 'The place of talk', teachers described some of the many different kinds of talk that usefully go on in school. One of the interesting things about that paper as a whole was the range of activities it revealed; and in this chapter, teachers continue to show that range, but this time by writing the different ways in which the tape-recorder can be used.

This issue has taken longer to appear than was promised by the editor, mostly because it takes so long to make transcripts. Some of the writers have probably forgotten they wrote these articles. I apologize to them; and I hope the next issue will emerge more promptly.

I thought it best to present the transcripts of tapes from the history department just as they are without any editorial comment. I think they might lead to better discussion if they are left to speak for themselves.

Anyone who would like to read the booklet that Ann Cadman writes about in this paper can order it from the publishers Ward Lock Educational.

The tape-recorder in modern language teaching
Graham Thompson

For the purposes of this paper, I have divided the uses of the tape-recorder into two broad categories: passive, where the pupils listen, and active, where they actually record speech.

Despite the fact that the tape-recorder has been accepted for over fifteen years as an integral part of language teaching, I feel that its full potential as a teaching instrument remains as dormant today as it did then. Familiarity does breed contempt. Perhaps tape-recorder is a misnomer; tape-player would be more exact. I would say that between 70 and 90 per cent of the tape-recorder's use in a language class falls into the passive category. Whether through choice or reluctant acceptance, language teachers seem to ignore the record button on their machines.

However, don't let me give the impression that the passive uses of the tape-recorder should be ignored.

At present, the audio-visual courses in the department fall into two types, Longman and Nuffield. The former, due to its age, uses the tape-recorder in a rather limited way as an alternative to the teacher's voice. The Nuffield course represents a 'second generation', and presents a more varied role for the machine.

The Longman method is based on the principle of 'over learning' structures. Each Longman unit contains a text in which a grammar point or structure is either introduced or developed; and the presentation of each unit follows a basic pattern of:

1 Watch (the filmstrip) and listen (to the tape).
2 Watch (the filmstrip), listen (to the tape) and repeat (in the spaces).
3 Listen and read.
4 Write.

Thus, a typical lesson of this type would be as follows. The teacher plays the tape through once, with the pupils watching the corresponding filmstrip frame; the filmstrip is rewound and the tape is played a second time, with the pupils repeating the phrases twice in the gaps; the tape is then switched off, and the teacher takes over initiating questions and answers to reinforce the structure introduced. When this has been consolidated, the pupils are introduced to the written text and have the opportunity to hear the tape again.

In subsequent lessons, when the material has been thoroughly digested, a tape of a conversation developing the text is introduced by the same method (with the exception of the visual stimulus), and this is perhaps dramatized.

I feel that the Longman method suffers from one inherent weakness. In relying heavily on the principle of establishing a pattern by repetition, it runs the danger of establishing the lesson pattern as a pattern. Pupils become 'conditioned' to the listen—listen and repeat—answer questions sequence, and through the 'practice effect' become quite proficient without necessarily associating the sounds they are uttering with meaningful communication. (For example, a pupil when faced with the question 'Who is late for school?' in connection with the text answers correctly 'Jean-Paul', but is incapable of answering the same question applied to a late arrival in the class! An extreme case, but essentially not an atypical one.)

The Nuffield course represents, in my opinion, about as far as it is practically possible to go in developing the passive role of the tape-recorder in modern language teaching: it is employed systematically in oral, reading and writing aspects of second language teaching.

Unlike the Longman course, where everything written has to be spoken first, thereby drastically limiting the amount of content in each text (and therefore interest), the Nuffield course uses the tape-recorder to aim at developing the pupils' skill in listening carefully and understanding immediately. The ability to repeat accurately receives a much lower priority.

Each Unit represents a situation showing some aspect of life in France. Through this, a limited number of sentence patterns is introduced. The situation is illustrated by ten posters. Before playing the tape, the teacher explains the background in English. Nuffield 3, Unit 4, for example, deals with the *Tour de France*. He also explains any of the technical vocabulary that will be met. The tape is then played through without stopping, the teacher pointing to the appropriate poster. A few questions are then asked to ensure that the children have understood. The tape is rewound and replayed two or three times, stopping in certain places to explain or make sure that the content is fully digested.

This differs from the Longman method in that, because the posters are on constant display, the pupils can 'see' the whole story; this also obviates the metronomic pip frame-change cue, which is a source of irritation and distraction. Content is enhanced by sound effects of the tape track — a technique employed on the BBC Radiovision programmes.

As the situation is too long to be repeated, specially prepared extracts of dialogue have been recorded. These are played with the appropriate poster as a visual aid, and perhaps dramatized when learnt. The sentence patterns in these extracts are re-developed through a number of dialogues which are prerecorded in spaced and unspaced versions. At the pattern is isolated in these dialogues it is intended that they be learnt by heart. The unspaced version is played several times, with any further explanation being given by the teacher. The spaced version is played with the children miming the actions while repeating the words in the spaces provided. Some children will eventually be able to produce the dialogues without the aid of the tape. At this point, the dialogues can be developed by making changes, first at the teacher's suggestion, then freely by the pupils. Then, reading is introduced. The text is a shortened, simplified, version of the situation displayed as a 40" by 30" poster. The tape of the text is both in unspaced and spaced form. After playing the unspaced version two or three times (indicating each sentence) the teacher plays the spaced version and invites some pupils to read the sentence in the space provided. When this has been thoroughly practised, pupils can read random sentences without the aid of the tape.

Reading in a foreign language is further reinforced in the Nuffield course by the planned introduction of readers, some retelling the situations, others presenting the same structures. All of these are prerecorded in an unspaced version so that they may be presented to the class as a whole.

Children reading in their own language are able to bring the correct intonation to a page of print. They do this through their experience of the oral language over a space of years, but they are unable to do the same in a second language. It is therefore important that they hear the stories read to them as they follow silently, in order to help them to bring meaning to the lines of type, as well as maintaining a correct intonation and a natural pace. The teacher plays the recording straight through, then replays it stopping to explain and ask questions. The tape is then replayed once more without interruption before the children read silently to themselves.

The recording is also used in conjunction with the reading text in the introduction of writing in a foreign language. The unspaced version is played straight through. When the spaced version is played, the teacher stops it from time to time. At first the pupils write down the last sentence that they have heard, then the next.

I feel that the Nuffield passive method with its accentuation of the development of listening skills has the advantage over the Longman course. The sentence patterns are introduced more subtly, and the uses of the tape-recorder are varied enough to conceal the underlying teaching pattern.

So far all the uses have been confined to the purely passive role of listening. No study of the use of tape-recorders in the modern languages department would be complete without mention of that super tape-recorder, the Language Laboratory. Contrary to popular belief this is housed in R 14, not room

101, and any high pitched sounds that are heard are of electronic origin and not the screams of some poor pupil being tortured for making mistakes with the pluperfect.

The majority of techniques described below are what I would describe as active uses of the tape-recorder, and could be adapted for use on a single tape-recorder.

Basically, whatever operation is being carried out in the laboratory has the underlying advantages of (a) privacy, enabling a shy pupil to work without fear of being laughed at for making mistakes, and (b) the self-correcting facility illustrated thus:

| Master programme | Stimulus | Corrected response |
| Pupil track | | Response | | Corrected response |

The main uses to which the laboratory is put are: the practice of rehearsed conversations in preparation for oral examinations; the practice of oral comprehension and description; and the practice of pattern drills. It is the last of these that has most relevance to years 1—3. No matter which method is being used, both call for the reinforcement of the structure by pattern drills. Apart from pure repetition, the drills are of various types, and can be combined to construct an oral worksheet for all abilities.

Whatever programme is being put out, the basic conduct of the laboratory lesson remains the same. The exercise is recorded from the master console on to the students' machines, either by prerecorded tape or direct from the teacher's voice. Once this operation is completed the pupils work at the exercise privately. (The master programme cannot be erased by the student.) The teacher can monitor individuals and correct them privately. I have also tried to encourage self-criticism within a group by hooking all booths into one recording (identity unknown) and allowing pupils to criticize each other's accent and intonation in complete anonymity.

I have dealt with the tape-recorder and the language laboratory so far only as modes for aiding language teaching. However, in the European studies department we are experimenting with other active uses of the tape-recorder. As the type of pupil taking this subject tends to come from the lower end of the ability range, often having problems with literacy, we have allowed, in the project work for the CSE Mode 3, taped essays to be submitted. Some of these are interviews and questionnaires and coupled with some written work. The results using this method have been encouraging and we are at present investigating the possibility of using the language laboratory for taped examinations. It would be theoretically possible, given the seating arrangements in R 14, to allow the pupils to choose, some completing the exam orally, others written.

I've confined myself to demonstrating the uses of the tape-recorder to teach language points, but I hope, that despite its specialist content, other departments will find in this paper something of use to them (if even a resolve to go no further).

Using the tape-recorder with less able pupils
Barbara Rees

David was a thirteen-year-old from a broken home. He had been to three infant schools, two junior schools, and this was his second comprehensive school. Was it any wonder that he couldn't read? His whole life had been a pattern of failure; he was desperately seeking success, but because of his disjointed education and his own lack of ability to concentrate he was often frustrated, and this led to discipline problems within his small remedial group. What could be done to help David? He needed individual attention; he needed success. David was allowed to choose books that he wanted to read. This was done with his teacher's help so that he chose books with an interest level for a boy of thirteen but which had a reading age of nine. The teacher took one book home, recorded it carefully giving all instructions, page by page, allowing time for turning over. At the end of each page, David was given instructions to point to certain words like 'shop', 'ship', 'church', before he turned over to the next page. He was then allowed to sit at the back of the class with his tape player, headphones, and reading book. He started to read with his eyes and simultaneously mouthed the words as the tape played them in his ears. His face lit up. Success! He could read! He went through the tape several times and then he'd had enough for one day. Another tape was made with blank spaces where the words to which David had pointed on the first page had occurred, and soon he had mastered this tape. He then decided to have a try reading the book without the tape, and this he managed quite well. He then recorded this story on another tape himself — success at last. He kept this tape and took it home to play to his 'mam', the first whole book he'd read himself. David read seven more books in exactly the same way, enlarging his sight vocabulary all the time; and then he found he could manage without the tape. He became an avid reader, and in the fourth year he joined a CSE group. At sixteen, he got five CSEs grade 3 and 4. But there is no happy ending. David is now on the dole thanks to the economic climate. I hope he is able to keep away from potential trouble, as he is still very volatile when frustrated.

It is said that practice makes perfect, and certainly with the child who is not a fluent reader frequent practice is needed, but there is not always a teacher, sixth-former, or parent available to listen and help. A tape-recorder can be used as a substitute, although it is not always satisfactory. I have used it with a group of girls — one girl was in charge of setting up a fresh tape every day and introducing it: 'Wednesday January 17th. Green group. Reading first Margaret Jones — Red Pirate page 9'. Then Margaret Jones would read as much as she wanted to, and the recorder was passed on to the next pupil. When the whole group had read, the girl in charge gathered all the reading books together, and the tape, and gave it to the teacher, who checked the reading after school, making notes of any child's particular difficulties. Not ideal, but better than missing the reading all together.

Listening is itself an art, and the skill of listening can be developed by using tapes. I have seen a very boisterous noisy class trained to listen by a teacher, initially through the use of tapes, and later by choosing suitable material to read to the class. This helped to develop a very studious attitude in many of the class.

Many stories have now been recorded by commercial companies, as well as by the BBC and by publishers, in association with their texts. Commercially produced tapes are also available for programme learning in different situations, and many of the programmes are very useful with the less able child who needs the reinforcement of sound. Children who have slipped through the education net, and who arrive at a comprehensive school without some fluency in reading, do sometimes respond to the structured learning situation where consonant blending and word building are concentrated upon with little regard for content and meaning. The added sense of sound does help many children, and often the newness of the approach provides an incentive for learning.

Some children have great difficulty in producing written work to satisfy teachers. Handwriting may be untidy, and spelling an unknown art. To be able to read their written work, which maybe only they can interpret, on to a tape and produce a satisfactory result, is a mark of success. It's only a shame that there isn't a similar method by which these children could produce the diagrams necessary for science or geography answers.

Instead of writing, children can record talks. Earlier this year my first year both gave and recorded talks, and the tapes and recorders were available for parents to listen to when they came to a first-year parents' coffee evening in the house in October. No longer 'Did you see my picture or read my story on the wall?' but 'Have you heard my tape?'

The fact that the cassette recorder is portable makes it very useful for children finding facts or asking questions from many people. Reminiscences of childhood by grandparents, for example, are very good source material for the young enthusiast with a cassette recorder. But all such work must be carefully prepared: questionnaires must be written and adhered to; each child must know what the purpose of the exercise is, what their aims are, and what they hope to achieve. Careful research is necessary by the teacher on any such project. It's no good just arming pupils with a tape-recorder and telling them to ask questions.

The practicalities of using a tape-recorder sometimes present difficulties. Batteries have become very expensive, and mains electricity is not always available. Where at Whitley is there a quiet room free from interruptions? I find that I have to record late at night after the television is over in a back room away from traffic noise; and when children record at school there is nearly always background noise.

When children are using tapes, I prefer the C30 cassette as I find that the risk of the tape unravelling increases with the length of the tape. Also there is less time wasted winding and unwinding, and finding the place. When children are listening to tapes, I use tape players whenever possible, as there is less chance of the tape being misused or wiped off.

Children today are becoming very familiar with these gadgets. They experience no difficulty in the mechanics, but they use them as toys in order to pirate *Top of the Pops*; to make up and record their own entertainment; to collect their own somewhat dubious jokes. If the cassette recorder is to continue to be used profitably in school, we must make sure its use is monitored, and that our tool is not going to be regarded as their toy.

Interviewing
Transcripts of tapes from a history field trip
1 Two girls interviewing passers-by. They have a sheet of prepared questions. There's the noise of heavy traffic in the background.

Q. Were you born in the village?
A. I was.
Q. How long have you lived here?
A. Now you want to know how old I am, don't you?
Q. (laughing) No . . . it's just work.
A. 56 years.
Q. Have you any grown up children?
A. Yes.
Q. Do they live in the village?
A. Two.
Q. Do you like living in the village?
A. Yes.
Q. Do you think the village has changed since you were born?
A. It has.
Q. Do you think it's better or worse?
A. Worse.
Q. Where do you or your husband work?
A. I don't work. My husband works at Ryton.
Q. How long does it take him to get to work?
A. About twenty minutes.
Q. How does he travel to work?
A. Car.
Q. Are there many new people in the village?
A. Oh yes, lots.
Q. Is there much contact between those who have been here a long time and the new people?
A. No.

2 The same two girls with the same questions. This time they call at a house and an old lady answers. She sounds kindly

but eccentric; speaks rapidly, often peremptorily, occasionally breaking into a girlish laugh.

Q. Were you born in the village?
A. Eh?
Q. (louder) Were you born in the village?
A. Yes.
Q. Have you any grown up children?
A. You'd better come in ... too cold ...
Q. ... Any grown up children?
A. Go on, sit down.
Q. Have you any grown up children?
A. Beg pardon? No no no, I'm an unmarried woman. I had other responsibilities that I stood up to and I performed them, and my conscience is clear, and I've no regrets. If I had my time over again I should do exactly the same. Any other questions about the village?
Q. Do you like living in the village?
A. Of course I do, I was born in it!
Q. Why?
A. Well ... I think it's like most village communities. There are good and bad everywhere, isn't there?
Q. Do you think the village has changed?
A. Eh?
Q. Do you think the village has changed much since you came here?
A. Oh, of course, yes. It's re-inhabited itself. (The clock chimes.) When I stand at my window and six people go by, there's five I don't know. There's few of we old Brinklow inhabitants left. Not above twenty or thirty. But at the same time change is bound to happen. Change and decay, the hymn says, is all around us every ... I don't think we've decayed, I think we've got on. Go on.
Q. Where ...
A. I'm a born pessimist.
Q. Where do you or your husband work?
A. Well I ... er ... well ... look, we occupied an old thatched house down the village 400 years old and Mrs Hazel Parkes, the newspaper proprietor, had another one built but it was burnt in ... er ... um ... bonfire night 1970, and was in (words indecipherable) in lodgings till '76. Then I came up here and I've made myself a new

home and I'm very comfortable. And you see my treasures, don't you?

Q. Yes.

A. I've got 500, 400, 500 books. I'm very bookish and they're wonderful company. Now carry on, because I want to carry on.

Q. Are there many new people living in the village?

A. Are there . . . ?

Q. Many new people . . .

A. They're all new people!

The interview continues: the old lady talks about the early days of cycling and the cycle trade; quotes Isaac Watts; lectures on enclosures. At one point she exclaims, 'I don't suppose you do any history nowadays, they don't teach you anything'.

3 Two second-year girls interviewing a woman in her home at Baginton. This is an extract from a long tape. There are several things that the transcript can't convey: the many murmurs of agreement and understanding from the girls; the relaxed pauses and moments of silence; the way the girls ask their prepared questions in a conversational way.

Q. Do you like . . . er . . . living in Baginton or would you rather live in a . . . large town?

A. Oh, I wouldn't want in a town now . . . I wouldn't want to live in a town.

Q. No.

A. No . . .

Q. Mmm.

A. I like to go into town to do the shopping.

Q. (softly) Yes.

A. You know, because you get a good variety, you see, but . . . the village shops are very convenient.

Q. Yes.

A. And they stock lots and lots of varieties of things . . .

Q. They're very good, yes.

A. . . . that you'd never think were in the shop until you went in it.

Q. Yes.

A. But . . . er . . . (laughs) of course, in the town you come across other people, you meet people you know, and it's more or less a little outing as well you see. (A pause)

Q. Is there . . . any particular reason . . . you like living in the area . . .

A. Particular reason?

Q. Mmm.

A. What in this . . . now?

Q. Mmm.

A. Well I'm really close to everyone I know through all the years, you see, and I'm acquainted with it. It's easy for me to get on a bus and go another connection if I want to visit friends, you know . . . although I've quite a few friends who'll take me, you know, for a ride in the car.

Q. Yes . . . (pause) . . . Is there anybody living somewhere else, you know, who can come and contact you . . . (tailing off)

A. What, my family? Yes. Oh I've got a daughter who lives in . . . er . . . the other side of the playing fields . . . and I've got a granddaughter and she's nearly sixteen. (pause)

Q. So . . . Baginton's quite a nice place for you then?

A. Yes . . . and of course they've got a nice playing field there, and there's a lot of children come from the town there in the holidays . . .
(She goes on to tell a story of a woman she saw with eight children getting off the bus, talks about the fort and moves on to the view from the back of her house.)

A. . . . I can look right over Coventry, and on a clear day I can look all through to Radford and Keresley . . . so you see what a beautiful view I have.

Q. The aeroplanes, you know, disturb you?

A. No, I . . . I don't hear much of the aeroplanes, and the airfield is just the other side of the fence, but I don't hear much of them.

Q. I bet you get a good view when it's the air show . . .?

A. Well I expect there will be because there's going to be a big one this year.

4. This is part of a half-hour tape made by two second-year boys. It's an investigation into two local ghost stories, and at times it has the quality of a good radio programme. The tape begins with a call on Mrs Claridge, who tells them to come back later. The boys then call on the vicar, via his housekeeper, and question him about the ghosts. Then they move on to Mrs Flowers, who tells them in intriguing detail the

story of the ghost she saw in the church. They question her, obviously interested in her story, but wanting more evidence. Then they return to Mrs Claridge. The tape-recorder is switched on as they knock at the door.

C. Right, will you come in. Last one close the door.
(Sounds of everyone coming in and getting settled.)
Now then before we start I just want to know what you want . . . you know . . .
1 Well we want to know if . . . about . . .
C. Are you all right there, because there's another chair there if you'd like to bring it over . . . Close the door and then you won't feel the draught.
1 You see we really want to know about the ghost you saw.
C. Just the ghost?
2 The story about it.
C. I see, from the beginning like. It isn't a very long one anyway. Are you starting?
2 Yes it's on.

(She then tells her story, very well! Many years ago, one September in the 1920s, she was walking along School Street on her way to fetch some milk. It was misty, and she saw a monk in a hood. There used to be a priory in the village. There's an appreciative pause at the end of the tale.)

1 What made you feel, you know, think it was a ghost?
C. Well, I saw it! But there was no footsteps, there was no . . . I couldn't hear anything, but I only saw this . . . this . . . the image of this. It had got a hood on, you know, like a monk's hood. And when I stood still . . . when I stopped that stopped, and . . . er . . . well now, how close would I be to it? About as close as you are.
2 Do you believe the story about the other lady . . . seeing the woman ghost?
C. That was the woman in the church wasn't it?
2 Yes, in the church.
C. Yes yes.
1 Could you describe the monk, what he was like, you know, what he was wearing, what colour?
C. Well, it was like a dark grey as near as I can tell you, dark grey. It wasn't light, it wasn't white. It wasn't a white

apparition, it was a dark grey, and it ... er ... shone up in the mist like, you know ... the mist ... as it came towards me it got clearer, you see. But what would have happened if I'd still kept going I don't know.

2 Could it have been blue?

C. Blue?

2 Dark blue.

C. Well, it could have been, either dark blue or dark grey, but it was a dark colour, definitely a dark colour.

1 Did you see his face? You know, what kind of face did he ...

C. No, I didn't, I couldn't ... it had got this hood on, you see, it had this hood ... monk's cloak ... it had a cloak with a hood on. No I didn't see the face.

1 About how tall was he?

C. Pardon?

1 How tall?

C. Well, I should say a bit taller than I am, and I'm not tall am I? But I think it was a bit taller than me, I should say a bit taller ... but it's as clear to me today as it was all those years ago, and that was in 19 ... early 1920s.

1 And you're quite positive you saw it?

C. I'm quite positive, yes, positive. And what convinced me, you see, was when this lady ... next morning ... told me that her grandfather used to see it ... that was in the same vicinity, you see, by the priory. He seen the same monk going to work only on misty mornings when it was getting light ... and this was ... this was dusk. It was dusk, you see, but there was a thick ground mist ... yes ...

1 Have you ever saw it again?

C. Never seen it again no.

2 Have you see any other ghost?

C. No I've never seen any others, no.

2 Did you believe in ghosts before ... before ...

C. No I didn't ... I didn't ... I didn't, and they tried to kid me that it was somebody dressed up as a monk but I shall never believe it was.

1 How long have you been living in Wolston now?

(The talk then moves on how Mrs C. came from London in 1911, when the Bluemel umbrella factory changed over to cycle accessories. There's talk of the past; what school used to be like; no electricity, water pumps, the old well.)

Talking about a poem

This is a transcript of a tape made by three fourth-year girls taking CSE English. In the previous lesson, the whole class had heard the poem, and the teacher had suggested various ways of getting to grips with the poem in preparation for a piece of writing. The girls decided to begin by talking about it in their group, and spent twenty minutes talking on their own in the corner of the house room.

The girls are Sally, Lynne and Lorna from Warwick House, and, if you know Sally, you won't be surprised to hear that she's the one who takes the lead. She begins by reading the poem aloud. (She reads it twice, because the first reading is interrupted. The girls are recording on Hood landing, and there are several interruptions from passers-by; but these are left out of the transcript.)

The Trap

The first night that the monster lurched
Out of the forest on all fours,
He saw its shadow in his dream
Circle the house, as though it searched
For one it loved or hated. Claws
On gravel and a rabbit's scream
Ripped the fabric of his dream.

Waking between dark and dawn
And sodden sheets, his reason quelled
The shadow and the nightmare sound.
The second night it crossed the lawn
A brute voice in the darkness yelled.
He struggled up, woke raving, found
His wall-flowers trampled to the ground.

When rook-wings beckoned the shadows back
He took his rifle down, and stood
All night against the leaded glass.
The moon ticked round. He saw the black

98

Elm-skeletons in the doomsday wood,
The sailing and the failing stars
And red coals dropping between bars.

The third night such a putrid breath
Fouled, flared his nostrils, that he turned,
Turned, but could not lift, his head.
A coverlet as thick as death
Oppressed him: he crawled out: discerned
Across the door his watchdog, dead.
'Build a trap,' the neighbours said.

All that day he built his trap
With metal jaws and a spring as thick
As the neck of a man. One touch
Triggered the hanging teeth: jump, snap,
And lightning guillotined the stick
Thrust in its throat. With gun and torch
He set his engine in the porch.

The fourth night in their beds appalled
His neighbours heard the hunting roar
Mount, mount to an exultant shriek.
At daybreak timidly they called
His name, climbed through the splintered door,
And found him sprawling in the wreck,
Naked, with a severed neck.

Jon Stallworthy

Sally reads the poem well, a bit melodramatically, and delivers
the last lines with relish. The group has already decided during
its previous talk to approach the poem by going over what
happens on each of the four nights, and they've already come to
some conclusions. They want to use the tape to put on record
what they think they have already decided.

Sally   What do you think Lorna? Lynne?
Lynne The first night, it was a dream, and he got woken up
        by it, and he thought it really was true, and it was
        true to a . . .
Sally   A certain extent, yeh . . .

Lynne But . . . er . . . I think it was something like a little
       wolf, and then he . . .
Sally His imagination . . .
Lynne His imagination ran away with him, and he slept on
       it, and come up with a monster.
Sally Yeah . . . Now, that's the first night. The second night
       it crossed the lawn (and she quickly quotes the rest of
       the second verse).
Lynne That was the wolf.
Sally Yeh . . . that's . . .
Lynne Yeh, that's the wolf.
Sally Yeah.

They've begun by putting forward together the idea which they
have previously formed: that there is no monster, but that there
is a creature of some kind which becomes a monster in the
man's imagination. But a doubt seems to creep in here: perhaps
their idea of the wolf conflicts with the lines that Sally actually
reads out 'A brute voice in the darkness yelled'. Sally turns to
Lorna, who's been keeping quiet.

Sally . . . What do you think Lorna? . . . Don't be scared.
Lorna I'm not scared. As I say I just don't like it.
Sally Yes . . . well . . . that's . . . that's happening, and he's
       waking up to find it's happening. 'When rook wings
       beckoned the shadows back' . . . yeah . . . er . . .
Lynne He stood there trying to catch the . . .
Sally Yeh, with his rifle against the glass . . .
Lynne Yes.
Sally . . . I don't know what that elm-skeleton is there . . .
Lynne No, nor do I . . .
Sally (mutters quickly the rest of the verse)
Lynne Yeh, I think that's kind of like flickers and things
       going round in the wood.
Sally Yeah, it's getting all hazy 'cause he's staying there so
       long . . .
Lynne Yeh . . . it's kind of like his imagination playing tricks
       on him again so that he's . . . gone a bit funny again.
Sally Yeh.

Lynne seems to misread the line 'And red coals dropping

between bars', and Sally brings in the idea of 'it's getting all hazy', perhaps misunderstanding the word 'leaded'. But they continue to make constant reference to the text, in a way that probably wouldn't come as easily if they had been writing; and they use the text to support their idea of the man's play of imagination. They're still supporting each other (No, nor do I); and Lorna, although not saying anything, is listening.

Sally ... the third night. 'Such a putrid breath ... ' (and quotes the next few lines quickly)
Lynne Well, that's if he lives near the woods and I think it's musty? woody smell of ... kind of like ... woods coming up.
Sally Yes, well, I think that's ... er ... the monster, well the fox, you know ... er ... made an atmosphere as thick, you know, coverlet, a horrible atmosphere ...
Lynne Yeah, but a fox couldn't do that ...
Sally Well, I dunno ... it's just imagination. He's thinking this, you see ... oh, I think this ... and he's making the atmosphere of a dog. While he's doing this, it amuses the man, you know, keeps him busy while he goes and kills his dog. That's what I think it is.
Lynne Mmmm.

What Sally is saying now is not so easy to follow as her words earlier in the tape: she's thinking aloud, working it out as she goes. They must now be talking about something which didn't crop up in their previous talk in the house room. The problem is the 'putrid smell'. Lynne wants to believe that there really is some kind of smell, and she thinks it's the kind of smell that she knows you get in a damp musty wood (especially in the early morning). Sally also thinks that there's a real smell, but she thinks it's caused by the 'fox'. Lynne, for the first time, disagrees — 'But a fox couldn't do that' — and Sally senses that she's right to do so. She changes tack, and argues that the smell is another part of the man's imagination. A new idea is beginning to form, but her meaning isn't clear: is she using 'he' to refer both to the man and the 'monster'? or is she suggesting the notion that the man kills his own dog — that the monster is the man himself? Whatever she means, Lynne isn't convinced. She gives a doubtful 'Mmmm', Lorna says nothing, and Sally quickly moves on.

Sally   What about the fourth night? They all tell him to build a trap don't they? So *they* think it's a real monster don't they?

The way she says this implies, 'If they think that, then perhaps we're wrong.'

Lynne   But maybe, you know what neighbours are like, you know, they hear something and they go 'Hahaha, oh go build a trap', you know, like that . . . give you a bit of a laugh . . . they think he's barmy or something.
Lorna   Think he's barmy or something.
Sally   Yeah. (and she laughs)

Lynne solves the problem of the neighbours: they're not really being serious in their advice. This amuses Sally, and seems to satisfy Lorna by the way she repeats Lynne's words.

Sally   'All that day . . . ' So he spent all day building a trap that's really massive and it's got claws and everything. It's a really good one and one . . . one . . . if you just touch it with a feather or something, it will snap and it will break anybody's neck. Now, the fourth night (and she quotes again from the poem). So he's . . . while the thingummybob was catching him he screamed didn't he?
Lynne   Yeah.
Sally   So . . . what do you think Lorna?
Lorna   (quietly) Yeah.
Lynne   Well, that's a bit stupid 'cause how did he get in his own trap? I mean, he must know it's there.

Again, Sally says, 'What do you think Lorna?' but this time her tone is more easy and friendly. Lorna is almost ready to take a more positive part in the talk. Meanwhile, it's Lynne who again poses the problem.

Sally   Well, he's probably forgotten . . . with fear . . . he's, you know . . .
Lynne   Running back to . . .
Lorna   (speaking very quickly) He's probably thinking, he's probably thinking the wolf's running after him and he

Sally	Yeah.

runs into his own trap . . . I think it's a bit like that.

Sally   Yeah.

Lynne   Yeah . . . Not unless . . . running round the back door . . .

Sally   I think he must have chased the wolf out, you know, I dunno, just went out of his imagination in his sleep-walking . . . yeah, yeah, sleepwalking . . . and he comes back into the house and he forgets the trap there.

Lorna   Yeah, he forgets the trap there and he's thinking that the wolf's coming after him and he runs into his own trap and gets his own death and solves it.

Sally   It's probably . . . they found him and he's got no clothes on.

Lorna   I wonder why he's got no clothes on.

Lynne   Well, maybe it's a warm night and he doesn't want clothes on.

Sally   Yeah, in bed, and he's woken up and he's run into the trap . . . Yes, *famous*! (and the tape is turned off)

'Famous!' says Sally — we've cracked it! They haven't, of course. They've raised more questions than they've answered, and they are not so much in agreement as they think. For example, both Sally and Lynne seem to agree with Lorna's explanation; but Lynne seems to have another idea in the back of her mind, and Sally brings in the alternative explanation of 'sleepwalking'. Lorna feels she has to restate her idea, and glosses over what is really a difference of opinion. The three of them are only prepared to go so far in their disagreement.

This was the first time that these girls had talked about a poem on their own, but they organize themselves well, and work easily together. They don't reach a full understanding of the poem, but they do learn that they have ideas of their own about the poem, and that there is more to say about it than they at first thought. By talking together, they raise their own questions, and begin to work out their own approach to a poem. Talking like this enables them, and makes them think in ways that writing, at this stage, would not allow. The questions they ask each other are not the questions the teacher would have thought of setting; but because they're not his questions but theirs the poem is brought more securely into their own experience.

Talk like this is inconclusive and time-consuming; and teachers have to keep in mind the amount of writing that children have to do for their CSE folders. The talk in this transcript is not extraordinary, and it's typical of the talk of which any average CSE candidate is capable. But there are ways in which even typical talk is remarkable, and it's for this that we should value it, and provide time and encouragement for it.

From information to understanding
A review by Ann Cadman

From Information to Understanding is a pamphlet, published by Ward Lock Educational and compiled by the Schools Council project team 'Writing across the Curriculum'. It aims to discover what is actually involved when children learn new ideas; but in this particular pamphlet the emphasis is on the part that talking plays in the learning process.

The method used was to take a number of children working in different school subjects at a point where information has been presented to them, and to record subsequent interviews or conversations related to this information.

It is difficult, without quoting at considerable length, to reproduce here any meaningful part of the conversations, because it is only as a conversation progresses that we recognize that the children are putting their new knowledge to use, exposing and then recognizing their own misconceptions, and finally correcting these — with or without expert help. However, here is a short excerpt from a long conversation between Robert and Terry.

They have been studying a worksheet on the Upper Thames area, and Robert is able to answer in writing questions in the following way:

> Chalk is a very soft limestone ... Limestone is a porous rock and it soaks up water ... The Thames valley was covered in thick forest and so were other places, but in the high hills there was chalk and limestone and the water was drained into low ground, so there were hardly any trees.

This account is reasonably accurate, and when he was questioned Robert was able to give a similar spoken account. We would normally assume at this stage that the boy understood the idea of porosity and move on to something else; but instead the teacher started off a conversation between Robert and Terry which included the following exchange:

Terry If there was a porous rock then lots of birds and that would sit on it to drink and that, and probably do their droppings, so that trees and plants and that would grow there. Instead of soaking right through you get some plants up there.

Robert You wouldn't get any plants up there because the porous rock would soak it through. It wouldn't stay at the top, so birds wouldn't be about, any moisture at all.

Terry Yes, well, some of the water might stay on top.

Robert No, not in porous rocks.

Terry Well how do you think the birds lived?

Robert Well, they would have gone down near the bottom of the hill, you know, or somewhere where the water comes out . . . where the water comes out . . . When it goes down to the bottom it soaks in so you'll find more forests at the bottom of the hill than the top of the hill, 'cause there's more porous rock at the top.

Terry Up to now there's lots of caves where the Stone Age used to live and mainly millions of years ago, these were made by water soaking through the rocks, porous rocks and that, and it made the caves in the stone.

Robert So water would soak through to the . . . er . . . to the, you know, hole, makes a hole in the, you know, soak through there.

Terry And it would come out somewhere and make a stream.

Robert And it would push, push, the water would push a great big gigantic hole in the rock and then stream down to the bottom of the hill.

It is very easy to become impatient with this kind of rambling conversation, and the urge to interrupt and correct is sometimes overwhelming, but just consider for a moment what has been achieved.

Terry has some idea that porous rock can hold water for birds to drink, and in order to challenge this statement Robert is forced to use the knowledge he has gained. He hasn't thought before about the presence or absence of birds, but he deduces from what he knows that there wouldn't be any. Now of course he is wrong, because the idea that all the water sinks through

105

porous rock is an oversimplification, but the important point is that this error has now been revealed and later in the conversation Robert is able to correct it for himself.

Robert goes on to suggest that the birds go to the bottom of the hill for water, but it is clear from the way he talks that he senses problems here, and although his 'There's more porous rock at the top' is not a solution, at least he has recognized a gap in his knowledge and later goes on to fill it.

Similarly, the talk about caves raises the incompatibility between water soaking through the rock and the kind of vigorous action required to make caves, and as in the earlier example, even when the children are unable to resolve these problems for themselves, they are now apparent, and can be corrected by the teacher.

The authors of this pamphlet make the point:

> Information is not taken on like cargo. Nor is it like being given something, as if now you have something where before you had nothing. When information is received it comes up against what is already there, and a process has to occur of marrying the new with the old . . . Often this involves shaking up and reorganizing a whole system of ideas by which we explain the world to ourselves . . .

and it is this process which is revealed in fascinating detail in the transcripts of recorded conversations in this booklet.

The value to the children who took part in this and other similar experiments is obvious, but I think there is a further benefit to the teacher, beyond the insights given into the process of learning. That is, by making talk like this a more regular classroom activity, we could more effectively direct our energies towards correcting misunderstandings and providing new information at the right psychological moment, rather than by relying on more formal methods of assessment — which tend not only to be less revealing, but are also unfortunately outdated by the time we manage to mark their books!

9 Is there room for reading?

Introduction

Earlier this year the Staff Association brought together a group of people to work on aspects of 'language across the curriculum'. Some of us were volunteers, and some of us were invited. We do represent different subjects in the curriculum, but we represent firstly each of the house staffrooms — places where talk between teachers of different subjects most easily occurs.

We decided to begin by collecting evidence about reading, and in our meetings we looked at reading diaries kept for one week by five pupils. The children were simply asked to keep a record for one week of everything they read both in and out of school. In the meetings we tried to read what the children had read during the week, but sometimes we couldn't conveniently collect all the texts. Sometimes, too, the children were not specific enough in their diary entries, though one of us did go through their diaries with them at the end of the week to clear up any doubts and to ask questions about titles, number of pages, and so on.

For the most part, the children enjoyed doing the diaries. In many ways, pupils are as interested in, and as interesting about, language across the curriculum as teachers.

We have looked at just one week's reading of only five pupils, and it's possible that the diaries throw up as many untypical as typical patterns. On the other hand, we did feel as we matched what the diaries told us against our own experience in the classroom that some kind of truthful impression came to light. This seems to be confirmed by what we've read of similar exercises in other schools, and by the findings of the Schools Council Reading across the Curriculum Project.

The reading diaries

The children were asked to keep a record for one week of everything they read, and what they each wrote is typed out here.

The group read the diaries in conjunction with as many of the texts as we could assemble. We hope it will be possible to arrange a display of what the children read to accompany the publication of this document.

1 *Paul*

Paul is in the upper middle band in the second year. These extracts from his English work diary give some idea of one side of his reading:

Today we finished *The Island of the Blue Dolphins,* and for me it was a relief that she had got off the island. I thought the book was over detailed. Every little movement Karana made was logged and spelled out. The bok also lacked much action, and I don't think I would have given it the Newberry Medal.

Other reading I am doing is done mainly at home. I have read Ronnie Barker's first book *It's Goodnight from Him* which is really funny in some places; others are not as good as the first one. This is one sort of thing which is better on television.

. . . I tried reading a book set on a Scottish isle about the time of the Romans. It was called *The Stronghold* by Mollie Hunter but I never finished it. I am now reading *The Midwich Cuckoos* and think it is very interesting. I have read about half of it and I should finish it before the holiday.

Here is his reading diary for the week:

Monday

before school	none
French	oral work
prep period	read geography exercise book to revise for a test
geography	copying from board information about raw materials in industry
English	read my own work and a sheet on King Arthur's death
history	information sheet on knight's armour
night	*Daily Mirror*

Tuesday

before school	nothing
PE	nothing
maths	textbook (various authors from different universities)
art	nothing
science	copied work on limestone off blackboard

108

night	*Daily Mirror* model instructions for Norton 750 commando

Wednesday

before school	nothing
French	copied questions on various things off board to answer them
history	*The Middle Ages* by R.J. Cootes and *This England* by I. Tennan
maths	same textbook by various university people
music	read one song from *Time and Tune book*
night	maths homework — used same book as in lesson that day

Thursday

before school	nothing
registration	read notice about bazaar bulletin *Birds of Prey* a Ladybird book
English	drama
French	worked out of Longman audio-visual Stage 1 by Moore and Antrobus and worked off blackboard
games	nothing
science	copied work on Epsom salts off the board
night	homework French. Read from same book as in lesson

Friday

before school	Top Trump cards
English	nothing
maths	same maths book, *Modern Mathematics for Schools*, by various authors. Copied work off blackboard
metalwork	nothing
geography	nothing
night	(this entry not completed)

2 Dawn

Dawn is in the lower middle band in the second year.

Having finished the diary she made a tape with her teacher in which she talked about herself and her reading. She spends some time reading at home, maybe a couple of hours on a Sunday afternoon if in the mood; she'd get through about fifteen pages of a paperback novel in that time. She visits the public library: she likes to read secretly the picture books in the section for younger children but doesn't like to be seen doing this. She borrows books from the classroom willingly, and reads stories aloud quite fluently though shyly. Recently she's taken small parts in class playreadings.

Here is her diary for the week:

Monday

Morning at home
This morning I sat up in bed and started reading a few pages in my reading book called *The Voyage of the Dawn Treader*. I have read three pages.

Morning registration
When I arrived at school I had my name ticked off the register and got a book off the back because I had forgotten mine and read four pages.

In French
Today in French I am working from a book called *Multiple Choice French*. I read altogether three units which is six pages.

Break
At break I did not read anything but the bulletin.

In PE
We did not read anything. We just done gym.

Dinner time
I did not read anything. I only played Chinese Whispers with my friends.

In English
Today in English I looked through my story and checked it for mistakes.

Break
In break I decided to read a few pages or rather a few posters on a disco, but I will not go to it.

In music
In music today all we done was to do a make-up kind of game. (Ed: this was a wordgame involving names of composers.)

At home
I have not read anything because I did not feel like it.

Tuesday

Morning at home
Got up late so there was no time for reading.

Morning registration
I read a letter for a vaccination of German measles. That is all that I read.

In French
Today in French we did no reading but we did learn a song. We looked and we read a song. (Ed: the song was written on the blackboard.)

Break
At break today I done no reading but I just looked at some pictures in R8 on the wall.

Maths
Today in maths we did not look at any books. We copied off the board.

Dinner time
I did not read any books. Me and my friends played a game instead.

Geography
In geography today we done no reading. We just copied down maps. The book was called *Location and Link (book 3).*

Break
At break today I read two pages of *The Voyage of the Dawn Treader*.

History
In history today we did do some reading. We read a page on Norman armour.

At home
At home I read five pages of *The Voyage of the Dawn Treader*.

Wednesday

Morning at home
This morning I sat up in bed and I read fourteen pages.

Morning registration
This morning I had assembly so there was no reading done.

In French
In French today I read a few sentences and a new book called *Pauvre Xavier*.

In prep
In prep today we done some work out of a book called *Multiple Choice French*. I done one and a half units.

In science
In science we read and worked out of a book but I cannot remember what this book was called. (Ed.: she read one page.)

Dinner time
I did not read anything. I played cards.

In maths
In maths today I read about half of a page about maths.

In geography
I read a very little bit from a book called *Location and Links* and I drew a map. (Ed: this was partly read by the teacher to the class.)

Monday   7th Nov

<u>Morning at home</u>
This morning I sat up in bed and started reading a few pages in my reading book called the voyage of the Dawn Treader. I have read 3 pages

<u>Morning Registration</u>
When I arrived at school I had my name ticked off the register and gota book off the back because I had forgotten mine. And read four pages

<u>In French</u>
Today in French I am working from a book called multiple choice French. In rather a few pages read altogether 3 units which is six pages

dinner time.
I did not read anything I only played chinese whispers with my friends

<u>afternoon Registration</u>
All I read in registration was to read a few names in the registration book.

<u>In English</u>
Today in English I looked through my story and checked it for mistakes.

<u>Break</u>
In Break I decided to read a few pages rather choose French. I read a few posters on a Disco but I will not go to it.

Thursday

Morning at home
This morning I got up late so there was no time for reading.

Morning registration
This morning in registration I just read the Bookworm sheet.

In English
Today in English we read a sheet and on the sheet was lots of titles and I chose one for a story and I read Gloria's story.

Break
I played cards so there was no reading done.

In history
Today in history we done no reading. (Ed: the teacher read briefly to the class before they copied drawings from the board.)

Dinner time
I just played cards with my friends.

In games
In games today I did not read anything. I just played hockey.

Break
I did no reading out of books but I did read a few posters inside the science block about safety in the lab.

In science
In science today I done no reading but I did draw out of a book called *Man and his Environment*.

At home
Today I read eight pages out of my book called *The Voyage of the Dawn Treader*. (Ed: this took her about an hour.)

Friday

Morning at home

This morning I done no reading. I got up late again.

Morning registration/English
We had drama so there was no reading.

In maths
I read a bit of history. I was playing this game with the class. (Ed.: a mystery! It may have been some kind of letter-count.)

In home economics
We done no reading today in home economics.

Dinner time
No reading done at dinner time.

In home economics
No reading again in home economics.

In art
Today in art I done no reading. I just drew a picture.

At home
At home today I read about seven pages from a book called *The Voyage of the Dawn Treader.*

3 *Stephen*
Stephen is in the top band in the second year.
He brought into school all the things he had been reading at home, and we were surprised to see just how demanding some of this was (e.g., the football encyclopaedia). *King Cinder* is a novel in hardback — a birthday present for someone very interested in speedway. He much prefers books of fact and information to fiction, and has only recently begun to be really enthusiastic about stories.
Here is his diary:

Monday

Bulletin	Two Roy of the Rovers comics
Enjoy Music page 34	Rugby team list for Saturday

History Test paper
(Tollund Man brochure)

Coventry Evening Telegraph
Last year's *Coventry and District Angling Association Book*
Two Speedway Star Annuals
1978 Shoot Annual
Hamlyn International Book of Soccer

Tuesday
Bulletin
Modern Mathematics for Schools Book 2
Open Field worksheet: history about an olden village: questions
Locust: Science. Had to read and draw. Nuffield Activity Booklet

5 Roy of the Rovers comics
Hamlyn Book of International Soccer Newspaper
Radio Times and *TV Times*
Angling Times

Wednesday
Rugby team list for Saturday's match v. Bluecoats
Off board. Questions about radius, circumference and diameters

Evening Telegraph, Daily Mirror
Hamlyn Book of International Soccer

Thursday
Bulletin

Had to read some poems out of *Living Language* BBC

French: had to read 9 sentences out of textbook
French: had to read two conversations and a description about a village

Two Roy of the Rovers comics
Newspaper
Five Speedway Star magazines
Six Speedway programmes
King Cinder
Hamlyn Book of International Soccer

Friday
Bulletin
Radius, diameters, circum-

7 Roy of the Rovers comics
Newspaper.

ference questions.
Science: had to read a sheet and then fill in questions and blanks.
Had to read a little about a French town.

Hamlyn Book of International Soccer.

Saturday
Before rugby match:
After match

Roy of the Rovers comic
Mickey Mouse comic
Newspaper
Hamlyn Book of International Soccer
King Cinder
The Hardy Boys

Sunday
Before dinner

After dinner

Newspaper
Roy of the Rovers comic
Mickey Mouse comic
Hamlyn Book of International Soccer
King Cinder

We listened to a tape of Stephen reading: he seemed to have more difficulty with an extract from *The Hardy Boys* than he did with the extract from the maths textbook, which he read with more fluency and sureness of meaning.

On pages 118–25 are reproduced some of what Stephen read in class during the week. There is a history worksheet missing, and pages from his French books; two of the items are reproduced only in part, the Tollund Man pamphlet and the poems.

We read these ourselves, experiencing some difficulty from time to time! We liked the history pamphlet especially, and the BBC pamphlet, though the text that the group felt was most difficult for them to read was the poem.

4 Gillian
Gillian is in the fourth year. She will probably be a CSE candidate in most of her subjects.

She's been issued with three textbooks: she is occasionally

Peter Tchaikovsky RUSSIA 1840-1893

1812 Overture

for full orchestra, military band, bells and cannon

In 1812, Napoleon's army advanced upon Moscow. Rather than suffer defeat by the French, the Russians burned their own city and withdrew. When the French army arrived there was neither food nor shelter. Napoleon was forced to retreat — defeated by the bitter weather rather than by the Russians.

Frozen, starving and exhausted, the French army limped across the snow-covered wastes. Many hundreds of soldiers died on the way. Here is how a survivor described the Retreat from Moscow:

'Whenever we stopped to eat hastily, the horses left behind were bled. The blood was caught in a saucepan, cooked and eaten. But often we were forced to eat it before there was time to cook it . . . The saucepan was carried with us, and each man, as he marched, dipped his hands in and took what he wanted; his face in consequence became smeared with blood . . . Those on foot dragged themselves painfully along, almost all of them having their feet frozen and wrapped in rags or in bits of sheepskin, and all nearly dying of hunger . . .'

68 years later, in 1880, the Cathedral of Christ the Redeemer in Moscow was nearing completion. It was to be consecrated in thanksgiving for the French defeat of 1812, and Tchaikovsky was asked to compose a piece of music for the occasion.

Realising that a rather spectacular work was called for, he composed a lengthy overture for full orchestra, military band, bells and cannon. (An operatic overture, such as *William Tell*, is intended to be played at the beginning of an opera; a concert-overture is a separate piece, usually opening an orchestral concert.)

The music has many contrasting themes: themes which Tchaikovsky may have based upon Cossack songs and folk tunes from the Novgorod region; exciting fanfares; an old Czarist hymn-tune; the French national anthem, the 'Marseillaise'; and the national anthem of Czarist Russia.

In a letter to his friend, Madame Nadezhda von Meck, Tchaikovsky described the overture as 'very noisy, with no great artistic value', having been composed 'without much enthusiasm'. But in spite of the composer's own comments, the *1812 Overture* enjoys great popularity all over the world.

Napoleon watching the burning of Moscow from the Kremlin.

'The Retreat from Moscow' by Meissonier.

34

10

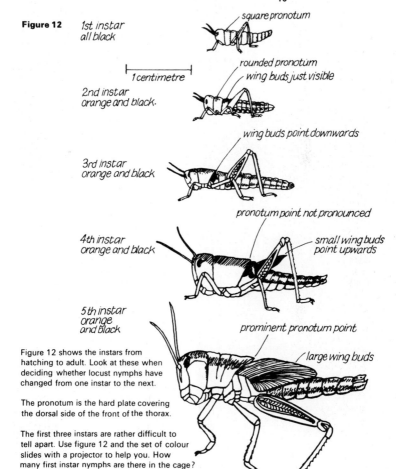

Figure 12

1st instar
all black

square pronotum

1 centimetre

rounded pronotum
wing buds just visible

2nd instar
orange and black.

wing buds point downwards

3rd instar
orange and black

pronotum point not pronounced

4th instar
orange and black

small wing buds
point upwards

5th instar
orange
and black

prominent pronotum point

large wing buds

Figure 12 shows the instars from hatching to adult. Look at these when deciding whether locust nymphs have changed from one instar to the next.

The pronotum is the hard plate covering the dorsal side of the front of the thorax.

The first three instars are rather difficult to tell apart. Use figure 12 and the set of colour slides with a projector to help you. How many first instar nymphs are there in the cage?

119

Often in history, as in detective work, the evidence is incomplete and the historian can never be quite sure that he has drawn the right conclusion. He or she must look at all the evidence that is available and weigh it carefully before deciding about what happened.

Now work as a historian and investigate the "Mystery of Tollund Man".

The first view of his face
Cover: The road to Tollund Fen

Setting the scene

An early Spring day—8th May 1950. Evening was gathering over Tollund Fen in Bjaeldskor Dale in Denmark. The evening stillness was broken now and again by the call of the snipe. Two men were cutting peat for the tile stove and the kitchen range. As they worked they suddenly saw in the peat layer a face so fresh that they could only suppose that they had stumbled on a recent murder. They notified the police at Silkeborg, who came at once to the site. Bit by bit they began to remove the peat from the man's body till more of him became visible. The man lay on his right side just as if he was asleep. He lay 50 metres out from firm ground and had been covered by about 2 metres of peat, now dug away. On his head he wore a pointed skin cap fastened securely under the chin by a hide thong. Round his waist there was a smooth hide belt. Otherwise he was naked. His hair was cropped so short as to be almost entirely hidden by his cap. He was clean-shaven but there was very short stubble on the chin and upper lip.

The air of gentle peace about the man was shattered when a small lump of peat was removed from beside his head. Underneath was a rope, made of two leather thongs twisted together. This was a noose. It was drawn tight around his neck and throat and then coiled like a snake over his shoulder and down across his back.

Who was this man? How long had he lain there beneath the earth? What was the cause of his death?

120

Scientific report
on the body

The body was removed from the bog and examined by doctors and scientists. They came to the following conclusions:

1 Date of burial
Underneath the body was a thin layer of moss. Scientists know that this was formed in Danish peat bogs in the early Iron Age, about the time when Christ was born. The body must, therefore, have been put in a hole in the peat roughly *2000* years ago in the Early Iron Age. The acid in the peat prevented the body decaying—it looked as if it had been recently buried.

2 Cause of death
Examinations and X-rays showed that the man's head was undamaged, and his heart, lungs and liver were also well preserved. He was not an old man though he must have been over 20 years old because his wisdom teeth had grown. He had therefore probably been killed by the rope round his neck. This noose had left clear marks on the skin under the chin and at the sides of his neck but there was no mark at the back of the neck where the knot was. It was impossible to tell if his neck had been broken because the bones were very crumbly.

3 His last meal
The stomach and intestines were examined and tests were carried out on their contents. The scientists discovered that the man's last meal had been a kind of soup made from vegetables and seeds, some cultivated and some wild, such as barley, linseed, "gold of pleasure", knotweed, bristlegrass and camomile.
There were no traces of meat and from the stage of digestion it was obvious that the man had lived for 12–24 hours after this meal. In other words he had not eaten for a day before his death. Although such a vegetable soup was not unusual for people of this time, two interesting things were noted:
a) the soup contained many different kinds of wild and cultivated seeds and some of them must have been gathered deliberately, because they were not always easy to find. The soup was, therefore, probably for a a special occasion.
b) the soup was made up from seeds which were connected *only with the spring*.

Acknowledgements
The authors and publishers are grateful to the following for permission to reproduce copyright material:
The Danish National Museum, photographs of Tollund Man; Earth goddess; Forhistorisk Museum, Moesgard, Denmark, photograph of Grauballe Man; Professor P. V Glob, Director, Danish National Museum, photograph of the sunken road and the Torc.

ISBN 0 7157 1572-0

© Schools Council Publications 1976

HOLMES McDOUGALL   EDINBURGH

Printed in Great Britain by Holmes McDougall Ltd.

b Use "Area of triangle = ½ base × altitude" to calculate the area of △ABC.

c Repeat *a* and *b* for triangles PQR and EFG in Figure 37.

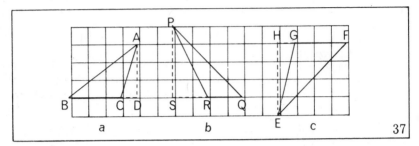

37

6 By drawing the surrounding rectangle for triangle ABC in Figure 37*a* can you explain why the formula '△ = ½*bh*' is true for this obtuse-angled triangle?

---

9 The construction of triangles

In this section we are going to examine just what information must be given in order to be able to construct a required triangle.

Suppose the teacher has a cardboard triangle ABC. You are to consider how to make an accurate drawing of it. You can ask the teacher for the length of any side you like, and the size of any angle you like; but you can ask for only one piece of information at a time, and you are to stop asking when you have enough information to finish the drawing satisfactorily.

Sometimes the teacher may be awkward and refuse to give you what you want, perhaps offering you something else. Take it if it will do, refuse it if it will not.

The object is to decide *how much* information is necessary; and whether, for example, if three items suffice, any three items will do.

This question is often important in practice: for example a map-maker wants to get an accurate map without the expense of making unnecessary measurements; an engineer building a structure involving triangles must specify clearly the shape and size of the triangles; a draughtsman in his drawings must include enough information about lengths and angles to enable the fitter to make the component the drawing depicts, and since every straight-sided shape can be built up from triangles, if we master the art of 'specifying' the data required for a triangle, we shall be able to cope with all other figures.

Exercise 9

1　Draw a line AB 7 cm long. Using your compasses, take centre A and radius 5 cm, and draw an arc above AB. With centre B and radius 4 cm, draw an arc above AB to cut the first one at C. Join AC and BC to obtain triangle ABC.

2　Starting with AB 7 cm long in each case, try to draw a triangle for each of the following:

First radius (centre A)	5 cm	5 cm	5 cm
Second radius (centre B)	3 cm	2 cm	1 cm

3　How can you tell by looking at the lengths of the three lines whether or not a triangle can be drawn?

*　　*　　*　　*　　*

4　Draw a line AB 6 cm long. At A, draw $\angle$BAX = 60°, with AX as long as possible. On AX mark C so that AC = 3 cm, D so that AD = 4 cm, E so that AE = 5 cm, F so that AF = 6 cm. Join BC, BD, BE, BF.

5　Given '2 sides and the included angle' as in question 4, can you draw a triangle in every case?

*　　*　　*　　*　　*

6　Draw a line AB 6 cm long. At A, draw $\angle$BAX = 30°, with AX as long as possible. At B, draw $\angle$ABC = 70°, $\angle$ABD = 90°, $\angle$ABE = 110°, $\angle$ABF = 130°, $\angle$ABG = 150°, $\angle$ABH = 170°, with C, D, E, ... on AX where possible.

7　Given '2 angles and a side', when is it possible to draw a triangle?

*　　*　　*　　*　　*

8　Draw a triangle with angles of 50°, 60° and 70°. Now draw another triangle inside the first with angles of 50°, 60° and 70°. How many such triangles do you think you could draw?

One evening in the bay of Lipari
on rocks that look over the harbour
    water
a man sits with his chin stuck into his
    shoulder
fishing for rainbow fish
with a long green rod and line.

Crouching in the pools behind him
we collect the rainbows in a beer
    crate
watching on that line.
The float dips. The man doesn't
    move.
We flick water across the fish to keep
    them fresh,
the sun still stands against the tower
and its shadow falls across the water.

Then the rod whips, up flies the
    float —
but nothing more. Thirteen
    rainbows, it stays.
We watch him roll a roll of bread in
    his mouth
to bait his hook again
and we duck
as past our ears go bread, hook and
    float
all on the end of that long rod and
    line.

Thirteen rainbows out of the sea.
It can't be bad. Fourteen would be
    better.
More fish: more soup. There's five
    middling,
five tiddlers and three whoppers.
Or if you stack them up the other
    way
three whoppers, five middling, five
    tiddlers.
We have a line too, because under
    these rocks
live moray eels.

Yards and yards of eel, writhing
    about
just where the round the edge

where the over the through the under
where there here, where we lower
    our hook
with a lump of raw rainbow dangling.

No sooner said
when yes he's slid out
and taken the bait. He's got it.
We've got it. He takes the bait
he takes the hook. He takes the hook
he takes the line — he'll have your
    fingers too.

Let go pull him
he pulls, pull him, I said. The line
    breaks,
and without a turn about or round
    about
he's in reverse and slides back along
    his tracks
to where it is his tracks back track
    to.

The sun sets behind the tower.
Three whoppers, five middling and
    five or four or five . . .
Four tiddlers —
Can't be bad.

The man's float still rises and falls.
He knows there's more where they
    came from.
He can feel them nibbling down
    there.
You can almost see them cruising
in a complete quiet
in the last rays of the day
the line dropping out of the light
    above
down to where they nudge about
    very cool
gliding round this right little chunk
of sweet nibble lump thing
that breaks off crumbs in the current
if you can bear to wait
if they can wait
we wait
one can't.
The whole lump he takes. The lot.

And up, up out of the quiet
into the sky like a silver bird
wey op wey op wey op
he's on the line
his last moment is a ride in the sky
wild, he flies on air with his fins
he must fall
and down he swings
once fast past the man's hand
once slap into it.
He holds that fish's wriggle alright
and takes his hook back
flings it to us on the rocks.

There's still life.
There's still heart and blood
the fins still stretch for the water.
He flips so strong
it could carry him to Spain and
    back —
underwater.
Here it turns him over and over
somersaulter
he keeps flipping.
Perhaps he can feel the smell of
    water
only inches away.
He keeps flipping for that water.
He could make it.
If we didn't like fish-soup
he could really make it.

We're on to him,
get our fingers round his belly
slide them down to that flashy tail
and crack his head against the rock.

Crack it again number fourteen
crack it once more and put him
    down.
Lie him down in the old beer crate.
He's middling.
Three whoppers, four tiddlers, six
    middlers.
Thirteen. Thirteen? I thought —
The old thirteen is being minced with
    line and hook
in a cold black crack by the moray
    eel
in the rocks somewhere.
Time for us to go.

As we leave, climbing over the rocks
back to the road,
the man looks out across the harbour
and near across a rubbish tip
where all the pots bottles boxes and
    crates in the world
have come.
He looks up the cliff above the tip
to the hotel that empties and drops
    the pots
and spits.

We'll have soup
so long as we've got fish.
Come on.

*Text from a 20 page illustrated
pamphlet accompanying the BBC
schools radio programme 'Living
Language'.*

125

asked to read a chapter at home in her geography and history books; her biology book she uses mainly in class, but did once look at it outside lessons for her own interest.

She always reads the *Coventry Evening Telegraph*, and reads *Jackie* every week. She occasionally reads a daily newspaper, but her parents don't have one delivered. She also reads her brother's soccer magazines. Most nights she reads in bed for half an hour before going to sleep.

Here is her diary for the week:

(On Monday, Tuesday and Wednesday she was absent from school.)

Monday
1.30	*Jackie* magazine.
4.15	the sheet about this diary
6.15	*Coventry Evening Telegraph*

Tuesday
8.40	Read a letter I got from a pen friend
11.00	Read *Marianne Dreams* for about half an hour — about 3 chapters
1.30	Read some more of the book, about another three chapters
6.00	*Coventry Evening Telegraph*

Wednesday
11.00	Read some more of *Marianne Dreams*
6.00	*Coventry Evening Telegraph*
7.15	*The Sun*

(Then she came back to school for two days before half term.)

Thursday
before school	none
registration	none
English	2 chaps. of *Marianne Dreams*
Games	none
lunch	none
Geography	sheet about nuclear power
Maths	none
HMWK	none

Coventry Evening Telegraph.
A few pages of *Marianne Dreams*

Friday

before school	none
registration	Grove House letter
geography	none
English	none
biology	none
HE	some sheets about nutrition
HMWK	none

Coventry Evening Telegraph
A chapter of *Marianne Dreams*.

(After half term)

Monday

before school	none
registration	none
history	CSE exam paper: questions on the First World War
biology	question sheet about respiration
careers	none
European Studies	answering questions from Spain textbook
HMWK	none

Coventry Evening Telegraph, some magazines, and a bit of a book called *Shake This Town*. This is a good book to read and I am enjoying reading it.

Tuesday

before school	note from pen friend
registration	none
maths	questions from textbook on cosines and tangents
geography	none
English	read work I wrote. Teacher read aloud short story.
history	read from textbook for about ten minutes
HMWK	none

Coventry Evening Telegraph, and a couple of pages of *Shake This Town*.

Wednesday

before school	*The Sun*
registration	none
maths	printed worksheet on cosines etc.
European Studies	continued work from textbook
HE	read a book about meat (O level Cookery, 2 pages)
HE	continued, and then went to another class to see what they had been cooking
HMWK	none.
	Coventry Evening Telegraph
	Read letter I wrote. Read couple of pages from *Shake This Town*.

Thursday

before school	none
registration	none
English	two chapters of *Shake This Town*
games	none
geography	blackboard information about erosion
maths	another worksheet on cosines etc.

5 Mindo

Mindo was in the fifth year, and wrote this in the term before taking her O level examinations:

Saturday

No reading at all until 6.00 p.m.

I did my French homework and for this I had to read a passage about two little boys and then I had to answer questions on this passage.

7.45 p.m. Read some geography notes from my own exercise book to help me do my homework — about pressure and wind.

Sunday

11.30 a.m. I started to read *The Farmer's Wife News and Views* paper. I went through all the recipes in it and then read the other miscellaneous pieces. Read for about half an hour.

1.05 p.m. I read some more geography notes from GCE O level passbook — notes on world climate to help me do my homework.

7.00 p.m. Read a few chapters from *Anatomy, Physiology and Hygiene* by J.K. Raeburn for own interest.

Monday

Maths	Read today's bulletin. Answered questions off the board.
French	Read off the board and a few words out of a textbook.
Geography	Read Chap. 14 out of *Human and Economic Geography* by Cain on iron and steel.
Swimming	none
Evening	*Coventry Evening Telegraph* for about ¾ hour. Read history book, a few pages, own interest. Read *A History of Modern Britain* by Peacock and made notes (finishing classwork) pp. 122 and 123.

Tuesday

Biology	Made notes on hygiene etc. from textbook — about 1 page.
English	none
Dinner	Read some notices in Warwick North
History	Read about Ireland and then did notes from the same section.
Maths	Read questions off the board.
Evening	Read two letters from India — one from my uncle and one from a family friend. Read and finished History notes that we were doing in class. Finished geography essay after reading some paragraphs from O level passbook. Finished English essay and read some of *Hobson's Choice* and some bits out of *My Family and other Animals*.

Wednesday

history	Read and made notes.

geography	none
dinner	Read bits of *Hobson's Choice* to prepare for essay.
English	none
biology	Read one paragraph on disinfection and made notes. Then I read off the board and copied the notes that were on it.
Evening	Read my brother's *Look-in* comic.

Thursday

French	Read a French conversation between a doctor, assistant and patient.
English	*My Family and other Animals* — small sections of it.
maths	none
history	Read notes off board.
geography	none
Evening	Read biology passbook for revision.

Friday

careers	none
study P.	none
games	none
registration	Read a letter about the teachers etc. and a bulletin type thing called Way Ahead.
French	Corrected a French translation.
biology	Copied notes off board
Evening	Read *Coventry Evening Telegraph*. Started to read *My Family and other Animals* from the beginning.

Books I have at home from school

English	*Hobson's Choice; My Family and other Animals; Huck Finn; Wilfred Owen poems; Voices 3; Modern Short Stories.*
geography	*The Foundations of Geography 1; Human and Economic Geography; World Geography 5.*
history	*Europe and the Modern World; A History of Modern Britain.*
French	*Audio Visual French* stage A 4; *Le*

Normally, I read much more than I did this week. I usually either buy a book or borrow one from the library and read that, and if it happens to be a very interesting book I usually get it finished within a week at the most. Recently I have been getting so much homework that I just don't have the time to read for my own pleasure. I've also tried to revise by looking through my old fourth year books; but because of the amount of homework, I can't keep to a regular revision time-table. However, sometimes it is my own fault that I don't get time to read because I let all my homework pile up on me.

My mum and dad don't buy the "Coventry Evening Telegraph" everyday because they don't read and I only happen to buy it if I feel like reading it and, that, isn't very often. We don't have a daily paper delivered either or a Sunday one except when one of us wants it. I don't read all the news in the paper: only if it looks interesting, normally I read just the horoscopes; take a little look at the sport and find out what's on television.

I've got loads of books at home; some of them belong to my brothers and sisters. Most of them are novels and storybooks but I also have books such as dictionaries, Geography books, encyclopaedias etc. Recently I have only bought "Geography and Biology 'O' level passbooks," and one that teaches you to type.

biology	*Français Aujourd'hui* 4; *Essential French Vocabulary*
	Life, Form and Function
maths	Log. tables; *Mathematics for Everyday Life.*

Some extracts

On these pages we give a very brief glance at some of the reading Gillian and Mindo have done. We hope books will be on display so that these extracts can be seen in context and within the form and presentation of the particular textbooks.

From *Europe and the Modern World 1870–1970* by J. and G. Stokes: page 120, a paragraph dealing with The Irish Problem.

Economic distress reached its apogee during the famine caused by the potato blight in 1846–48. By 1851 Ireland's population had dropped from over 8 million to 6½ million. Half a million, perhaps more, had died of starvation or typhus or dysentery. The rest had emigrated to the New World. In their new homes rancid memories stirred them to support, financially and by word, nationalists left behind in Ireland. Irish immigrants in the United States, like immigrants of other nationalities, tended to form a block, very interested in what went on 'at home'. This being so, politicians in the United States found it expedient to seek Irish support — much as later Woodrow Wilson was to pay attention to the demands of Czechs in Chicago and elsewhere.

From *Geography of the British Isles* by Graves and White: page 39, the beginning of Chapter 5, The Great Port: Liverpool.

A The Nature of Liverpool's Main Function

The towns we have studied in this book have been examples of settlements in which one *function* tended to give the town its main character. For instance, Edinburgh is dominated by its *administrative function* as the government centre for Scotland, Hexham by its *function* as a market for the surrounding area, Canterbury by its cathedral which attracts many visitors. Such towns are called *central places* in the sense that they tend to be centres performing services for surrounding areas — Liverpool is hardly a town in the centre of an area (see Fig. 1.2), and yet it acts as a *central place*, this time one in which its function as a port tends to distinguish it from other large towns. Table 5.1 and Fig. 5.1 show what has happened to Liverpool's trade in recent years.

From *Voices 3* edited by Summerfield, page 166.

165 At Day-Close in November
    The ten hours' light is abating,
      And a late bird wings across,
    Where the pines like waltzers waiting,
      Give their black heads a toss.

    Beech leaves, that yellow the noon-time,
      Float past like specks in the eye;
    I set every tree in my June time,
      And now they obscure the sky.

    And the children who ramble through there
      Conceive that there never has been
    A time when no tall trees grew here,
      That none will in time be seen.

Thomas Hardy

From *Introduction to Biology* by Mackeson page 102, from the chapter on Breathing. (There are 5 diagrams on the page and these words apart from captions and labels.)

Lungs (Fig. 20.1)
The lungs are two thin-walled, elastic sacs lying in the *thorax*. They can be expanded or compressed by movements of the thorax in such a way that air is repeatedly taken in and expelled. They communicate with the atmosphere through the wind-pipe or *trachea*, which opens into the *pharynx* (Fig. 18.3). In the lungs, a gaseous exchange takes place; some of the atmospheric oxygen is absorbed and carbon dioxide from the blood is released into the lung cavities.
Lung structure. The trachea divides into two *bronchi* which enter the lungs and divide into smaller branches

called *bronchioles* (Fig. 20.2). These divide further and terminate in a mass of little thin-walled pouch-like air sacs or *alveoli* (Figs. 20.3, 20.4 and Plate 23).

(a) AIR PASSAGES. Rings of cartilage keep the trachea and bronchi open and prevent their closing up when the pressure inside them falls during inspiration. The lining of the air passages is covered with numerous *cilia*. These are minute, cytoplasmic hairs which constantly flick to and fro. Mucus is . . .

From an examination paper, AEB, Ordinary Level November 1977, English Language Paper 3 (The 'comprehension').

Read the passage carefully and answer the questions that follow.

One of my earliest memories is that of a small boy sitting in our village street surrounded by a group of grey-whiskered old men. Bored and fidgety, he is reading aloud in fluent sing-song the war news from a tattered newspaper. This boy and I were of one generation and we shared the same trick of enlightenment. We were both the inheritors after centuries of darkness of our country's first literate peasantry. My mother and father read well and were largely self-taught. But their parents could do little more than spell out their names, and if given a book were likely to turn it over in their hands, cough loudly, and lay it aside . . .

. . . From my earliest years I was at home only with those particular classics which approached in style our country speech and the Bible. The three books that continue to stand out are *Pilgrim's Progress*, *Robinson Crusoe*, and *Gulliver's Travels*. I was at the village school when I read these books (having bought the three of them at a rummage sale for a penny). At the school itself there were few books, except things about Cats and Mats, or terse little pamphlets stating that Jill was Ill and Jack had Broken his Back. Those were innocent, monosyllabic days, of which I was the last to complain.

Laurie Lee

The comments of the group

After the fourth meeting of the group, each of us went away and wrote down our thoughts so far. These are reproduced in this section. We realize that some of the time we repeat each other, but we decided that we wanted to preserve the conclusions that each of us came to, and to give the sense of several voices rather than just one.

LAC thoughts

Apart from the general feeling of surprise common to the group as a whole about the small amount of reading done by many pupils, both in school and at home, I have found the meetings rather revealing at a personal level. I am now much more aware of the reading tasks I set my classes, and the need to make them more meaningful.

The use of scientific language in written material presented to the children concerns me. Very often, by misunderstanding one key word, a passage becomes meaningless. One possible solution to this might be the setting up of classroom scientific dictionaries, perhaps as a wall-chart for ready reference and access.

The lack of suitable textbooks within the Science Department, especially in lower school and CSE classes, presents a real problem. There is evidence from the reading diaries that science textbooks can be used just for drawing diagrams, rather than for the text they contain.

Note-taking and making is a problem closely associated with the use of textbooks. Many children find this an almost impossible skill to master and perhaps they need much more help in acquiring proficiency. Too often they are simply told to 'read and make notes'.

Alida Burdett

Language across the curriculum

The points which left thoughts in my own mind were probably:

(i) The alarmingly small amount of reading undertaken by the pupils we sampled. This seemed to decrease as the age of the pupils increased. This worried me and disturbed me. It worried me because without the basic skills partly acquired through reading, and without the desire to find something out by reading, and without the ability, perhaps, to know

135

how to use a book, it seems apparent that as a pupil moves higher up the school, the more we as teachers will inevitably have to supply the information that is required. It disturbed me because, at a personal level, I was previously critical of shortcomings in other people's lessons which I am now aware that I do myself.

I refer pupils to books perhaps without adequate guidance and help; I expect pupils to know how to use a book, and I assume they know how to research a topic. It is a vicious circle. Many of our pupils appear not to read a great deal of anything, certainly not material of quality for most of the time, and so we endeavour to correct this deficiency by giving them material ourselves. Perhaps we do not encourage them to read, or is it that what we do ask them to read is negative, uninspiring, and written in a language that is too specialized?

(ii)   We assume that our pupils understand everything we tell them and show to them. Because we have spoken about a topic in the classroom, perhaps we assume that we have expressed ourselves clearly, concisely and imaginatively. Do they always understand our turns of phrase? How should we decide that our lesson has been understood?

(iii) A number of the textbooks we use in school are colourless, uninteresting to look at, and written in a style which is either boringly full of factual data, such that it is meaningful only to a scholastic pupil, or they employ words and phraseology which would leave almost any pupil puzzled as to the meaning. Sometimes there is a dearth of textbooks. Is a child likely to read or show more interest in a subject because he possesses a textbook to look at, or is he happy to receive an endless succession of carefully duplicated handouts? I do not think we provide sufficient textbooks for children to use and take home, and that our departments, in the main, prefer to build up class sets of books — sets which are usually only used within school. I realize that this situation is dictated by the lack of funds to purchase large numbers of books, and where costs have escalated alarmingly in recent years.

(iv)   We expect a great deal in the way of literary skills and understanding, and yet we make few provisions to acquire these skills. Do we perhaps not assume that a child can read a chapter, or a book, properly? Do we not believe

136

that anyone can make notes? Why are we often frustrated when a pupil merely copies out chunks from a book, word for word as written, or they cannot select material from various parts of a book in order to answer a particular question?

(v) Underlying so much of our efforts within the school situation is the quality of the home background. Many homes will have books, but others will be devoid of books and magazines, devoid of incentives, and lacking interest in their offspring's educational progress. We are in a TV watching age, although this can be a rich source of language and knowledge, but it does so often strike me that a pupil's absorption of a programme is frequently superficial. As an example of what I mean, I wonder how many pupils could indicate the location of Argentina or Zaire on a world map?

(vi) Even though despair and despondency flowed through my system at times, I did also often remind myself that I probably did not read any more than some of our pupils do when I was their age. What expectancy do we have of the children in our charge? Do we not make too many assumptions? I, too, was spoonfed, nor did I know how to make 'proper notes'.

Although there are exceptions, visually the inside of Whitley Abbey is dull. Classrooms lack display material to look at and to read, and certainly it is lacking in those places accessible to pupils in their free time. On the credit side, however, we have a library where so much excellent work is being done by the staff who use it and by the ancillary staff who work there.

David Cleasby

Comments on LAC group
I have found the reading diaries produced by pupils very interesting and enlightening and a valuable part of this enquiry, but I do feel that other aspects of language should be investigated also. Home economics is a subject which allows a lot of verbal contact between teacher and pupil, and I feel that language can be helped greatly by talking and developing ideas orally rather than by the written word. I should be interested to discuss the oral side of language development in the classroom and also

137

have the opportunity of discussing the amount of 'talk' possible during other lessons. The use of tape-recorders could be very helpful in this research, not only to assess the pupils' verbal capacity, but also the relevance of the information passed on by the teacher!

Pat Gandy

Notes on reading diaries

In all of the diaries that we studied, I felt the single most important factor to emerge was the surprisingly sparse reading demands made on the children in school, and the nature of the reading actually done in lesson-time. Much of this, although linked to the current topic, was not read in the sequential way, but as an isolated page, passage or blackboard notes. As this was invariably 'fed' to children, I wonder how valuable it is, either in teaching the child to read selectively for himself, or in encouraging him to wonder what came before, or comes afterwards. Following on from this, I wonder how many children, whose reading is not reinforced at home, ever really see books and reading as something which they can control and develop themselves; how many, in fact, who once school stops 'feeding' them in this way, ever read constructively again!

On the other hand, something which struck me about several of the diaries was that some children seem to have a positive hunger for reading, which is sometimes being satisfied, and sometimes not. The top band boy, for instance, read compulsively about topics which interested him — most of his reading was very factual, and even the comics and stories pertained to factual interests — Speedway magazines and comics, for example. From his list, it seems obvious that literature is freely available at home. The lower middle band girl, however, although from her diary a compulsive reader of posters and notices, seemed to have no such abundance of reading matter at home. She compiled a very detailed list, and this in itself struck me as interesting. Apart from her library book, she too seemed to have few reading demands made upon her in school. She was said to be a willing reader, and enjoyed 'younger' books. I wonder if she was being offered enough interesting, but easier, material to satisfy her own desire to read, and which would counteract any tendency to feel that 'reading' is difficult. I wonder if there are assumptions made about lower band children; they do not achieve with the sometimes difficult reading matter given to them, therefore reading is 'too hard' for these children. Perhaps if there was more reading in school, of a more suitable nature, such children's willingness to read could be channelled more constructively. The upper middle band boy also seemed to read very little in school, although he read a textbook for homework, and model-making instructions. His reading seemed largely to be linked to a purpose – in that case, should the 'purpose' not be created more frequently in school?

In addition to this, I noticed the following points, some of which are questions which occurred to me.

1 Children *do* read notices – this seems to be an obvious opportunity in school – if the notices are interesting and changed frequently. (Also newspapers, magazines etc.)
2 School must compensate for any lack of reading at home by actively bringing reading to children's attention, not just by providing a library.
3 Is copying notes off a blackboard quite the same as reading a chapter, then making notes? Bearing in mind the difficulty some children find with this, and also the volume of facts needed in some subjects, shouldn't we give more help to children in the lower school in their note-taking and make them more aware of the techniques as the need arises naturally in project work and other situations – some of which we might deliberately devise for that purpose?

Diane Lindsay

LAC notes

The amount of reading the children do, both in school and at home, is considerably less that I would have expected. There is a wide variety of reading, but it appears only in short extracts.

e.g. 'read *some* Geography notes'
'read *a few* chapters'
'read *one paragraph* on disinfection'

We often issue books to the children and expect them to read passages, and 'understand' what they have read; perhaps with not enough forethought on whether certain words, which *we* may use regularly, will mean very much to the children.

We have seen a variety of ways of presenting work in a reading form, and I feel that we often place more emphasis on the actual subject matter contained in the passages, than in how interesting the work is to the children, both in how it looks and how it reads.

> e.g. I found the folding history leaflet much more interest-
> ing and more involving than pages x to y in a 200 page
> book.

Is it another of our faults that we refrain from supplying reading matter of any kind in certain lessons because the teaching and learning process will take too long?

> e.g. making notes from a book — another assumption in
> itself?

Ken Russell

Some thoughts on LAC

1 The amount of reading carried out generally by children in the school is surprisingly small. This is true of children of all abilities and of all ages. From looking at the children's reading diaries it would appear that the children are not encouraged to use books or information sheets themselves (one wonders if there is possibly an overemphasis placed on 'talk and chalk' in the classroom) or to carry out research on their own. Are we perhaps spoon-feeding our pupils too much?

   This becomes worrying when we consider that in many cases school should be compensating for a lack of suitable reading material in the home. Certainly the establishment of class libraries could go towards helping the children in their reading.

2 Much of the reading material that the children are presented with is usually boring. All too often a child can reject reading material because it does not 'appear interesting'. This is true of information sheets as well as a page of the textbook.

3 How many children know how to use a textbook? It is far easier to ask the teacher where a particular piece of information is than to use an index. Suddenly in the fourth and fifth years children are expected to be able to research information on their own and transform that information into a readable narrative in their exercise books. How often does 'Make notes on the Franco-Prussian War' become a copy of the information in the textbook? Children are not helped to acquire the skills that they need.

4 Textbooks themselves must come under close scrutiny. How suitable are many of the books used in the school? Many subjects that make up the curriculum have developed a

specialized language of their own but all too often we seem unaware of this. Several passages that the group read appeared difficult to us yet we expect 14—16-year-old adolescents to be fully conversant with the specialized language of seven subjects. The children may be able to read the textbooks but do they understand what they are reading?

5 I feel that this should lead us to re-assess the examination courses that are offered in the school. Since the raising of the school leaving age far more children than ever before are taking examinations but I wonder what efforts have been made by examination boards and teachers to accommodate these children? Do we just push these children into CSE examinations hoping that they will obtain a grade 4 or 5 when the examinations do not really cater for the needs of these children?

Barry Spring

Some thoughts on reading

I have made the following observations from the evidence collected from pupils of various ages and abilities.

1 The amount of reading done in class and at home is minimal and in some cases is non-existent.

2 From these diaries, it seems pupils below the top band classes read very little for enjoyment.

3 The reading material given to some pupils is beyond their reading age and understanding.

4 Frequently, the reading done seems only to be a reinforcement of the material already taught by the teacher.

5 The format of reading material is often unappealing, e.g. The 'Tollund Man' pamphlet ensures immediate interest in history, whereas many history textbooks fail to inspire.

6 Occasionally, books may be used in class as the lesson itself where the class is at the mercy of the set of textbooks. This will be ineffective in an unstreamed first-year class and may be unsuccessful in a broadly banded class. The lower ability child will doubtless be lost, whilst the higher ability child will fail to be stretched. Books in this situation should be used as information books only.

Suggestions on improvement of reading (purpose)
1 It would be helpful if departments were to examine their reading material by Cloze procedure or Fog index to estab-

lish its true reading age and readability. Publishers' propaganda may often be inaccurate.

2 Regular interchange of book information between teachers in departments should be possible.

3 Departments should build up resources of small topic books and textbooks for pupils' own research as outlined in the article 'What is a horse?' (*School Librarian*). The school loan library can help with this as loans are available on a termly basis. Information book collections can promote reading for enjoyment.

4 Reading is increasingly used in the upper school for the purpose of making notes. There is a need for the teaching of note-making as this presents difficulties.

5 Subjects in school seem each to have a language of their own. Each subject requires a new kind of literacy. As adults we often find it difficult to read new kinds of printed materials, so we must appreciate how much more difficult it must be for children. We found in the group difficulty in reading texts brought by other subject teachers.

June Whiting

Conclusions and resolutions

We've found ourselves asking, 'How often do children read in my lessons?' and, 'How long do they read for? How much at a time?' and 'What sort of material am I asking them to read, and what sort of sense are they making of it?'

We'd say we feel guilty about the answers to that, though we think we're probably in good company?

We now say definitely that there must be many more chances and occasions for children to read in our lessons, and in our homeworks, and in our tutor periods; and we should read to them more often, too.

Other questions cropped up:

How often do I let children find something for themselves in a book, and help and encourage them in this? What's the alternative to saying, 'Turn to page . . .'?

How often do children get the chance to browse through a book in my lessons, and how often do they borrow a book from me?

How often does a child go to a library in connection with my work?

How often do children read, or hear me reading, really

interesting material in connection with their work?

We think that if these things aren't happening then what we recognize as real reading isn't happening either.

Are textbooks real books? We've looked at quite a number: some are very good but there are lots we'd much sooner not use. We imagine there are many of us who are unhappy with the books we're using: how do we manage, and what kinds of help with the text do we give children?

We think there's a lot of scope for teachers to write core material themselves for their own children; and from our experience of looking at each other's books and sheets we think that a teacher of another subject can often help us to see difficulties in a text that we wouldn't have noticed.

We think, too, that more money should be spent on setting up classroom collections in all subjects of 'real books': both in the form of class libraries for browsing in and borrowing from, and as collections in support of core texts for particular topics and units of work.

We've noticed children reading a lot around the school: posters, bulletins, magazines, displays, letters, timetables, charts, and so on. We think there could be much more up on the walls in rooms and houses; and that tutors could make good use of much of the printed material (bulletins, newsletters, information sheets, forms, letters to parents, appeals, newspapers, comics) that comes to the classroom every day.

Much of this material provides a kind of reading that doesn't crop up in the normal run of lessons.

Just what are the children we teach reading at home? What's involved in reading a comic or magazine or football encyclopaedia? If we knew more about children's reading habits and interests, couldn't we capitalize upon this? For example, it's possible that children could bring books to the classroom as well as take them away — be lenders as well as borrowers.

We suspect that we often make wrong assumptions about children and their reading outside school.

When we thought about the kinds of writing children do in association with what they're reading, we came up against the old problems of copying straight from the book or the board and of making notes.

We felt we didn't give enough guidance about notes, but felt we ought to because of the difficulties it creates. It's just that we don't know what's the useful thing to do or say.

We think a group of teachers should look at this, and see what are the different kinds of note-making and note-taking that occur in subjects, and the purposes they serve. Perhaps if pupils can understand more clearly why they're making notes they might find it easier to do. We think that opportunities for this kind of work arise naturally in the course of work in the lower school, and that we should make use of these as they arise with an eye on later difficulties.

Finally, we arrived at these resolutions for the new school year!

1 When we want to present something for children to read we shall try to figure out what difficulties it's going to create, and sometimes ditch it before going any further.

2 When we're thinking of asking children to read something in our lessons, we'd like to feel sure in our own minds just why they're doing it, and how it fits in with the sequence of work and learning — and we'll try and get this across to the children as well.

3 Children are going to read more in our lessons, and we'll try to make this an interesting part of their work.

But the trouble with groups like ours is that it's one thing to arrive at statements like these — though not easy — but it's another thing actually to put them into practice in our own teaching. We're willing to try, but it won't in all honesty happen overnight, and as teachers we all need the support of ongoing discussion within our departments and across departments. We're aware of big problems lurking beneath the surface of all this, that need to be brought into the open and patiently discussed.

What is the place of books and what is the place of reading in my subject and my lesson?

What is it that makes some reading difficult, and what are the helpful things that teachers have done and are doing?

In what ways does a child become a better reader and what's my role in that?

Recommended reading
We've done some of our own reading, too, and recommend these!

1 'The Language of Textbooks', by Harold Rosen in *Talking and Writing* ed. James Britton.

2 *Reading after Ten* by Colin Harrison and others, published by the BBC in conjunction with a series of programmes on Radio 3 earlier in the year. Chapter 1 reproduces some reading diaries kept by children in a comprehensive school with extracts from texts.

3 The Bullock Report: *A Language for Life* in particular, the beginning of Chapter 21: Books; paragraphs 7 and 8 in Chapter 12: Language across the Curriculum; parts of Chapter 8: Reading: The Later Stages; and Chapter 4: Language and Learning.

4 'What is a Horse?' an article about topic books by Margaret Spencer in *The School Librarian*.

5 *Language across the Curriculum* by Michael Marland, especially pages 80—129.

SECTION 4
CONSULTING PUPILS

It isn't surprising, really, that pupils should have strong and useful views about how they work best, and helpful insights into how it feels at the other end. They are, after all, the reason why the whole thing's there at all: schools and teachers exist for the benefit of pupils. So it ought to be commonsense to involve students in decisions about what goes on.

But it's inevitably more complicated than that. Firstly, it hasn't always been clear whether pupils are being asked about *how* or about *what* they should be taught: and a good deal of public anxiety about the curriculum seems to have been caused by worries about whether young people were altogether the best judges of *what* they should be taught. In addition, there is the basic clash between two fundamentally different points of view. One view would see pupils as necessarily less experienced and knowledgeable than teachers, and argues that because relevant knowledge has to be transmitted from a knowing to an ignorant generation, the teacher–pupil relationship needed for that transmission symbolizes the necessary authority relationships of society itself. This view would not see consultations with pupils as either necessary or desirable.

On the other hand, there is the view at the centre of 'language and learning', that teaching and learning is a partnership, and that the pupil's job is not just to take over someone else's preformulated information, but as Michael Armstrong puts it, to 'reconstruct knowledge'.[1] In this view, the teacher feels that the pupils are nòt passive recipients, but active participants in the process of learning, and therefore, the process needs both acknowledging and exploring. Thus, trying to discover jointly the best ways of working is seen as a necessary condition of successful teaching.

It is clear from this very sketchy description that these are not only different views of teaching and learning, but also different political positions – in the sense that 'politics' is to do not with political parties, but with the distribution of power and decision-making. But it should also be clear that by deliberately polarizing them like this, I have wildly oversimplified the complexity of people's actual responses and relationships. One of our schools did involve pupils in its initial survey: there was a fiery staff meeting about it. But later, the working party in the same school put together some of the comments it had collected from pupils. As you see, the comments are not just perceptive and thoughtful, they achieve several important things.

1 They allow teachers the valuable shift of viewpoint, to see things from the pupils' point of view.
2 They show that pupils can think clearly about what happens to them, and that therefore their opinions can be taken seriously.
3 They do propose, implicitly, ways in which a teacher might actually improve his or her own success as a teacher.
4 They give insights into what's happening inside pupils, insights which are rarely available to teachers. Particularly interesting are comments B3, 4 and 5.

We feel that discoveries like this are intrinsically valuable, and therefore worth looking for.

Children have many important things to say about Language across the Curriculum. It is worth the initial antagonism to use them — for instance, in fact-finding projects.

Note
1 In 'Reconstructing Knowledge: an example', in *The Countesthorpe Experience*, ed. Watts J. (Allen & Unwin, 1977).

10 The pupils' view of school

In the course of the Bullock Committee's work, we have collected a number of comments by girls about the way they see school. We feel that these comments are interesting enough to share with others.

A. Firstly, we talked to the girls who did the survey for us. Some of their comments are as follows.

1 They had equated 'whole class discussion' with 'listening to the teacher' because in those discussions not many girls talk. Real discussion, they said, 'doesn't happen much'. The main reason for not talking in whole class discussions was that they 'don't know what to say'. Sometimes they don't know what answer the teacher wants, or what the question means; but they find it difficult to say that. It depends a lot on what kind of teacher it is as to whether they are able to say they don't understand.

2 They defined a good teacher. It is someone who:
   won't snap at you if you get something wrong
   helps you over the problem
   lets you talk, rather than insisting on silence
   makes you interested, by being interesting about the subject, and interested in you.

3 They discussed dictation and copying from the board. Copying from the board can quickly become boring: they prefer dictation because the class is together as a group. Sometimes, they added, they can't read the teacher's handwriting.

4 One girl remarked that a subject can be boring if 'you haven't got any confidence in yourself'.

5 A comment about teachers: 'They just go on and on, and you can't get a word in edgeways.'

6 They were asked about talking in class, and about the aspect that worries teachers — that pupils will gossip and chat. One said, and the others agreed, 'If you can do the work and it's easy then you don't talk about it, you just chat; if it's hard and you can't do it, then you talk about the work.'

7 The girls were asked how they preferred groups to be formed. They said they would most like to work with 'people the same as you', 'people with more confidence

than you', 'friends'.

B. Secondly, we had interesting comments about the homework survey [see Section 7]. A fifth-year class had the following points to make:

1 It always takes longer than teachers think it should — 'I am often told by my father to put my books away'.
2 'I put off my homework till the weekend and then I can't get out, but my parents think I don't get enough.'
3 'Homework is supposed to be for only 35 minutes a night and if I'm anything to go by when I do the homework I can spend as much as the whole night on one subject, which is absolutely ridiculous but it is true.'
4 'At the moment, I find I am being pressured and end up worrying for days on end after the homework has accumulated. Judging by my classmates, I find I'm not alone in this point of view.'
5 'What's the use of giving me homework when I can't do the classwork?'

C. Thirdly, there were the perceptive comments made by pupils in general, which have caught our attention.

1 When you're really working hard you need a kind of coffee break, when you can chat and joke. That's what we were doing in the middle of the lesson — having a rest.
2 When you're in a lesson you don't really remember what the teacher says even if it's interesting at the time. You remember the bit you say yourself — oh, and the little bit that comes just before and just after what you say.
3 Mrs X's lessons are really good. You have these big discussions and really you don't think you're learning anything, but at the end of the lesson you know ever so much more than you did before.

We have found pupils' comments very helpful and perceptive. They have often said things which seemed obvious, but were new to us. It was as though the girls were showing us something which had been under our noses but unnoticed till it was pointed out.

There is a natural next step to consulting pupils, and that is to make explicit basic processes that the teacher is conscious of. The one major difficulty with this is that we ourselves may not always be fully conscious of what these basic processes are. For instance, some of the most commonly used processes of learning — note-taking, note-making, summaries, revision and the writing of essays — are exceptionally complicated; and although we may cheerfully tell a class to 'revise for a test', we may not find it very easy to explain *how* to revise. (See Section 7, page 257.)

There has been a surge of work on reading in the last ten years, spearheaded by the Open University's very influential Reading Course PE.261. But other areas still remain to be considered. In one of our language packs I included an example of work from outside our authority, by a head of a humanities faculty explaining to his pupils how to set about projects, by making explicit some of the existing theories about writing and learning.

11 How to do a project – Medway's method

Many projects are a dead loss because they're nothing more than information from books or pamphlets. Who'd want to read them when they could go to the books or pamphlets and get it straight from the horse's mouth?

These projects seem to be pretending to be books – all about transport, history of fashion, etc. But books are to *inform* people who are going to buy them or get them out of libraries. Projects aren't for that at all – they're a way for *you* to learn. So why write them as if they're phoney second-rate books? (Whoever saw a book written in biro?)

These projects-pretending-to-be-books aren't any good for CSE or GCE assessment either, because they don't show that you know anything or have thought about anything. The only ability they demonstrate is the ability to put other people's words into different words – when the other people's words were probably perfectly all right to start with.

So, these suggestions are for the purpose of making projects more useful. To follow them, you need to understand something about different sorts of writing.

1 Books are written to be read by anybody. That's why they're written the way they are. The man writing the book doesn't know who's going to read it or where or when. The audience he's addressing is the public. And he's addressing them for a very clear purpose – to tell them things he thinks they'll want to know.

2 You know more or less who your readers are going to be – your tutor, maybe some other people in your year, an assessor. When you're writing to someone you know you don't write the way book-writers do. You know you can just be yourself and you don't pretend the whole world is going to read your words. Think of the writing you do in your log books, those of you that use the log as a way of talking to your tutor. Some of the best writing that gets done is in log books – because it's honest and relaxed.

3 Sometimes you write only for yourself. That's a different sort of writing again. Say you're making notes on a book, and you know the only person those notes will be useful to is

you, later. You won't need to spell everything out, you can use symbols and abbreviations and shorthand. This is writing for an 'audience' of yourself.

Now to your project. Let's say you've already got together the books etc. that you need. Here's how to organize it.

Have three sections. Start Section 1 and Section 2 at once. Start Section 3 later.

The differences between the sections are that they are written for different 'audiences'.

Section 1

Audience: your tutor — a particular person whom you know and who knows you, so you won't be writing as if you're writing a book. It will be more like your log book. Your teacher will write back and you can have a sort of correspondence.

Start Section 1 by telling your tutor why you want to do the project and what you want it to be about. Tell him the sort of things you know already about the topic and the sort of things you'd *like* to know. Say how you think you'll go about it — i.e. map out your plans. Say what problems you can see coming up. Ask any questions you want to. Say how you *feel* about starting the project.

From then on, write in Section 1 very frequently. Make it a running commentary on how your project's going, what you're thinking and what you're learning. You'll be talking to your tutor but at the same time you'll really be talking out your own thoughts for yourself. His replies should help you along.

Ask questions; note down ideas for things you might do later; record your reactions to the material; let off steam when you get frustrated; think up theories and explanations; talk about worthwhile things you're learning; record any changes in your original plan.

(Although it's personal between you and your tutor, the assessor will see this section. From it he'll be able to learn a lot about what you've got out of the project, and what you've put into it.)

Section 2

Audience: yourself.

This section is your *notes* on the books etc. you're using. This is where you record any information you need to record. It should be in *note* form, arranged on the page in shapes that help you to understand the material at a glance. It should not be in continuous prose.

Full references should be included to the sources — author and title of book, date of publication, page numbers.

Also in this section would go any other writing which isn't *mainly* intended to be read by someone else — ideas you want to note down, reminders to yourself, questions that occur to you.

In many *bad* projects the information *is* the project. In *this* method it's only one part. An assessor *will* be interested in it, but he'll be just as concerned about what you've done with the information once you've got it and how you've gone about getting it and what thoughts you've had about it — and he'll learn about those from the other two sections.

Section 3
Audience: public.

It isn't actually going to be published but write it as if it were. It *may* well be seen by other students and teachers, and some projects do get typed out and circulated.

This section will contain polished, well-presented, worked-over, public writing (if it *is* writing — it can be other media such as tapes). In it *you* have to be saying something yourself — not just repeating information you've got from the books. The information may not be original but what you do with it should be. What you've learned should be put to use, not just written out.

You may want to do one single big piece of work for this section or a collection of pieces. You can include stories, poems, and other fictitious writing, imaginary arguments and letters, reports, leaflets to push through letterboxes — or you can write a book. That's OK as long as it's a *real* book, that provides something for the reader that he can only get from you and *couldn't* get in a better way from other books.

Obviously you need to know a bit before you start Section 3, but you need to be thinking about what will be in it from quite early on. Record your thoughts, ideas and plans in Section 1.

SECTION 5
EXAMINING PRACTICE

Traditionally, 'research' into what goes on in the classroom has not been held in very high esteem by the teaching profession. It's difficult to see completely why this is so: but the reason may be that a good deal of research has concentrated on things that teachers themselves have not thought to be centrally important. To put that differently, the questions that researchers have asked are not always those that teachers want answers to.

What happens then, when teachers start doing their own research? The first thing is that 'rigorous' methodologies are not necessarily searched for. (See comments in Section 2, p. 29.) Scientific objectivity is not totally desirable if what we are talking about is the surprise of encounter when a teacher first begins to explore his or her own teaching. What is wanted, apparently, is a more sensitive and flexible way of coping with the experience. Because, after all, what is going on *is* sensitive. A teacher considers his or her own teaching: the shock can be quite disturbing, as you will see below. The teacher then has to transmute that shock into a form which will both cope with the teacher's private responses, and yet make available to colleagues, the essential guts of the experience. And then, finally, the practice of teaching itself has to change. I say 'has to' because it does seem that once a teacher has looked squarely and honestly at the reality of classroom experience, it is almost inevitable that he or she tries to change. And change is not a pleasant or comfortable process.

The two pieces that follow are both very similar and yet fundamentally different. The similarity lies in the form — both were published as pamphlets in the schools, and then distributed in the authority — and in the way teachers put their own teaching under the microscope. But the difference is important. 'Making choices' is concerned with what pupils do, and there is a healthy curiosity in experimental strategies and different experiences. 'Asking questions', however, is far more personal: it is not the pupil who is under the microscope, but the teacher, and what is being exposed, with sometimes searing truthfulness, is the vulnerability of *all* teachers. These teachers here are not beginners: they are experienced and competent heads of department: yet they are led towards painful conclusions *about their own teaching* as they examine a brief stretch of transcript.

It seems that it is much less threatening to the individual teacher if what is being examined is the pupils' performance in language: groups have examined tapes of pupils on their own and in groups, and have looked at pupils' writing. But shift the attention to the teacher's language, and inevitably it becomes both harder and far more painful. Perhaps this suggests that beginning by paying attention to the language of teachers is not a good idea, and that this should only be embarked upon when everyone is ready for it. Having said that, the power of a tape-recording to change or affect a teacher in a very particular way when he or she is 'ready' to listen to himself or herself, is unique. It enables a teacher to make perceptions about his or her own language in the classroom and how it affects pupils' language; and if a teacher has really listened to himself or herself, then it becomes possible to listen to other teachers, too.

The problem is that it is dangerously easy to be critical of someone else's — or indeed one's own — performance, and to level severe charges against it. What is never visible is the fact that no one *chooses* to be a bad teacher: at the time, what one does is done in all good faith, and enthusiasm. The point of balance between devastating criticism and supportive encouragement is invisibly delicate sometimes.

The two main modes of language in school are explored in these two pieces. 'Making choices' was produced by the Bullock group in one school: it looks at writing, in the first, third, fifth and sixth years, and sees that offering a choice of styles of writing to pupils is a useful and valuable thing to do. 'Asking questions' examines teacher-talk by concentrating on short extracts of transcript.

12 Asking questions

Introduction

A group of six teachers from the Art, Home Economics, Biology, Technical Studies and English departments, met irregularly to talk about the use and effect of oral questions in the classroom. We talked about the theory of it but decided to tape our own lessons to hear just how we approached matters.

It was daunting looking at the expression on colleagues' faces as they listened to our feeble attempts. But here we were, experienced teachers, including heads of department, using words which pupils could not comprehend, asking impossible questions, playing the game of 'read my mind', and generally not listening to the pupils, while, of course expecting them to listen attentively at all times to us.

After making transcriptions of parts of the tape, we talked and listened as a group, adding our comments and suggesting alternative methods, questions and approaches. We had to justify the content of a lesson to each other, why we had set about it in a particular way, how we had followed the lesson, what the writing was for, and so on.

So really, Language across the Curriculum has made us think about ourselves as teachers. It's a form of self-induced change; and there's much more to do still.

1.T.   Now Loraine what did we do not last week but the week before? Without looking in your book, think.

2.P.   Spending money.

3.T.   Yes we started thinking about spending money and how we spend our money. What was th . . .

4.P.   Miss, I need a new book please.

5.T.   Er, you'll have to go at break and get one. You'll have to use some paper now you can't stop in the middle of the lesson.

6.P.   Ahh.

7.T.   Here we are and we'll staple it into your book when you've written on it.

8.P.   I'm not stapling it into my book.

9.T.   Well I don't mind.

10.P.   I do.

11.T.   Are you going to copy it up then into your new book?

12.P.   I've got a little bit of space here.

13.T.   All right then use that space. We thought about what you spend your money on, now next we are going to think about where you go to spend your money and usually when you spend money you go to a — shop (pupils all join in with the word 'shop') You can buy things in other ways without going to a shop. Who can think of another way that (14.P. A club) you can buy. Don't call out! Yes Loraine?

15.P.   A club.

16.T.   A club, yes. What do you mean by a club?

17.P.   You know a . . .

18.T.   No I don't know you tell me.

       (Pupils answer generally)

19.T.   Loraine is answering

20.P.   You have a catalogue and you buy things. You know pay weekly.

21.T.   How do you get the things?

22.   Pupils in general: Order them.

23.P.   Through an agent.

24.T.   Ah, but how does the agent get them?

25.P.   She sends away for them (Various other answers offered.)

26.T.   Shh! Don't call out! Loraine,

27.P.   She sends them out to these places.

Commentary

A potential discipline situation which has to be avoided —
'I don't mind' (9)

The pupil is placated.

Obviously I have something in mind which the girls will have to
guess at. 'Who can think of . . .' usually means *'I'm* thinking of
. . . you have to work out *what* I'm thinking of.'

28.T.   Because she gets them . . .? How? How do they get to her?
29.P.   By parcel.
30.P.   Through the post.
31.T.   Right we've got there they come through the post. So you can buy things by sending away and they come through the post. Is there any other way you can buy things? Yes?
32.P.   A van. A vegetable van coming round.
33.T.   Yes, rather than you going to the shop, the shop can come to you in the form of a van.
34.P.   They're dearer, they are.
35.T.   Usually yes they are more expensive. Can you think of a reason? Loraine can you think of a reason why a shop that comes to your house is more expensive than one you go to?
36.P.   Because you have to pay for the petrol.
37.P.   Because you have to pay for the petrol.
38.T.   That's right you've got to . . .
39.P.   VAT
40.   . . . pay for the petrol. Pardon?
41.P.   VAT
42.T.   What's VAT? What's VAT Jackie?
43.P.   I dunno.
44.P.   It's where you add more money on to what it is.
45.T.   Do you know what VAT stands for?
46.   Chorus: Value added tax.
47.T.   Value added tax. The tax which is added to the value of the goods and there are different amounts of tax added to different things depending on whether it is considered to be a luxury or a necessity, something you really need. Now all things usually have some sort of tax, usually value added tax so that doesn't really apply particularly to something that comes to your home in the form of a mobile shop. How else can you buy something apart from going to a mobile shop, or going to an ordinary shop or having it through the post? Another one? Yes?
48.P.   HP
49.T.   Well you usually go to a shop to organize hire purchase don't you? even though — er — HP isn't really a different place of buying it is a different way of paying for something isn't it?

160

It's taken all this time to get where we wanted. It's longwinded and boring, this 'guess the right answer' game; but what's the alternative?

Random comments, at 32 and 34, are woven in, rather than dismissed.

Is this definition of 'necessity' really necessary? Perhaps it is and perhaps it isn't.

Missed opportunity here, for talking further about hire purchase.

50.P.	When they come to your house like Avon.
51.T.	Like an Avon lady that's right. You can buy things in your own home or in somebody else's home.
52.P.	Like the Avon lady
53.T.	Apart from Avon ladies what else can you buy in your own home or somebody else's home. Jackie Chisholm.
54.P.	Tupperware.
55.P.	Tupperware.
56.T.	Tupperware right.
57.P.	And jewellery.
	(Various suggestions offered)
58.P.	You can have Pandora parties as well.
59.T.	What do you buy at Pandora parties?
60.P.	Linen and jumpers and —
61.P.	And you can have them jewellery ones.
62.T.	And pottery. In fact there is no end to the type of parties you can have.

162

Did this pupil miss what the other said (at 50) or was she simply not paying attention?

This is the kind of innocent remark you can so easily make in class without realizing the un-innocent interpretations possible!

English: practical criticism in the Lower VI form

1.T.   'When air rang to a cock's crow
           As a glass to a finger nail.'
        Erm — well 'as a glass to a finger nail' — we'd think of
        that, *I* think of that as an effective simile describing the
        cock's crow because if you have a nail on a piece of glass
            (gets up from chair)
        I don't know if I can do it
            (runs finger along glass window pane)
        no — but you remember when I used to do it on black-
        boards well it's that
            (Laughter. silence: class watching)
            (Runs nail down wall, making scratching noises)
        That — that doesn't capture the shrillness of a cock's
        crow . . . I mean I can't do a cock's crow at the moment
            (attempts a cock-crow)
        You know, it's not shrill enough is it?
            (returns to seat)
        But I think he's trying to put over this er shrillness
        which again complements — the brittle landscape . . .

2.P1.   I don't think it means that — you know.

3.P2.   I put glass is sharp and clear.

4.T.   Glass is sharp and clear and I think that's what he wants
        to bring over. Yes?

5.P2.   . . . finger nail is dull.

6.T.   Finger nail is dull?

7.P2.   Yes — not very — sort of — sort of (?)

164

Commentary

I am myself sorting out what I think. I'm appealing to the class to come with me, ('We'd think of that . . .') but I'm really thinking aloud, trying to understand the image in the poem.

I'm doing all the talking in the mistaken belief that I'll get them to respond. Mistakenly, too, I thought of glass as glass in a window pane, rather than as a wine-glass or whatever.

Presumably, having trapped myself in this situation, I'm trying to liven it up. I have, of course, completely misunderstood the meaning of the image, as the comment about blackboards shows.

Crucially, at (2) I completely miss the girl's attempt to disagree. Although on the tape her comment is clear (it comes between my words 'complement —the brittle'). I disregard it completely, and indeed, did not hear it at all. How often do our pupils say something important, only to have it apparently ignored like this?

My repetition (4) of the pupil's answer shows me hunting around for something positive to say about his reply. The open-ended 'yes?' is another of my favourite non-questions which hardly deserves recognition.

The pupil is obviously having difficulties, because he is trying politely to disagree with my interpretation. Not realizing this, my comments, instead of helping him to say what he thinks, only confuse him more. My rather aggressive and surprised repetition (6) again throws him, where an intelligent question on my part might have helped him.

165

8.T.   Well, yes, yes but . . . we've also got 'When the air rang'
        Air seems to be, what . . . full of the cock sound of the
        cock. It's ringing with it. So we . . .

9.P1.   It's like when you tap with your finger on a glass with
        your finger nail you get that sort of rhythm
             (taps finger on table)
        and it stays in the air afterwards, well, that is like a
        cock when it crows especially that still sharp cold air —
        you know.

10.T.   Well now, might it also, you see we're thinking of
        window panes aren't we? Like you know when you
        get a glass and you just run your finger round at it
        creates a set of —
             (runs finger around imaginary claret glass, making
             vibrating hum)
        Yes? And that highlights the ringing doesn't it of the
        cock's crow. And of course in this subdued, paralysed
        landscape any sound would I suppose be very resonant
        and reverberating, wouldn't it? Mmm? So do we like
        that comparison? Do we think it's effective? Yes?
             (Class nods — general 'yes')
        Well we need someone very brilliant to say why Julie
        and to express why

11.P3. Well the . . .

12.T.   The simile is effective yes.

13.P3   The air is cold and sharp so no sound can be heard.

13.T   Yes (willing her on) . . .

15.P3. So . . . um . . . it really can be heard throughout the land
        a sharp sound as though you have tapped the glass
        which stays in the air.

16.T.   You just tap it — yes it does (imitates Ting!) doesn't
        it? Almost an icicle sound (pause). So, so far we're
        reasonably impressed, aren't we?

Apparently not getting anywhere with the simile, I change and focus attention on 'rang'. Teachers are, after all, professional silence-breakers! Only one pupil has, apparently, spoken so far, because I missed utterance 2. In my despair, I come out with the classic line 'full of cock'. A suitable comment!

At 9, the pupil who spoke at 2 at last helps out. She has not only had the courage to talk at all in this difficult situation, she is also strong enough to persevere with her alternative interpretation. Tapping her fingers on the table threw me. She's right, of course, in what she says, but I'm still so fixed in my own interpretation that I can't really hear what she says. I was still thinking of window-panes. I respond (10) to what I think she has said, and make a mass assumption about what everyone's thinking: 'You see we're thinking of window panes, aren't we?' Then, realizing my mistake, I now take up her suggestion quickly by demonstrating it — and I suppose demonstrating too that it must have been my idea! Conscious of the lack of response (and of the tape-recorder) I look for responses — 'Yes? ... doesn't it?'

Again, at the end of 10, I ask the non-question 'Yes?' to end my canter.

Receiving only a class nod, I pick on someone to answer my very difficult question . . .

. . . but even then I blunder in (12) and stop the pupil from talking freely.

However, at 13, the pupil finally makes a simple and accurate formulation. What a long way from my original misunderstanding! It's taken all this time to discuss one of the points of the two lines out of the whole poem.

In retrospect, my last observation is ironically crushing.

I've finished up learning something from the pupils (though I didn't realize it at the time: I only saw it by studying this transcript). But what have the pupils learnt?

Woodwork: first-year class

The class has just had a short demonstration using a piece of jelutong (a type of wood). They had been told and shown in a previous lesson that they were using this timber, with no comments made about the timber itself. On this occasion the teacher wants to make the children aware of different types of wood and hopes that by the end of the group of lessons they will be able to recognize about six different types of wood.

1.T.   What wood do we use. Yes?

2.P.   Jelutong.
3.T.   Yes jelutong. Good girl. Does anyone remember where in the world this wood grows. Yes?
4.P.   Malaya.
5.T.   Malaya. Good lad. How do you know it's jelutong. Yes?
6.P.   Sir because it carves easily.
7.T.   Oh so do a lot of other woods. You all put your hand up and said jelutong but how do you know this is jelutong?
        (he picks up a piece of beech)
        Is that a piece of jelutong?
8.P.   No.
9.T.   (Picks up piece of jelutong) No. But this you say is a piece of jelutong.
10.P.   Yes.
11.T.   So how do you know that's jelutong? Yes.

12.P.   It's softer.
13.T.   But how do you know it's softer. You've not carved that piece but you said straight away that it wasn't jelutong. Right?
14.P.   Looks like jelutong.

15.T.   It's what?
16.P.   It looks like jelutong.
17.T.   It looks like jelutong — but why does it look like jelutong?
18.P.   Last week we used jelutong.

168

I hadn't planned this. It simply happened, as things do, in the course of the lesson.

It's a correct answer, number 6 — but not what I wanted!

When I heard the tape, I was shocked to hear how aggressive I sounded, at 11 for example. I don't know if I usually do or not! Maybe I was cross because what seemed to me to be an easy question wasn't answered quickly.

This is closer. It's the appearance I'm after. Now, looking back, I can see that my question at 5 was too vague.

18 is a very sensible answer! — she's hunting around for something that will satisfy me.

19.T. Sorry?

20.P. Last week we used jelutong.

21.T. Well all right so I won't use a piece of jelutong, I'll use this. Is this jelutong?

22.P. No.

23.T. How do you know it's not jelutong?

24.P. Sir, jelutong you can't — it hasn't got so deep crease things in, marks.

25.T. (With relief) Grain.

26.P. Grain.

27.T. Grain. Anything else different about it?

28.P. It's a different colour.

29.T. Yes a different colour. What colour is it?

30.P. Yellowy colour.

31.T. Yellow colour. And what colour is that?

32.P. Brown.

33.T. Yes a light fawny browny beige. So we know that's jelutong by the colour, the fact that it's soft, and the grain. Can we remember this? OK back to work.

I still don't ask the clear question that's in my mind, about grain and colour.

Finally at 24 a boy gropes towards the answer. He hasn't got, or can't remember, the word 'grain'.
That's it! They've got there. This is what I had in mind all along.
When (27) I ask a specific question, I get a rapid and clear answer.

What a description!
Interesting: way back at 12 they said it was soft, but although that was right, I rejected it in a way, because it wasn't what I was thinking of. Ironic that at the time I didn't see this talk as being 'work'.

Looking at it now, it's quite clear that I'm asking the pupils to read my mind (I'm thinking of something, and you have to guess what it is) and that I see so clearly the answer I want that I can't understand why the pupils can't see it too.

I hope I don't always sound this aggressive!

Biology: fourth-year CSE rural science

We had discussed the structure of the earthworm, by holding one (each) and looking at it in some detail with a hand lens. The basic ideas — of a muscular body wall, made up of longitudinal and circular muscles, and bristles (chaetae) — have been established. In the follow up — on tape — I am trying to get this pupil, who won't work with anyone else, to use this information to observe accurately and to explain how the worm moves.

1.T. What's happening now?

2.P. It's crinkling up because its longitudinal muscles come together —

3.T. Good.

4.P. — and they're making the outer ones push out and that makes it move — and it puts its — what do you call it?

5.T. It's all right you can say wrinkles. Now watch this bit. Now just that bit just that bit there. What muscles have contracted to make it long and thin?

6.P. The long — the longitudinal muscles.

7.T. No the longitudinal ones are like this — when they shortened —

8.P. Oh the outer ones come out and the circular ones come out.

9.T. Now let's do it again.

10.P. Ah look they're squashed together now because the longitudinal ones have gone in like and then — it's going to stretch now.

11.T. That's it. Which ones have contracted to make it stretch?

12.P. The circular ones — look if you're looking you can actually see them.

13.T. Yes that's right.

14.P. It's a good worm (affectionately).

15.T. Now I want you to tell me now why when it stretches out why does it stay in its new position. What anchors it to its new position?

16.P. It's the — what're they called again — you know . . .

Commentary

He wanted the word bristles, or chaetae: my misunderstanding!

The boy is encouraged to use his own language: understanding is more important than knowing the scientifically correct word.
The worm is moving as I talk.
I drew them quickly.
He may not have expressed it 'scientifically' but he's certainly understood it. This is a moment of breakthrough for him, when he sees it all very clearly.
At (9): I didn't say 'well done' or anything, because at the moment, we're both involved in a real dialogue about the worm.
At 8, 10, and 12: the pupil makes his first formulation very much in his own words. To insist at this moment that he should be scientifically correct would perhaps have got in the way of his understanding.

The pupil (12) seems to see the situation not as one in which he is being examined, but as one in which two people are sharing an exciting experience. I think he's more likely to learn new things in this relaxed situation.
He's obviously quite deeply involved in a living experience, and has become quite fond of his worm!
15: what a sentence!

16: A long question, I've noticed, often gets a short vague answer.

17.T. You try.

18.P. (looking in book) Tell you when I find it — caters, bristles.

19.T. Chaetae.
20.P. Chaetae.
21.T. Chaetae.
22.P. Chaetae.

He's worrying a bit about the 'right' word: I don't mind how he says it as long as he's got the right idea, and would be happy if he said it in non-scientific language.

The boy is encouraged to use his book to find the answer. What's the use of having it written down if he can't go back and use it? You couldn't expect him to memorize such a difficult word yet.

Finally, he uses the correct scientific word. I help him to pronounce it properly, too. I'm very pleased: not only has he observed very closely, he's also understood what he's seen, and been able to use both his own words, and, where appropriate the correct word.

13　Making choices

Introduction
Mike Torbe

Writing is so common an activity in our classrooms that it's something we rarely think about in much detail. We take it for granted. Yet it is the major way in which information is communicated, the main way in which our culture transmits itself both to our own time and to future readers. A glance at the range of writing around us in our everyday life can be almost bewildering: newspapers, books, colour supplements, posters, weather reports, comics, statistical surveys, political propaganda — so many different kinds.

In school, the range of writing is not so varied. Essays and notes are the commonest kind of writing: add to them things like write-ups of science practicals, stories and copying, and you've covered most of what exists. But what kinds of writing actually help our pupils to learn and understand the new ideas they are constantly meeting?

It is this topic that the Bullock Committee has been exploring. As Alison Jones points out, the two questions underneath all that follows are to do with how much experience of different kinds of writing our pupils have, and what the effect is of these varying experiences? We hope that this pamphlet will be found useful by departments and individual teachers.

Home Economics
Ros Grey

I deliberately structured my recent lessons with first years, on the topic of bacteria, to emphasize practical investigation and oral work, rather than writing. This was to see if it would enable the girls to accept more readily and understand the need for hygiene in the kitchen and identify the potential areas prone to contamination. When we had thoroughly investigated, researched, observed and discussed, I felt confident that they had really made the knowledge their own and were ready to write about it.

My group is mixed ability so I organized three different levels of work:

1 To the less able I gave specifically structured work cards, e.g.

Hygiene in the Kitchen 2
1 Study the pictures.
2 Discuss them with your friend if you wish.
3 Write the title 'Do's and Don'ts when handling food'.
4 Make a list of six.

2 The middle group were expected to show more thought.

Hygiene in the Kitchen
1 Study the picture.
2 Write a side heading — food.
3 These foods are all perishable. What does this mean?
4 List those most likely to be affected by bacteria.
5 List any other perishable foods you know.

3 In order to give the able girls scope, I gave them the following card, but because we had already discussed at length, I deleted the verbal option.

Hygiene in the Kitchen
1 Read *Food and Nutrition* by L. Ganthorpe pp. 99—101.
2 Discuss the subject content with your friends if you wish.
3 Plan your own informative article on this subject. It can be verbal, written, illustrative or a combination of two or more of these techniques.

The girls were given one period during the lesson and were asked to complete it for homework. All attacked the work enthusiastically. I was delighted when I began to mark it because it proved convincingly that they were writing with a knowledge and understanding that was genuinely their own.

I talked with Mike Torbe about it, and showed him photostat copies taken from books belonging to some of the able girls. He commented that it was written in continuous prose containing disjointed ideas, and would have been better set out in note form. There were no paragraphs.

e.g. When cooking use clean utensils and wear your hair back. Do not lick your fingers when cooking as there are germs in your mouth and you will put them on the food causing food poisoning. When you transfer your rubbish from the kitchen bin always wash your hands because dustbins are very dirty and encourage bacteria. When you have transferred your rubbish make sure you put the dustbin lid on securely as cats may come searching for food and then bring all the germs from the dustbin into the house. Always wash round dustbins as well, to keep bacteria away. Do not blow your nose in the kitchen because you cannot trap all your germs in the handkerchief and they may fly on to food or you might forget to wash your hands.

I immediately recognized the validity of these statements. I had never really put specific emphasis on types of writing, some being more appropriate forms to use than others on occasions. I usually concern myself with assessing the number of correctly reiterated facts.

In subsequent lessons I included in my observations forms of writing. In particular I focused my attention on the interpretation that children made of my instructions, regarding written work.

When I asked for a list, many wrote a string of words across the page — despite my expectations of columns, down the page. When I asked for a recipe to be written down, and specifically showed them the way to do it, many still wrote a string of ingredients across the page.

These observations confirmed to me the need to very carefully consider the written form that we encourage the girls to use and it has sensitized my awareness to considering its appropriateness.

I decided to attempt to achieve a more planned piece of work from one of the original girls whose work I had photostated. Explaining to her that it read as though she had sat down and simply neatly written the various thoughts as they had come to mind, I invited her to read it through carefully and try to re-write it in a more organized way.

Her second attempt was much improved. It was set out in paragraphs and read much more coherently. I did notice however that the paragraphs were set out with the first word near to the margin and the subsequent lines indented, instead of the reverse.

e.g.   When cooking use clean utensils and wear your hair back.
       Do not lick your fingers when cooking as there are
       germs in your mouth and you will put them on the food
       causing food poisoning.
   Some bacteria are not dangerous, they come in different
       shapes and we cannot see them.
   It is vital that cuts are cleaned quite quickly in case it
       closes up with all the dirt still in it, so it is a good idea
       to keep a first aid box in your kitchen.

When I had re-read her second attempt, several times, I felt
she had achieved a further stage towards writing notes. I con-
templated inviting her to make a third attempt with this piece,
simply for my benefit, in order to discover if this might be a
way of teaching note-making.

My final request was to ask her to look at each paragraph,
think of a title for it then to list briefly the points to include.

This was part of the result:

Bacteria
Some bacteria are not dangerous, we cannot see bacteria,
they come in different shapes.

Cuts
Clean cuts quickly before they close up with dirt in them.
Keep a first-aid box in the kitchen.

To achieve this had been a tedious process for the child, especially at first-year level although it was completed over a
period of six weeks. I do think that I could adapt the idea to
use in a class situation to teach note-making.

On reflection, it is obvious that some forms of writing are
better used as means of recording or ways of communicating
than others.

Geography
Alison Jones

Initial questions
How much are pupils encouraged to use different forms of
writing?

How much do pupils learn from different types of writing?

Classroom method

Two second-year classes were involved in a piece of work which required them to use a form of writing other than continuous prose. One of the classes was given a free hand to choose any form of writing they wished, while the other class was advised to choose from four suggested alternatives. They were asked to describe the summer and winter monsoon mechanism and the resulting weather conditions.

The latter group were given the choice of a table, a flow diagram, a cartoon, or part of a log book. Initially, they were not sure how each of these might be used and therefore examples of each method were either shown or explained to them. The other group was given little specific help, other than an oral list of at least twenty possible alternatives. The piece of work, based on material they were already familiar with, was set as a homework in order to minimize collaboration in the classroom.

Resulting work

Most of the girls in the class given four alternatives chose the flow diagram and the cartoon. The use of illustration was evident in all but six of the pieces of work. In the other class's work there was a much wider range of presentation and a number of points were noticed:

(a) Nearly every pupil in the class combined illustration and writing in one form or another.

(b) The range of writing forms included (i) notes, (ii) annotated diagrams, (iii) stories, (iv) poems, (v) tables, (vi) cartoons, (vii) flow diagrams.

(c) The influence of television weather cartoons had a very great effect on the choice of illustration.

Follow-up lesson

Each class was organized into friendship groups and each group was asked to write a written assessment on three or four of the pieces of work of other members of the class, commenting especially on the content of the work:

(a) Most of the groups were able to come to a soundly based conclusion about the factual content of the work:

'She forgot to put in that the wind picks up moisture from the sea.'

'She shouldn't have included the intense heat in the winter as there isn't any.'

'This is a good account, but could be neater, and in the winter it doesn't explain why the cold sinking air makes wind.'

'It's funny and colourful and tells about the weather, but does not tell about the pressure and wind.'

(b) Certain comments were obviously mindful of teacher's clichés:

'Could have done better.'

'She hasn't taken a lot of time over this piece of work.'

'You tried Karen.'

'This is the same as Mary's.'

(c) Some of the pupils commented on the appropriateness of the form of writing and presentation:

'It isn't a table but a description.'

'Lin, you could have used the paper better.'

'You should have concentrated on neat and clear description, rather than drawings.'

In the discussion that followed a number of pupils commented on the fact that they had to know the work first, before they could mark the sheets. They also found it interesting to look closely at the work of other members of the class, whose books they did not normally see.

There were occasions during the group assessment when pieces of work were passed from one group to another, and the second group felt strongly that the first assessment had been very unfair. They were extremely conscious of the fact that a piece of work should be justly assessed, and initially unaware of the fact that there might be differing standards between groups.

Reaction to lesson (two months later)
The classes were asked to comment on:

(a) The topic or piece of work that they remembered best about monsoon lands.

(b) Why they thought that this was the most easily recalled.

The number of girls from each group, who recalled the topic (which involved choosing an appropriate form of writing), varied. From the one class, which was given four possible alternatives, only 17 per cent recalled that particular topic. The other class was asked to choose any forms of writing and 57 per cent of the girls recalled this topic.

Their reasons for recall varied, though some mentioned the use of different forms of writing while others attributed the recall to the amount of time spent on the topic.

Implications

(i) Given the opportunity pupils will happily choose from a number of different forms of writing, other than continuous prose. Each pupil may choose the mode that she finds most appropriate or easiest to deal with.

(ii) A flexibility of choice, rather than a rigidly imposed form, may have had some effect on the interest the pupils had in a piece of work.

(iii) Some of the pupils felt that organizing their work in a form other than continuous prose helped them to consolidate information that they had previously encountered.

(iv) In order to mark each other's work, pupils needed to know the topic fully themselves. It was not therefore a beneficial exercise for the least able, other than giving them the opportunity to see work produced by more able members of the group.

Business studies
Rose Maden

At the end of each topic I traditionally set either an essay type question or a more structured 16+ examination question to test students' understanding of that section of the work. The disadvantage of this type of assessment is that it tends to be a test of factual recall of knowledge and in marking the work it is not easy to be able to identify areas of work that students find difficulty with.

This year with the present fourth year at the end of the section on Banking I asked them to imagine they were opening a Branch of their own bank within Coventry, and to write a letter to potential customers indicating why people should bank with them as opposed to any other bank.

This exercise took a double lesson and for the first fifteen minutes most of them were showing a great deal of anxiety, I suspect because this was not the kind of task that either they were expecting or were accustomed to doing. By the end of the lesson all had finished between half-a-side of A4 and one and a half sides.

About 50 per cent wrote offering the traditional banking services, and only the name of their bank was different from one of the 'big four'. The remainder made a much more imaginative attempt to provide services which were better than the traditional services.

The exercise showed me two major things. Firstly, this form of written work showed me quite clearly that certain students did not understand some of the banking principles which they had earlier studied. The traditional structured essay does not show this; it tends to show omissions of knowledge but not understanding. Secondly, I found it much more difficult to mark. How do you compare the work of someone who clearly understands the principles of banking but who only writes about two or three of the bank's services as opposed to the candidate who reproduces seven or eight banking services but in a sterile, factual account?

History
Adrian Booth

As a result of discussions on different forms of writing, and their appropriateness, the lower sixth-form history students were asked to conduct an experiment.

I asked them to set out a piece of writing on the Constitutional Crisis of 1909—1911. This was not to be in continuous prose or note form.

I made no suggestions as to how they should go about this, although I did justify its value as I saw it, within the context of their A level history course.

The following is a transcript of a tape completed after the

experiment, in which they discuss what they did and its usefulness.

Joan Foley, Sandra Burke, Tina McDonnell.

Joan   We are three lower-sixth-formers taking A level history. We were asked to write up the constitutional crisis, in other ways than note forms or essay form.

Tina   We sat around together and decided what methods we would use. Once we decided what methods we could use we all went away and each person chose one of them. I chose to do it as newspaper clippings . . .

Sandra   I chose to do it in diagrammatic form.

Joan   I decided to do it in an imaginative way.

Sandra   Once we decided what to do, we all wrote it up by looking up in our notes, and in different books, to find various opinions about the constitutional crisis, which we could include in what we did.

Joan   When I wrote the memoirs of a fictitious peer, I found that I had to really know my notes well, and I also found that I had to look in a number of books to find out different opinions of the constitutional crisis; and then I had to think of how a Liberal would look at the crisis at the time it occurred. After that I wrote it up. Tina!

Tina   When I decided to write mine up as a newspaper clipping, first of all I had trouble deciding how I was going to start. I solved this problem by putting each section of the constitutional crisis under different headings. Then I had to decide whether I was going to be a journalist who would be for the Parliament Act, or against it.

Joan   How did you decide which argument you'd take?

Tina   Well, I tried to be as unbiased as possible, because I felt when I'd read all my notes and books, that it would be better if I could put it down in an unbiased way; but in the times you would have to have been biased towards the Lords.
Yeah . . . Yes

Sandra   Well! when I did the diagrammatic form, I found that I had to know my notes really well, so that I could put them down. I had to put them down in point

	form virtually, so there was no opinions as such, although there were general opinions for and against the arguments.
Joan	I found when I was writing the memoirs, that in the same way that Tina was slightly biased towards the Lords as she was writing from *The Times* point of view, I had to be biased towards the Lords as well. I had to think of how a Lord would react to the crisis, what his thoughts would be. I found this slightly difficult because in some ways I was on the side of the Liberals' government, wanting to get rid of the House of Lords' power in the way that they did. So I found that quite difficult. But on the other hand, that helped me to learn all my notes more than I would have done otherwise. It forced me to go and look in the library in different books, to try and find other opinions by people of that time.
Sandra	Well I had to have an unbiased opinion because I was just putting it down in note form. I had to look in all the books to find out as many arguments as I can for and against, which meant that consequently I learnt my notes better. And as they are down in print form I can learn them better than if they'd been written out fully in an essay.
Joan	So you find that note form in points is a lot easier than essays?
Tina	Yes, yes.
Sandra	Much better than essays because you just have to read the points and then you could dig around those points. Whereas if you have to learn all the waffle beforehand, it's a bit difficult, so in that way it's a lot better.
Joan	I remember in the first, second and third years that we used to have to write something from history from our point of view, as if we were for example a Roman soldier or a serf. That helped as well. Even though I find notes a lot easier to revise from, I also find imaginative work helpful, because you've really got to know the work before you can put down the opinion of something of that time.
Tina	Yes, you've also got to know the other side of the story so that you can pit your arguments against

theirs.

Joan So which would you think is the easiest to revise from, to actually learn your notes as you're going along in note form, or writing up in an imaginative way?

Tina I think they both help you a lot.

Sandra Personally I think it depends on the person: note forms are easier to revise because they're just points, and then I can build up around those points later.

Joan Yes, I think I feel that as well. What do you think Tina?

Tina Yes I agree with that.

Sandra It's a very useful exercise.

Tina I think as well if you're writing in an imaginative way you've got to read a lot of information before you can do that, and then sometimes you get bogged down with so much information that you're totally confused.

Joan And you don't know which way to turn.

Tina Yes. So if you've just got notes, it's straight and clear whereas if you've got a lot of information I find I get bogged down, because there is so many different opinions around.

Joan When I was doing O level history I had two sorts of notes, I had the essay type, and the notes that were in point form, and I always found that when I came to revise, I revised the point form rather than the essay.

Tina It's difficult for us to go through a whole load of different pages all on about the same thing, whereas if you've got it out in point form, it's a lot easier.

Joan But I think what we did was very helpful. I think it's a very useful exercise as Sandra said before.

Sandra Because you had one argument leading on to another and you can see how the whole thing followed through and came to the conclusion that it did at the end.

Joan I think it, it breaks up the monotony of having to write up note form all the time and then presenting an essay, say every four weeks or whatever it is.

Tina Yes it breaks up that monotony doesn't it?

Joan Do you feel the same?

Sandra   Yeah, definitely, of course, yeah.

The discussion revealed the following points:

1 (i)   A definite attempt to examine conflicting evidence and discriminate as to its usefulness for their writing purpose:

      Joan   'I had to think of how a Lord would react to crisis what his thoughts would be . . . It forced me . . . to try and find other opinions by people of that time.'

   (ii)   It also led to an attempt to clarify evidence:

      Tina   ' . . . I solved this problem by putting each section of the constitutional crisis under different headings.'

2 (i)   The discussion also revealed that their work had encountered problem — bias.

      Joan   'I had to think of how a liberal would look at the crisis at the times it occurred.'

      Tina   'I had to decide . . . who would be for the Parliament Act and who would be against it.'

      Sandra   'Well I had to have an unbiased opinion (?) because I was putting it down in note form.'

3 (i)   All through their discussion the problems of research were commented on.

4 (i)   The work also led to an interesting questioning of their roles as writers. This in turn led to a more discriminating examination of the evidence available to them.

      Joan   'I found when I was writing the memoirs that in the same way Tina was slightly biased towards the Lords, as she was writing from *The Times* point of view . . . I had to be biased towards the Lords as well.'

The discussion further includes comments about revision and what processes they find most useful.

Since the work has been completed the essays they have handed in have contained less narrative and more selective comment.

Afterword

In general, there are several points of interest raised by this work.

1 It seems, from all the work, that when pupils were allowed a freer choice of how to deal with ideas they understood them much better.
2 Significantly, pupils had no difficulty in finding appropriate ways of writing, although we may have expected them to struggle.
3 The comments by the sixth-formers seem to make explicit (because of their greater maturity) what happened to all the girls: that they had to understand the work fully to do this, whereas very often what they had to do they could write without necessarily understanding. It seems then that when the girls had to *handle* information in some way, and not simply reproduce it, they were forced to learn it properly.
4 Ross's point is important: that when pupils write in these more open ways, what one learns above all is what they *don't* understand.

Finally, a point of some elegance: the four teachers writing here all chose quite different ways to present their thinking. That in itself suggests that the choice of form is controlled not only by topic and content, but also with *the way in which the writer thinks*. If we always choose for our pupils the way they will write, perhaps we are preventing them from full development as writers and thinkers.

Kinds of writings

diary	story	questions	questionnaire
poem	labels	reports	crosswords
logbook	jokes	comics	captions
newspaper	scripts	lists	letters
notes	instructions	quizzes	broadsheets
circulars	manuals	catalogues	summaries
advertisements	indexes	signs	notices
	recipes		
graphs	maps	networks	flow diagrams
matrices	cartoons	branching	plans
topic webs	process	diagrams	sectional
tables	diagrams	Venn diagrams	drawings

SECTION 6
LANGUAGE AND THE SUBJECTS

It's paradoxical but perhaps inevitable that the course of development of language across the curriculum has been oddly circular. Its beginnings are charted elegantly by Harold Rosen, talking of the English teachers who started it all, back in 1966 and earlier:

> For many years we busied ourselves with our own fascinating specialist concerns with what did or would happen in the two hundred minutes per class of curriculum space allocated to us by the timetable. Increasingly, however, we found ourselves being pushed beyond the boundaries we had come to accept or perhaps helped to create. We found ourselves discussing the relationship between language and thought, how language represented experience, the functions of language in society, different kinds of language and how they were acquired, the difference between talking and writing, the nature of discussion and group dynamics. Inevitably we started to trespass in areas marked 'Keep Out', though some colleagues waved a welcome from the other side. There were others peering over fences, those engaged in integrated studies, group work, enquiry methods, environmental studies, social studies and innovations of all kinds. Some of them, though not many, were also concerned with questions of language. Soon we found ourselves talking about 'language in education', or 'language and learning', and finally about 'language across the curriculum'. We felt sure that language was a matter of concern for everybody, that if children were to make sense of their school experience, and in the process were to become confident users of language, then we needed to engage in a much closer scrutiny of the ways in which they encountered and used language throughout the school day. For this we needed all the help we could get from other subject teachers.
>
> *Language, the Learner and the School*

So the move was away from subject departments, and towards

the 'across the curriculum' view which has been so influential.

But what has begun to be apparent, at least to us in Coventry, is that although some teachers have always been interested in the wider aspects of what was going on, for most secondary school teachers, the response has been much more cautious. When it comes down to it, a subject teacher asks, 'What will these theories do to my lessons in geography? history? science? maths?' and so on. And, after all, why not? These are very real and proper questions.

There have been several initiatives in Coventry. In addition to the two illustrated here, there is a group of history teachers who have met to discuss language and to make video tapes; a group of science teachers who met for a year examining talk and discussion in science lessons;[1] a group of maths teachers who met to talk about the relationship between language and learning in maths. There have been courses for teachers of modern languages and English and discussion of tapes and transcripts by PE teachers. There needs to be this steady inter-relationship between the across the curriculum aspect and the more specific subject-based work of which you see examples here.

Note

1 Published in the ASE study paper *Language and Learning in Science*

14 Language: Humanities

This is a report of a course on language and classroom organization held for history, geography and social studies teachers in the Spring Term of 1977.

The course was organized by the Officers of the Geography Teachers' Association and the Local History Teachers' Forum who arranged and led the course with the assistance of Mr D. Maund, Educational Adviser in Secondary Humanities.

Aims and objectives of the course
1 To bring together teachers from history, geography and social studies disciplines to discuss common problems of language.
2 To highlight some of the problems associated with language, such as readability, use of work cards, teaching in a multi-cultural society and classroom organization.
3 To introduce skills of measuring or objectively assessing the depth of the problem (e.g. the use of indices to measure readability and the assessment of the suitability of work cards).
4 To enable departments to share the experiences they have had in the beginning to implement language policies.

The classroom problem – Session I
The first meeting was devoted to a simulation exercise (Document 1.1). A typical classroom situation was presented and resources provided for a lesson on coal-mining which was to be given to a class of second-year mixed-ability pupils. Resources consisted of a textbook (Document 1.2), a worksheet based on a set passage from the textbook (Document 1.3) and a map exercise from the same book, for which a badly-produced map outline of the British Isles, containing contour lines and grid numbers, was prepared.

The meeting divided into groups to consider the situation presented and to write a brief critique of the lesson resources with particular reference to the problems of language and classroom organization which might arise. Each group was invited to devise an alternative lesson strategy. Chance cards were also issued to provoke discussion of typical language and learning difficulties.

In general, comments on the resources were highly critical.

Although the textbook was visually pleasing the illustrations were frequently unlabelled and lacked descriptive detail. The book was marked for mixed use in the second year but it was felt that the language would be difficult for many pupils and the passage was too long for sustained interest. There was felt to be an imbalance between the high level of interest initially aroused and the low level of information provided. Many terms were mentioned but not fully explained and much of the passage needed fuller explanation from the teacher and elucidation of problems by pupil/teacher discussion. The textbook could not be used as a resource in isolation nor could it be used as an introduction to the subject of coalmining. Most teachers felt that the material required considerable editing before sections of it could be used and then only as a reinforcement of earlier information introduced by the teacher and developed by the pupils.

The worksheet was criticized both for presentation and content though some credit was given for the attempt at graduated questions. All groups agreed that it was badly produced and difficult to decipher. The length of the exercise would discourage the less able pupils and the more able would skim through the text in order to find the information in the required time. There would be no extension of pupil skills; the extraction of information, problem solving, simulation or imaginative writing. To quote one group; the worksheet was 'a comprehension test and badly organized at that − suitable for a teacher who puts his feet up and sits back'. Poorly defined terms in the set passage made certain questions difficult to answer without prior knowledge. There was no indication of key words or ideas which the teacher was aiming to instil or reinforce by means of the exercise; the worksheet lacked continuity and unity.

The map exercise was particularly criticized for its poor presentation. Most groups preferred an outline map without the distracting contour patterns and grid numbers. The map was too small for accurate observation to be recorded.

For alternative strategies a number of approaches were suggested and certain solutions proved common to all the groups. Most teachers recommended introducing the subject through the medium of the pupils' own experience; the pupils' knowledge of coal and its uses; current mining/coal production issues and their understanding of these via the various media; possible involvement of family/relatives/friends in coalmining; comparison between their own life styles and expectations of those of a miner in 1841. Simulation and role play were also suggested; the dramatization of a pit accident; the experience of working underground by adopting a cramped position in a confined space for a short time or sitting in total darkness. The visual approach was also popular as a teaching method; showing a few slides was suggested and inviting children's comments to increase observation, reporting and interpretation skills. All groups agreed that the textbook should only be used as one resource among many and that key ideas could be originated by verbal introduction from the teacher and developed by the interchange of pupil/teacher ideas or by group discussion.

As part of the simulation chance cards (Document 1) were introduced to facilitate discussion.

The following are some of the points raised or solutions offered by the groups in discussion.

Late arrivals — the teacher should try to find time for private explanation if possible; a little time could be used for revision of the lesson for the benefit of latecomers and reinforcement of knowledge of rest of class; make late arrivals copy summary of work from board.

Insufficient extension of individual pupil's abilities — develop a more flexible and open-ended approach to content; develop parental trust by consultation and a sympathetic understanding of their aspirations; provide additional work at a higher level; critically examine interaction between pupil and teacher; pupils should be allowed a freer and wider choice of topic.

Problems of minority having Polish as a first language — make special arrangements within the school for a crash course in English; look critically at the curriculum and justify its relevance to a cultural minority; do not concentrate on the minority to the detriment of the majority as this will emphasize differences; enlist children's help in explaining instructions to increase communication; use visual material wherever possible; are all teachers also teachers of English?

The development of a language policy within a department — development should be via departmental discussion with reference to the Bullock Report's recommendations; a possible start could be made by considering the media by which language is conveyed within the department.

Classicists' complaints about the inclusion of modern history within the syllabus — if the syllabus aims at the extension of pupil skills and the teaching of basic historical concepts then surely any period of history is relevant and suitable for inclusion?

African studies — there should be departmental consultation when a syllabus is prepared; should all departmental members be obliged to teach all aspects of the syllabus within the department?

DOCUMENT 1.1

The Havens comprehensive school second-year lesson simulation
The Havens is a typical large city comprehensive school. In the second year the classes are organized on a mixed-ability basis with all the inherent advantages and problems. There are about thirty-two pupils in each class which meets for seventy minutes per week in both history and geography. It is assumed that children with severe reading problems have been withdrawn into a remedial unit.

History and geography are taught in the type of classroom common to most secondary schools. The double desks are arranged in three rows facing the blackboard at the front. Blackout facilities are at hand in two of the department's three rooms while display boards are mounted in all rooms. There being no actual storage area, equipment such as film strip/slide and overhead projectors, screens and tape-recorders are stored in cupboards in various classrooms and are available for use if arranged in advance with the head of department. Resources such as textbooks, worksheets, maps and so on are similarly stored.

The general policy of the department is to attempt to provide a core of textbooks so that all pupils have some common core of knowledge. Departmental policy is discussed at regular fortnightly meetings.

Lesson — coalmining
Children are asked to read pp. 40—42 of the textbook provided

and then to attempt the worksheet. After this they answer the map exercise on page 45.

Task Using the set of course materials provided for the teaching of a lesson within the above framework give a brief critique of the lesson, considering the problems of language and class organization which may arise.

Devise an alternative strategy for the lesson/group of lessons.

Chance cards

A number of children arrive later, with good reason, after the worksheet has been introduced by the teacher.

The parents of a girl in the class come to school and complain that the child is being held back by not being given sufficient work to extend her.

A group of children move into this school whose first language is Polish.

The head teacher calls for a statement of the departmental policy on language.

A new member of staff, a classicist, maintains that too much time is spent on recent history.

A member of staff refuses to take seriously a course unit on African studies.

DOCUMENT 1.3

Coalmining

Read pages 40–42 carefully, then answer the following questions.

1 Where was coal first found?
2 How was coal first found?
3 Why did coalmining become necessary?
4 How were accidents caused in the first coalmines?
5 What was a winder?
6 Describe the various ways in which life became harder for coal miners before 1842.
7 Draw a summary in pictures of the things girls had to do in coalmines before 1842.
8 Explain what you understand by the term 'Knockers-up'.
9 Explain what would happen in a 'Tommy shop'.
10 How did miners safeguard themselves from the dangers of methane gas?

196

He knew that some people were using coal instead of timber but the new coal mines were so far away. He often saw long strings of pack horses trudging along the rough old roads into the town. They could not bring enough coal for everybody, however, because each horse could only carry 125 kilogrammes of coal. Although his son had told him about the 400 coaling ships which could carry nearly fifty tonnes of coal each, and which regularly beat down the North Sea from Newcastle upon Tyne to London, he wondered if they could carry on because he also knew that people were dying of starvation in the streets of Newcastle. Would workers become too poor and weak to mine enough coal? He had realised that every town needed help from other towns but how could help be given and the new crafts fed with enough fuel?

30 A drift coal mine and coaling ships
31 Mining coal in 1810

TASK A

1 Why was Queen Elizabeth alarmed that so much forest land was being cut down? (*Clue*: island, defence)
2 Why was Queen Elizabeth pleased to see more ships being used to carry coal, and more fishing boats making long voyages across the Atlantic Ocean to Newfoundland? (*Clue*: training, defence)
3 A salt industry grew up on the coast near Newcastle. Why was coal needed for this? (*Clue*: -v-p-r-t-)
4 This second Elizabethan Age is also a time of great change. Deduce or find out what recent changes old people consider to be:
   the most surprising.
   the best.
   the worst.

Solving the Fuel Problem

Coal has been used in parts of Britain for over 2,000 years. It seemed that there was plenty to be picked up on the sea shore or the mountainsides. Monks used it in their workshops and people burned it in their homes. When it had all been used, workers only had to dig into the mountainside to find plenty more. As more coal was needed, the holes or pits became deeper. Even then many men dug their own pits. In the Forest of Dean a man could dig his own pit anywhere provided he was 'one rubbish throw's' distance from the next hole.

As the holes were deepened it was natural to treat them like wells. Workers were lowered in buckets and the coal was pulled up in the buckets. The ropes soon wore thin and sometimes broke.

40

197

The handle sometimes slipped out of the winders' hands and tragedy followed as the bucket went crashing to the bottom.

The miners learned to live with danger which grew worse every year as more risks had to be taken to hew more coal. During the early part of the 18th century, coal miners were highly regarded skilled workers who employed their own helpers. Gradually, however, they became poorer and life became harder as they worked for wealthy pit owners instead of for themselves. The women began to earn a little extra money by carting away the coal which their menfolk had hewn. Life became harder and even the children went down the pits to help their mothers. Four-year-old children opened and shut the trapdoors along the dark galleries, and kept the rats off their fathers' food. As they grew older they helped their mothers to pull the trucks instead. This was not stopped until 1842 when Parliament was told, 'Girls regularly perform all the various offices of trapping, hurrying, filling, riddling, tipping and occasionally getting, just as they are performed by boys.

'One of the most disgusting sights I have ever seen was that of young females dressed as boys in trousers crawling on all fours, with belts round their waists and chains passing between their legs.'

The pit owners employed 'Knockers Up' who went around the miners' homes calling each worker by name. After a meagre breakfast the miner and often his family went to the pit. They wore as little clothing as possible while they worked in the hot poorly ventilated galleries for one and a half pence an hour. Even then they had to buy their own candles and equipment! The miners were given a free house and coal, but some owners made certain of getting most of the miners' wages back. Some men were given 'Tommy Tickets' as part of their wages. These could be taken to the local 'Tommy' shop and exchanged for goods. Of course the shop belonged to either the mine owner or his friend and the prices were always very high, often fifty per cent higher than normal.

The miners knew that they were always risking death and it took many years to solve their safety problems.

Their only form of lighting until 1813 was ordinary candles. At first the miners could not understand why there were often gigantic explosions. Even when they did realise that the explosions were caused by 'fire-damp', or methane gas, life was still very dangerous. When they smelt the gas the miners ran out of the gallery and pushed a flame into the gas-filled region. The gas exploded and the miners knew they were safe for a few more hours. However, they did not always smell the gas in time . . .

On May 25th, 1812, ninety-two men were killed down a good mine near Sunderland. Many people were appalled. They appealed to the scientists for help. Eighteen months later Sir Humphry Davy had made a new safe lamp, and said, 'I have never received so much pleasure from the result of any of my chemical labours; for I trust the cause of humanity will gain something by it.'

Miners had also been killed by poisonous gases such as carbon dioxide. The obvious answer was to pump fresh air along the galleries. Giant bellows were tried but a better idea was to sink two mine shafts. Fresh air was pumped down one shaft and the old poisoned air rose up the second shaft. This was not efficient enough. In 1798 John Buddle of Wallsend invented a powerful fan which sucked the poisonous air out of the mine.

The fuel problem had begun to be solved. Factories everywhere were using more every year, and large country houses used as much as a tonne of coal every day. The miners were meeting the growing needs but only at the cost of terrible suffering and danger.

32 Explosion!
33 Using an early Davy Lamp. The cauldron of burning coal was used to create air currents
34 Newcomen's steam engine

32

TASK B

1   Look at Figure 33.
    How did the fire cauldron help to ventilate the mines?
    (*Clue:* hot air)
    Why was this a bad idea?

2   Look at a map of Britain. Why was it natural to expect a person from a place like Wallsend to invent the fan?
    (*Clue:* know, problem, think, work)

3   Why was it accepted as normal for young children to work down the mines? (*Clue:* mother, care)

33

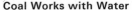

Coal Works with Water

For many years it seemed as though coal mining would have to be stopped. The deeper the mines were sunk, the wetter they became. Many miners were drowned in the flooded mines. Buckets could never bail the water out quickly enough and prospects seemed hopeless until mining was saved and the world changed by the invention of the steam engine.

In 1708 Thomas Newcomen invented a type of steam engine which could raise 45 litres of water 45 metres at one stroke and make twelve strokes every minute. The engines pleased the miners and were used by the richer mine owners. The only trouble was that they used so much fuel and could easily explode! Someone was needed to improve the idea; that person was James Watt.

Although he was quite a weak child, James Watt was very determined. As a boy he worked with his father using pullies and ropes. He then trained to be an instrument maker.

A model of a Newcomen engine was brought to him to be repaired. Although he knew nothing about the engine, he studied it and noticed that it did not work efficiently. He tried to improve it but made a new type of steam engine instead.

He was not a rich man and therefore he could only make a model of his machine. A business man at Birmingham named Matthew Boulton went into partnership with James Watt in 1776 because he realised that the nation was accepting steam-power for its industries. These successful engines were used all over the country. Iron foundries also used them to pump air into the blast furnaces.

Coal was the fuel of the machines which had saved the coal mines. As more engines were needed, more iron was needed to make them and the machines they powered. By the end of the 18th century many people were spending their lives making things which helped other people to work in a different way. Life had changed a great deal!

34

11 Write a letter of protest to a newspaper on 25 May 1812 about the appalling hazards in coalmines.

12 Describe and illustrate the miners' safety lamp invented by Sir Humphrey Davy.

13 What did John Biddle invent? How did this improve safety in coalmines.

14 Turn to page 42 and answer the map exercise, question 2, Task B.

15 When you have completed these questions turn to page 45 and attempt the map exercise.

Readability – Session II

Mrs B. Armour (Woodlands School: geography department) led the meeting and began by introducing the course members to two approaches to assessing readability, the Fog index and the Cloze procedure. The meeting then divided into groups to apply these techniques.

The difficulty of a passage from a biology textbook (Document 2.1) was assessed, using the Fog index (Document 2.2). The groups then simplified the passage (Document 2.3) by splitting long sentences, removing grammatical complexities and substituting short and familiar words for long and difficult ones. The readability of the groups' passages was then assessed and compared with a version provided by Mrs Armour (Document 2.4).

The original extract from the biology textbook was found to have a readability suitable for fifteen to sixteen-year-olds. Simplified versions were produced by the groups of which the following is a specimen.

The Skin

Take a look at your skin, using a magnifying glass. You will find hairs of many sizes and furrows crossing the surface.

On the tips of the fingers there will be ridges which will help you to grip. These make a different pattern in each person. This is why finger prints are studied by detectives.

Inside, the skin is made up of two main layers. They are called the epidermis and the dermis. On the hands and soles of the feet the epidermis is very thick. Everywhere else the skin is very thin, only 1/10 mm deep.

The dermis is much thicker and is made up of different

fibres. There are blood vessels and nerves in the dermis. These help you to feel pain, warmth and cold and give you the sense of touch.

Hairs are special parts of the epidermis. Each hair on your head grows about 0.3 mm a day. After a few years it drops out and a new hair grows in its place.

When your body is hot, it is cooled in two ways. Blood vessels, or capillaries, open fully. This allows more blood to reach the cooler surface of the skin. This cools the blood in your body. Also your body sweats. This sweat evaporates and cools your body.

In cold weather the blood capillaries narrow, making you look paler. Your body must keep warm. It does so when tiny muscles pull hairs upright. They trap warm air around the body.

This simplified version was found to have a readability suitable for pupils aged ten to eleven. The version provided by Mrs Armour was found to have a readability level suitable for eight-year-olds.

The Cloze procedure was next attempted (Document 2.5) and, as expected, it was found that difficulty varied from passage to passage according to the knowledge, experience, vocabulary and comprehension of the reader. The following conclusions relate to both Fog and Cloze procedures and were arrived at by the groups.

1 Oversimplification of reading matter may destroy the original meaning of the passage, resulting in the loss of essential concepts or key ideas. The prepared and simplified version of the biology extract is an example of this. It avoided explanations of difficult mechanisms relating to the composition and the heating and cooling processes of the human skin and the absence of paragraphs results in a lack of cohesion and the logical development of ideas.

2 The length of a word does not necessarily indicate its difficulty: some three syllable words are simpler to understand than words of one syllable e.g.: 'animal' as compared with 'truth'. A more effective way of assessing readability might be to consider the complexity of the sentence by counting the number of subordinate clauses.

3 There are dangers in using the Cloze procedure when no

reasonable consideration is given to the variety of alternative words which might be employed. A reader ought to be able to make a reasonable attempt at a passage and use a number of synonyms. The main criterion should be comprehension; has the reader produced a reasoned development of the passage and shown comprehension by adding words which indicate its sense?

4 The course members were interested in the two procedures and thought that their application could assist in the assessment of readability. Resources could be assessed and their reading levels could be recorded on a card retrieval system with easy access by members of staff wishing to locate material suitable for the different reading levels within their classes.

Note
One school, Tile Hill Wood, did attempt to use the Fog index to assess certain geography textbooks after the meeting and found that a number had surprisingly advanced levels of readability.

DOCUMENT 2.1

The Skin — more than just a covering

Inside your skin

Take a look at your skin, using a magnifying glass. You will find regularly spaced hairs of various sizes and numerous furrows criss-crossing the surface. On the tips of the fingers there will be distinctive ridges, which, like the tread of car tyres, improve the power to grip. These form a unique pattern in each person, which explains why fingerprints are studied by detectives.

Inside, the skin is made up of two main layers: the epidermis and the dermis. Except on the hands and soles of the feet, the epidermis is very thin, just about 1/10th mm deep. At its surface, dead cells are being continually rubbed away, and new cells move out from the living layer inside to replace them.

The dermis, is much thicker. It is made up of a meshwork of tough white fibres and springy elastic fibres. Between them run many blood vessels and nerves which are connected to tiny organs responsible for sensations of touch, pain, warmth and cold.

Hairs

Hair are specialized parts of the epidermis and they grow from the base of hair follicles. Each scalp hair grows about 0.01 inch (0.3 mm) every day for three to six years, rests for a few months and then drops out as a new hair starts to grow in its place. The waxy secretion of the sebaceous glands oils the hairs, and also provides food for the follicle mite, a minute spider-like animal that lives in many people's eyelashes.

Temperature control

In cold weather tiny muscles pull the hairs upright, trapping a film of warm still air around the body. The blood capillaries in the dermis narrow, so that the skin looks pale. In warm weather these capillaries open fully, to allow more blood to reach the cool surface of the skin, and the sweat glands pour out a clear salty liquid, which evaporates, cooling the body.

In the armpits and genital areas are special sweat glands called apocrine glands, whose products smell strongly under the influence of local bacteria. These may have helped our animal ancestors in sexual attraction. Today, however, man self-consciously suppresses them with deodorants.

DOCUMENT 2.2

Measuring readability using the Fog index

The instructions for calculating this index are as follows:

1 Select a number of samples from a text whose difficulty you wish to estimate. Each sample should contain 100 words. You might, for example, take the first 100 words from every tenth page, starting with the first complete sentence.
2 Count the total number of complete sentences in your sample. Count the number of words in these complete sentences. Then calculate the average sentence length by dividing the number of words by the number of sentences.
3 Count the number of words of three or more syllables in the total sample. Divide this number by the number of 100-word samples. This gives the percentage of long words in the sample.
4 Obtain the Fog index by adding the:
   (a)   average sentence length, and

(b)   percentage of long words

Then multiply this total by 0.4

This figure represents the grade level for which the material is appropriate in terms of difficulty. The age equivalents are as follows:

Grade:	1	2	3	4	5	6	7	8	9	10	11	12	13	14	15
Age:	6	7	8	9	10	11	12	13	14	15	16	17	18	19	20

Example One

1 Let us say that you decide to take a sample from pages 10, 30 and 50, of a book of 60 pages, i.e. three 100-word samples.

2 The number of complete sentences, and words in those sentences, might be as follows:

Sample	Complete sentence	Words in complete sentences
1	6	98
2	8	93
3	7	97
	21	288

Average sentence length = $\frac{288}{21}$ = 13.7

3 The number of words of three syllables or more might be:

Sample	Words of three syllables or more
1	2
2	4
3	3
	9

Percentage of long words = $\frac{9}{3}$ = 3%

4 Average sentence length plus percentage of long words = 16.7

Fog index = 16.7 x 0.4

$\qquad$ = 6.68

Thus, this text would be considered suitable for pupils in the sixth grade, i.e. children aged 12+.

Example Two

1 Let us say that you only wish to assess the readability of a particular passage, then you would only consider one 100-word sample, as follows:
2 The number of complete sentences, and words in those sentences might be as follows:

Sample	Complete sentences	Words in complete sentences
1	6	98

Average sentence length = $\frac{98}{6}$ = 16.3

3 The number of words of three syllables or more might be:

Sample	Words of three syllables or more
1	2

Percentage of long words = $\frac{2}{1}$ = 2%

4 Average sentence length plus percentage of long words = 18.3
Fog index = 18.3 x 0.4
= 7.32
Thus, this text would be considered suitable for pupils in the seventh grade, i.e. children aged 13+.

DOCUMENT 2.3

Instruction sheet for workshop on readability

1 Use the Fog index to assess the readability of the passage 'The Skin'.
Choose three 100-word samples from the text.
Refer to the salmon-coloured sheets for instruction on how to calculate the Fog index. (Document 2.2).
2 Rewrite this text, using such techniques as:
(a) splitting long sentences into two or more.
(b) reducing the grammatical complexity of sentences by:

(i)   removing ambiguity, for example, restoring deleted
      words, as in the sentence:
      'The assistants were paralysed with wonder; the
      boys with fear' which becomes:
      'The assistants were paralysed with wonder, and
      the boys were paralysed with fear.'
(ii) removing clauses in sentences, which have been
      inserted between the verb and the subject, as in
      the sentence:
      'The girl standing behind the lady had a blue dress'
      which becomes:
      'The girl had a blue dress and she was standing
      behind the lady.'
(iii) removing concealed negatives, as in the sentence:
      'Tom's mother was anything but pleased.'
(iv) removing grammatical and stylistic features which
      do not occur at all or only rarely in speech.

(c)   Omit long, difficult and unfamiliar words, and substi-
      tute shorter and more familiar words.
3   Use the Fog index to assess the readability of your simpli-
    fied passage.
4   Obtain the published simplified version of this passage
    from your team leader. Calculate the Fog index for it, and
    then compare it with your simplified version of this text.
5   Discuss, to decide the advantages and disadvantages of the
    Fog index as a measure of the difficulty of a text.
6   Complete the Cloze texts, by filling in the blanks (blue
    sheet)
7   Collect the answers to the Cloze passages from your team
    leader, and then score your sheet as follows:

  Score: If 40 per cent—60 per cent of the responses are cor-
         rect you have no comprehension problems.
         If less than 30 per cent are correct, you are having
         problems, and you may be using material which is as
         yet too difficult for you.
8   Discuss to decide which of the following conclusions you
    would subscribe to:
    (a)   Readability measures and Cloze procedure are of no
          value
    (b)   These techniques are interesting but impractical in

the classroom
(c)　These techniques can be used
(i)　on your own
(ii)　with the help of your class
(iii)　with the help of colleagues who are prepared to undertake a wider-ranging study of materials in common use in schools.

If you subscribe to conclusion (c), write brief notes on ways in which you would organize this kind of study. Note the way in which you would indicate the readability of the books themselves, how you would record the range of readability levels in each subject area, and how you would use the information.

9　If time permits, use the Fog index to assess the readability of the passage on 'Solving the Fuel Problem' — pages 40—42 of *The Developing World*.

10　Rewrite the above text, in simplified form, and then assess its readability using the Fog index.

11　Repeat tasks 9 and 10 for any textbook you have with you.

DOCUMENT 2.4

The Skin

The skin
The skin has two layers.
The outside layer
is called the epidermis.
It is thin,
but it protects the body.
Dead cells wear off, and
new ones take their place.
Dead skin is thickest
on the palms of hands
and soles of feet.
The inner layer of skin
is called the dermis.
It has fibres,
blood vessels and nerves.
The nerves make us feel

heat and cold,
touch, and also pain.
There are many fat cells
under the dermis.
These store food.
They also help
to keep the body warm.

Hairs
In very hairy animals,
such as cats and dogs,
hairs also help
to keep the body warm.
In cold weather,
small muscles
make the hairs stand up.
This keeps warm air
close to the skin.
In warm weather,
sweat glands near the hairs
make sweat.
This cools the skin.
Oil glands give out oil.
This makes hair soft.

DOCUMENT 2.5

Measuring readability with Cloze procedure

Text 1 (from the *Sunday Mirror*, 10 October 1976)
It is the politicians . . . have failed. The 15 . . . cent Bank Rate
is . . . disaster. Inevitable, no doubt. . . . a disaster. It has . . .
up the cost of . . . . If it lasts, it . . . force down investment in
. . . . It will throw people . . . of work. It is . . . monument to
the failure . . . the politicians. The nation . . . made great
sacrifices. Because . . . pay has been frozen, . . . of our most
useful . . . — managers and highly skilled . . . have had their
standard . . . living slashed. Trade unionists . . . surrendered
their right to . . . in the open market . . . .

Text 2 (from the *Sunday Times*, 10 October 1976)

It is the worst . . . Denis Healey has given . . . in his Chancellor-
ship. The . . . priests of monetary theory . . . burn celebratory
incense, but . . . we can get away . . . the arcane algebra of . . .
and M3; and look . . . factories and people at . . . , the reality is
that . . . squeeze is a major . . . for the Healey policy, . . . we
have always supported, . . . building on the twin . . . of the
social contract . . . industrial regeneration. We have . . . the
slightest sign of . . . on real resources. We . . . factories half
idle and . . . out of work, and . . . rates at a very . . . level, with
investment and . . . only just reviving.

Text from *The Developing World* — History Two
The towns grew unchecked. . . . warehouses and houses were
. . . together as closely as . . . . The nation grew richer . . . with
the towns it . . . a different story. Mothers . . . see that a third
. . . the children died before . . . age of five. Older . . . noticed
that townsfolk seemed . . . be dying younger than . . . did. In
fact that . . . life span in Manchester . . . 1840 was only seven-
teen . . . . A farm worker, however, . . . expect to live thirty . . .
years and a 'gentleman' . . . -two years!

Although many . . . had been attracted to . . . towns in the
hope . . . high wages, they found . . . the higher wages were . . .
swallowed up. In the . . . there had been more . . . to prepare
soups and . . . , to take bread and . . . beer. In the towns . . . ,
it was necessary for . . . to work long hours . . . six days a week.
. . . were therefore usually snatched . . . from the cupboard.
Sunday . . . the one day of . . . week when time could . . .
spared to cook meals. . . . , bacon and tea formed . . . main
part of the . . . .

Cloze procedure: words omitted
Mirror: who; per; a; But; forced; living; will; industry; out;
    a; of; has; there; many; people; workers; of; have; bar-
    gain; place.
Times: news; us; high; may; if; from; M1; at; work; the; set-
    back; which; of; pillars; and; not; pressure; have; people;
    interest; high; growth.

The Developing World:
    Factories; clustered; possible; but; was; could; of; the;
    people; to; countryfolk; average; in; years; could; eight;
    fifty; workers; the; of; that; soon; country; time; broths;

brew; however; everybody; on; Meals; quickly; was; the; be; Bread; the; diet.

Work cards and questioning — Session III

Mr John Wright (Elm Bank) led the meeting and talked briefly on work card composition and the type of exercise/questions which should be included in order to develop the skills of the pupils to whom the work was directed.

The skills he defined as desirable came under four headings:

1 Literal comprehension
2 Reorganization
3 Inferential comprehension
4 Evaluation

In practice, comprehension is the most frequently used form of questions. Many worksheets omitted any type of question which would involve the pupil in the processes of comparison and inference or the evaluation of ideas from a variety of sources in addition to those in the text. (See Document 3.1. This is based on Barrett's Taxonomy.)

Presentation was very important in motivation of the pupil and variety and open-endedness also very necessary (Document 3.2). Mr Wright showed several examples of an open-ended work card which could stand by itself as a teaching resource to which a number of exercises could be applied.

The meeting then considered a number of worksheets on a variety of topics; as part of the worksheet the Group were also asked to rewrite the original worksheet on coalmining (Document 1.1) and to include examples of every type of question specified in the skills sheet (Document 3.1).

Examples of questions are given:

Literal comprehension
   reorganization — Rewrite in your own words the sentence which first mentions dangerous conditions within the coal mines.
   recall — Which of the following statements is true?
Four-year-old children began to help their mothers in the pits.

	Miners began to work for the pit owners.
	Women began to work in the pits.
	Children began to pull trucks underground.
	Miners employed their own helpers.
inferential	An imaginative exercise or role play
evaluation	A letter-writing exercise in which the pupil would treat the same subject from different angles and viewpoints.

Groups indicated the difficulty of classifying questions into one special category.

In view of the large number of work cards available for examination, most groups had time only to consider a small number. The following comments were made.

Schools Council Moral Education Project This was praised as being sufficiently open-ended to suit all levels of ability and a wide range of ages. Visually the material was unexciting though it might be argued that its starkness provoked automatic comment.

The Litter Kit The material was very varied in quantity and quality so that it was difficult to assess its overall impact on the pupil. The pack was criticized for setting some impossible tasks.

Macmillan History Workshop Some tasks set were unrealistic and insufficient detail was provided for drawing exercises; it was felt that these were bad drawbacks which were not compensated for by the attractive print and format.

Street Pack This was an excellent example of an open-ended teaching pack which could stand independently of any other resource; the visual impact was excellent. Some of the course thought that teaching difficulties might arise regarding values and attitudes.

DOCUMENT 3.1.

Appendix III

Purposes of reading and teachers' questions.

1 *Literal comprehension*
   (i)   Recognition. The pupil works with the text and is required to reproduce specific words or passages of the given text.
   (ii) Recall. The pupil works without the text and is required to reproduce as accurately as possible specific words or passages of the given text.

2 *Reorganization*
Reorganization requires the student to clarify, summarize and synthesize ideas stated in a given text. This may involve quoting verbatim or paraphrasing the text without expressing any personal opinion.

3 *Inferential comprehension*
Inferential comprehension requires the student to understand the ideas and information in the text and then to use his own thinking, experience and other reading as a basis for personal conclusions relating to the text.

3 *Evaluation*
Evaluation involves comparing ideas presented in the text with other ideas, experiences, knowledge or values presented to the pupil from other sources and making decisions about them.

DOCUMENT 3.2

Work cards: a guide to evaluation
The following points are intended as a framework for work card analysis. All are important, but some are more important than others, e.g. 'Information' and 'Questions and tasks set'. It is the balance between all the points that will make a work card a meaningful resource in the classroom situation.

1 *Initial impact*
The initial impact of a work card is dependent mainly upon the visual appearance and this impact helps to gain the interest of the pupil to the task embodied in the work card.

The work card should look 'professional' and not too casual or apparently ill-conceived as this may encourage a similar response from the child. The 'professional' appearance is achieved through a combination of initial impact, choice of print and illustration, presentation, and most important, layout.

2 *Illustration*

An illustration in the form of a diagram, line drawing or photograph can be used to impart information to support the key ideas of a work card, as well as adding impact.

The real effect of the illustration depends upon its clarity and relevance, this being more easily controlled by the use of a diagram or line drawing. Photographs may be used to good effect but it should be remembered that they often include much extraneous information and consequently need to be cut down to focus the pupil's attention.

3 *Print*

(i) The type of print

A work card should minimize any potential reading problem for a pupil by using a legible and appropriate script. A handwritten script is quite acceptable providing that it does not ask the pupil to decipher personal handwriting idiosyncracies. e.g. — r or v? — o or a?

These problems can appear insurmountable to à child with reading problems who is attempting to build a word by looking at each letter, resulting in an annoyance to the teacher who may be constantly interrupted to act as interpreter.

(ii) The amount of print

To many children a page or work card of closely packed script is a daunting prospect and does not invite further involvement. The use of space and/or illustration between paragraphs can enliven the page and create a less demanding appearance.

4 *Layout*

Layout is the arrangement of titles, headings, blocks of print and illustrations upon the card. A successful layout helps to achieve impact.

The layout of a work card should be logical in the sequencing of the components already mentioned. This ensures that the pupil may easily follow a predetermined path through the tasks set. The inclusion of illustrations or diagrams can easily result in confusing a pupil by having a work sequence that progresses horizontally, diagonally and vertically on one card.

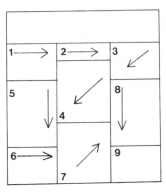

5 Presentation

(i) Durability

The durability of a work card is an important factor, as whether money for commercial cards or teacher time for school-made cards is invested, the work card should withstand use. The quality of card and some kind of protection (lamination) are crucial.

(ii) Storage

When constructing your own work cards, size will be a determining factor as a work card that is too large or too small may result in it being unacceptable to a storage system already in operation by a school or department. Storage will also need consideration if the work card relates to another medium, e.g. slides, tapes, etc. and needs to be stored together.

6 Information

The information on a work card may be presented by an illustration, the written word, or the spoken word. (A teacher introduction or an associated tape etc.)

Care should be taken to match the relevancy of the information to the task in hand and the intended ability range. Of equal importance is the need to match the appropriate language level for the intended ability range (Appendix 2).

A failure to meet these important criteria can easily nullify the value of the work card.

7 *Questions and tasks set*

Some of the most important aspects of a work card are the questions asked and the tasks set to the pupil which will identify:

(i) The pupil's approach to the work
(ii) The learning value of the work card to the pupil
(iii) A means of assessment for the teacher that the objectives of the work card have been achieved.

The number of tasks and the inherent work load should be also carefully considered to ensure that they are appropriate for the intended ability range. Many commercially produced work cards include tasks apparently to suit a variety of ability levels, often resulting in pupils having to tackle tasks below or above their own capabilities.

Tasks should be realistic and justify the time taken, e.g. many commercial work cards include the phrase 'Make a model or paint a picture about . . . ' an unrealistic task in a classroom not suitably equipped and also in terms of the time that can be unnecessarily taken over something that is secondary to the objectives of the work card.

Questions asked on a work card should extend and involve the pupil at an appropriate ability level. Wherever possible questions should be structured to be open-ended, asking the pupil to prove an understanding of the ideas and information given by using experience and thinking to draw personal conclusions and decisions. The learning value of the questions asked is crucial and meaningful investigation can be minimized by questions that do not involve the pupil or pre-empt the response from the pupil.

A work card needs to be explicit and not ambiguous, as it cannot answer questions posed by the child.

Multicultural education and the humanities – Session IV

At a time when Britain is beginning to submerge its interests with those of its immediate European neighbours; at a time when the visit of an American President brings to London the leaders of the industrial heavyweights, it is inevitable that long perspectives of this country are re-examined. Dean Acheson's comment that Britain had lost an Empire and failed to gain a role is underlined by the euphoria for our imperial traditions generated by the Jubilee celebrations.

Like all Empires the British collapsed towards the centre and this has been accelerated by the need, shared with the whole of Western Europe, for an unspecific workforce willing to undertake the jobs in the economy which education has made the indigenous workforce unwilling to do. Technology has played its part rendering as irrelevant the physical boundaries that once kept peoples apart, though we must remember that it was the horse that began the process! Commerce has similarly blurred the economic boundaries.

From these positions the teacher of the humanities is obliged to seek a new personal or pedagogic standpoint through which to interpret the forms of human involvement to his children. Quite likely the teacher in the classroom has to operate against an educational background which has offered him little help in gaining other than a white, Christian, European vantage point. His class of white, black and brown children make enormous demands on him unless he is to peddle the myth that civilization has been carried forward on the shoulders of the white population. The idols, heroes, inventors, innovators, discoverers, in sport, medicine, architecture, law, engineering, chemistry, of the teacher's childhood are generally incredibly white. The periods of history were the white periods as he wandered across the stepping stones marked monastic system, feudal system. Tudors and Stuarts, the age of (white) discovery, the French and industrial revolutions and the causes and outcomes of the great world wars. Asked to relate non-white people who contributed to mathematics, law, architecture, medicine, navigation, philosophy etc. most of us demonstrate just how 'snowpake' is the world we view.

With about 3 per cent of our school population from non-white families the responsibility is relatively small. But in the inner cities where very much larger percentages are from non-white backgrounds (in Coventry 14 per cent) the responsibility is very much greater. Because of the increased attention given to migrants' children there is a pattern developing of increased success but these children are in danger of losing a lot of themselves as the price of educational success. Faced with a curriculum which is selected and directed by teachers who inevitably lack any deep awareness of the cultural or historic roots of these children it is inevitable that the children go through a culturally *white-loaded* experience. They emerge seeing the world through blue eyes, not brown, and see civilization as largely a white construction in which Asian and African have played no part.

Each teacher is at the mercy of his own education to a substantial extent. The role that Britain played in the prewar era in which most of our teachers were educated was an Imperial one and the education system reflected this. It is to the credit of so many teachers especially in the humanities area that they have begun to seek ways in which to crack this imperial mould. I would not suggest that the imperial message (or its colonial equivalent) survives anywhere but its consequences will linger on for several decades in our school libraries, in our perceptions of pigmentation, in our attitudes to non-Christian religions but more than anywhere in our ignorance of the perspective of the Caribbean or Asian. Our ideals, beliefs, frameworks, knowledges are particular; we should not fail our new society by them but more likely by default in not widening these to incorporate the contributions in the past as well as the present of the black and brown forebears of many of the children in our schools.

We look to the reluctant universities and to the colleges to set about the development of research programmes that will assist us in this but they are too trapped in the culture mould and in the interim we will have to begin the reinterpretation of society in the classroom and on the resources of our own service. As elsewhere, educational change will have to work upwards. Outside the cities as well as in their suburbs the population of our schools is ill-served by a curriculum which ignores the role in world and national affairs of the black and brown majority. All our children are going to live in a multiracial society and in it no particular group can claim to have an exclusive contribution to make.

The twentieth century is one in which the world population is moving. The states of America have reluctantly learned to cope with this diversity, given a great deal of pressure from their minority groups. The states of Europe, faced with the same challenge, must inevitably respond and Britain is already in a position to show a new strength which will redirect old energies, in a social revolution as effectively as it directed its energy in an industrial revolution.

(This is a synopsis of the talk given by Mr Feeley, Educational Adviser, on the multicultural dimension.)

Teaching procedures — Session V

Mr D. Maund (education department) began the session by showing ideas on classroom activity and the organization of language within the teaching situation (Document 5.1.). He presented a grid system (Document 5.2) on which he suggested that it was possible to plan a lesson in a variety of ways, employing different combinations of teacher/pupil/class/groups and different types of language use; talk/writing/reading/listening. The groups were then asked to plan a lesson using the grid system and prepared resources.

Discussion resulted from the grid system. There was also interest in the question of the proportion of teacher time allocated to the different pupil levels within a mixed-ability situation.

It was agreed that the check-list on classroom organization presented a good picture of possible teacher/pupil combinations within the classroom but drama should be included as a language activity distinct from talk, writing, reading and listening. The following situations were defined as teaching situations in which the teacher talked to the whole class; discipline, giving information, discussion, question and answer, instruction.

One group considered three of the resources presented and made the following observations:

The Yellowstone National Park; extract from the Schools Council's Geography — 14—16 Project.
Lesson aims — to teach the concept of planning; planning solutions and conflict situations arising from these.
Organization — whole class: groupwork.
Talk — role play: expression of pupils' ideas.
Writing — expression of pupils' opinions.

The Hales inventory — select transcript No. 2; Archive Educational Service.
Lesson aim — to give some idea of the content of a Tudor/ Stuart household.
Organization — whole class; group work.
Talk/reading/writing — groups to make inventories of their own houses and compare them with the Hales inventory. As an alternative strategy the class could start with a visual approach; an illustration of the house or a plan of it.

Report of the Watch Committee — select transcript No. 6.

In its existing form the transcript would not be suitable for direct use by lower/middle school pupils but various items could be extracted, such as pay, equipment, duty rotas.

Organization: group work; the role of the police; wages/prices for comparison between 1977 and 1836; present-day police-wages problem.

         — individual work; topic/project work

Language use: not specified

Two problems were discussed; the readability level on which opinions differed; the relevance of archive material to children who related to the modern police force as shown on current TV programmes.

DOCUMENT 5.1

A way of looking at classroom activity is to classify the forms of organization and the media through which interaction takes place. Usually the system works by the setting of tasks which result in some outcome or product (Document 5.2.)

One familiar form of organization is where the teacher's purpose is to deal with the class as a whole. Interaction takes place through talk, writing, reading or listening but normally the teacher is the focus of whatever activity or task has been set. Thus the teacher may give oral instructions to the class whose task is to listen, absorb and possibly later recall whatever has been said. Alternatively, there are occasions when the teacher's role is like that of a chairman and the class task is to participate in open discussion. Another, frequently seen, example is where the teacher has set a worksheet containing questions and the class task is to answer them. This is not individual work as is so often claimed since the only individual element is the rate at which the questions are completed. There are many examples of this form of organization and each has its place. It would be interesting to list them all and to categorize them according to their purpose. In this way it might be possible to make clearer the choices open to teachers.

A much less frequently seen form of organization is where small groups work towards a single task. Obvious examples of these are the use of geographical and historical games. Sometimes children are put into groups to decide upon the strategy for a particular task such as a group project. One of the major advantages of this organization is that it permits children to talk in their own language forms in addition to assisting with the more social objectives of cooperation.

The final form of organization is seldom seen. This is individual work where children are working on quite individual tasks. Examples might be the CSE project work which is sometimes required. Where individual project work is undertaken there is the danger that children will merely transfer information from one book to another unless the task is very carefully structured so that this does not happen.

The grid shown on the diagram can help either in the planning of work or in the analysis of what is happening in a classroom. There is no set starting point — although the notion of task is an obvious one. Some of the skills and ideas discussed during the course can be fitted into the grid. Thus, problems of questioning either written or oral can fill several of the cells. In fact, some of the tasks given on work cards would fit the cell for group/talk. The point is that each of the cells can be used depending on the purpose of the activity and the task which is set to achieve that purpose.

TASK
1 What do you think of this as a check list of classroom activities?
2 What kinds of teacher talking to whole class situations are there?
3 Use the resource to set up an example of each type of organization.

TASK

	talk	writing	reading	listening
Teacher to: whole class				
group				
individual				

PRODUCT

Points for consideration
Culled from the group reports are the following suggestions. Some may appear to be rather self-evident but, nevertheless, can be overlooked in classroom practice and lesson planning. Certainly they may be open to discussion. The points are loosely grouped under the headings of language and classroom organization but in no particular order.

Language

1   The teacher teaches by example.
2   A relationship exists between the quality of worksheet presentation and effective learning.
3   How important is the teacher's own legibility on blackboards and worksheets, etc.?
4   In worksheet layout, what is the maximum amount of acceptable handwriting or type?
5   Continuity and grading are important features of all worksheets.
6   A visual mess is offputting.
7   Illustrations as decorations are of little value.
8   The length of a passage to be read by pupils is geared to age and ability.
9   Many worksheets are better reorganized as a series of small cards but guard against worksheet phobia.
10 Refresh the class by telling a good tale.
11 Drama, in addition to role play, might be more usefully employed.
12 Do we all regard ourselves as teachers of English?
13 Skilful question and answer technique continue to be highly effective teaching medium.
14 Crosswords and cartoons could be more fully utilized.
15 Do we know the reading ages of our textbooks or our pupils?
16 Are questions set for which there is no answer in the text?
17 Are instructions in questions suited to the pupil's level of ability — 'summarize', 'describe and illustrate', 'give a reasoned account of . . .'?
18 Long reading passages cause the more able to 'skip-read' and give bare answers while the less able simply flounder.
19 Understanding is rarely achieved by copying text.
20 Simplification of passages can destroy meaning or dilute key-ideas.

Classroom organization

1 Group work is the key to successful teaching of the less able.
2 Lessons should achieve a balance between level of interest and level of information; too little of the latter frustrates the more able.
3 The personal experience of students should be capitalized upon.

223

4 Assigned tasks should be geared to specific key ideas.
5 What do parents and teachers mean by 'stretching' the more able?
6 Is the teacher the main resource?
7 Do teachers overlook the fact that most desks are mobile and the implications of this?
8 Resources; a correlation exists between their accessibility and extent of use.

Criticisms and comments on the course arising from discussion
1 The course was not aimed at providing solutions to the many problems of language. The objective was to highlight some of the problems and encourage open discussion.
2 The second and third meetings, on work cards and readability, were found to be the most useful and concrete.
3 It was thought that it would be advantageous to continue the same small groupings for discussion throughout all the meetings. This would help to continue links and continuity of thought and discussion from one meeting to the next. The group leader could be a different person at each meeting.
4 It would be useful to send out a questionnaire to all Coventry secondary schools to ascertain how departments are organizing language policies, if at all.
5 A request was made for more of the time available to be devoted to lectures and less of the time to be devoted to workshop and discussion sessions. In some situations, discussion was thought to be too theoretical, thus avoiding the practical problem or task.
6 With reference to the first session, when the 'Havens Comprehensive School Simulation' was undertaken, a few criticisms were expressed about the type of resource used. The inadequacies of the resource were too obvious, and a need was expressed for using a resource, or a number of resources, with both good and bad qualities.

SECTION ONE

Minutes of a meeting held on Tuesday 1 March 1977 at Elm Bank Teachers' Centre

The implementation of a language policy within a department

A joint meeting of the Geography Teachers' Association and Local History Teachers' Forum was held at Elm Bank Teachers' Centre on 1 March 1977. Although this meeting was not part of the language course mounted in January/February 1977 it was felt that many of the observations made during this meeting had relevance for the Language bulletin. The meeting highlighted many of the language problems encountered in schools and an opportunity was given to teachers to discuss constructive ideas for language policy already in process of implementation in Coventry schools. The meeting was chaired by Mr D. Maund, Adviser in Secondary Humanities, Coventry Education Department.

Mr R. Eddowes, head of geography department, Cardinal Wiseman (Boys) School
The departmental policy was derived from a general school committee of approximately twenty members of staff who met once a month to consider the Bullock Report's proposals and their application to school policy.

It was decided to look at first-year mixed-ability groups and identify language problems by testing the readability levels (Fog index) of all first-year resources; textbooks, work cards and blackboard work. The reading ages of pupils were also assessed by careful testing and their results compared with the levels of readability discovered in the teaching resources. In this way it was possible to give teachers tangible evidence of language problems.

The procedure emphasized the difficulties of the less literate pupil and there was a tendency for the language group to concentrate on the remedial child. One solution seemed to be the withdrawal of remedial children for extra tuition but it was decided to attempt a revision of work cards which would be tested and graded for readability to cover all levels within the classroom.

Mr J. Brodie, Mr T. Haley; geography department, remedial department, Foxford School
The geography department at Foxford School is organized within the humanities faculty. Teaching takes place within mixed-ability groups. The geography department became aware that worksheets were presenting pupils with language problems and it was decided to invite a colleague from the remedial depart-

ment to look at language within the teaching situation and suggest an alternative language strategy.

The remedial colleague identified two areas which needed restructuring; the form and content of worksheets and the teaching aids used for subject development. Structured worksheets were abandoned as they led to streaming within a class. It was decided to prepare worksheets on a team basis with careful attention to language. The material and content were to be applicable to all levels of ability but extra teaching aids such as language master cards, OHP cells and taped transcripts of the subject core, presented in story form, were to be made available for the use of pupils with language difficulties.

Mr D.F. Waterhouse head of geography department, Woodway Park School

The department as yet had no defined language policy but discussion had resulted in the testing of the readability levels of the worksheets and textbooks used in the department. The remedial department had been interested in contributing to the department's efforts by looking at first-year resources and producing a book on 'weather' for pupils with language difficulties. It was felt, however, that most textbooks could be used with most groups if there was adequate pupil guidance from the teacher and methods appropriate to particular groups were first sorted out. Pupil involvement was very important and the department was now more aware of the part that 'talk' played in lessons. Resources which stimulated talk and discussion were increasingly used; film-strips and other visual aids including mounted photographs on card and exercises in the completion of sentences.

Mr W.A. Shields head of humanities faculty, Alderman Callow School

Mr Shields began by questioning the assumption that literacy was necessary or desirable in the modern industrial technological society. He was able to quote good authorities to strengthen the argument that reading and writing were becoming outmoded by typing and recording techniques and arithmetic redundant in the face of modern calculating devices.

At Alderman Callow School, integrated studies were taught to mixed-ability groups for the first two years; in the third year, individual subjects were taught. As a result of integrated studies, the humanities team consisted of teachers from a number of different disciplines and English teachers worked in close liaison with colleagues from other departments. This liaison facilitated the introduction of common standards and policy throughout the lower school.

At present, Alderman Callow was looking closely at language problems, especially the problem of pupil/teacher talk but no definite policy had, as yet, been developed.

Miss S. Morgan head of history department, Tile Hill Wood (Girls) School
Miss S. Morgan was unable to be present but the following statement was submitted on her behalf by Mrs E. Castle, secretary, local history teachers' forum.

The introduction of a language policy within a department entails a cooperative effort to discover the best and most successful ways which enable pupils to learn about history. Current teaching methods within the department need to be explored and their effectiveness examined. The teachers have to become more conscious of how learning actually operates through the different uses of language and these areas require careful analysis.

Talk is one of the most important language areas and should be examined on the following points:

1 the effect of teacher talk both in the lecture situation and the informal 'story' situation of the 'good tale well told'.
2 the way in which the teacher talks to the pupils; does teacher/pupil talk make the pupil feel confident and secure by the process of the pupil accepting information, listening to the teacher's talk and understanding it?
3 the encouragement of purposeful talk among pupils; at what point should pupil discussion be introduced as a valuable contribution to the pupils' understanding and discovery of knowledge.
4 the use of pupil talk by the teacher; how does the teacher monitor, reinforce and reflect back to pupils the valuable observations they make and so demonstrate to the pupils what they have learnt?

Writing is another area which needs careful examination. Pupils do not move directly from the introduction of new ideas to the process of formal writing about them so that it is difficult to get accurate and publicly acceptable writing from many children. Writing exercises are part of the learning process and the formal writing can be usefully capitalized on by the pupil.

Reading is the third definable area of language. Certain reading procedures (Cloze system) can be used as ways of teaching and learning. Survey and resource skills can be taught and also the collation and evaluation of evidence by the use of several different sources of information. Readability cards should be tested.

Generally pupils should have some explanation given about the purpose of basic techniques such as the taking of notes and writing of essays. It is desirable to explore by discussion with the pupils the consequences of various modes of history teaching and to discover how the class feels about the different techniques being used.

To put a language policy into practice, cooperative discussion is needed to identify the areas to explore. There should be agreement to test out agreed procedures and report back on them; this should lead to a genuine shared approach to the various problems identified and a policy should then naturally develop.

Points arising from discussion
1 The different standards of language operating within the various departments of a school and the need for closer liaison between departments in promoting a common language policy.
2 The importance of teacher talk especially in the history narrative which can involve pupils in personal decision making.
3 The need for more continuity in the teacher/pupil relationship. Groups of pupils are allocated to one teacher for pastoral care; would it be possible to apply the same principle to the development of the pupils' language by having one teacher teaching the pupils most of the subjects within the curriculum.
4 The transfer of skills from one subject to another by the pupil. Why do pupils write well in one subject and poorly in another? Is this solely a matter of pupil motivation? Would teachers' expectations of pupils' language capabilities be increased by a greater appreciation of their potential in other subjects?

5 The problem of 'switch-off'. Do pupils 'switch-off' when motivation declines or is 'switch-off' a natural reaction to sustained study and a period of marking time while ideas germinate?

SECTION TWO

Comments by M. Torbe, curriculum development officer, Elm Bank Teachers' Centre
I have been asked to make some comment about the meeting of 1 March and to do so is a pleasure.

There are some general points I'd like to make.

1 I was struck by the comment from Rob Eddowes that a 'language policy' was seen by many to refer to pupils with problems and by his phrase about being 'bogged down talking about remedials'. It does seem to happen that staff feel that only the 'remedials' have a language problem and that it takes a major shift of emphasis to see that *all* pupils have language problems because it is through language that they learn. The recognition that a problem with language means a problem with learning ought to be balanced by the equal recognition that a problem of learning, with sixth forms, O level pupils and first years, is also a language problem.

2 The comment from Foxford School speakers which I recall most clearly was that they have found it necessary not only to simplify worksheets but to pay attention to the 'instructional' language, that is the way in which instructions are actually given to pupils. This most important point extends past worksheets, of course, to the way in which teachers talk to pupils, i.e. to spoken instructions.

3 Doug Waterhouse, despite his modest disclaimers that nothing much was happening, actually seemed to me to be defining the way a language and learning policy ought to operate — by a growing consciousness of such things as the importance of talk, or the inappropriateness of commercial materials for the real pupils in one's classes. His comment that the way a teacher talks to pupils, or uses books, is intuitive is, I think, only partly true; it is important to become conscious of what the characteristics of good practice are, so that the good can become the norm, rather than a happy

accident.

4 Bill Shields, in his impish talk, brought home powerfully to me the relativity of knowledge, by his story about changing as a boy from a Northern Irish to a Southern Irish school and discovering, in a history syllabus picked up at exactly the same stage, that 'overnight the heroes had become villains and the villains heroes'. It made me realize the absurdity of presenting anything about history as a *fact*.

5 Sandra Morgan's comments about consulting pupils for their views I support entirely. I am consistently impressed at the insights pupils have into their own learning. Pupils in a fourth-year history group remarked to me that they remembered what they said themselves rather than what the teacher said 'even though it makes sense at the time'. They added that they also remembered the bits immediately before and after what they said.

6 There were other points, arising from discussion, which I have remembered. The recognition, for example, that to get purposeful talk, you have to have something to talk *about*. The fact that even the most purposeful talk meanders and digresses. The problems for the teacher of measuring the quality of talk — how can you tell when it works? The point about talk, I take it, is that success is when pupils say something they didn't know they knew, and that the teacher's job is then to make the pupils aware of what it is they have said.

Someone commented that the process by which you arrive at a decision say, in the Iron and Steel game, is more important than the decision itself. And another point was that the teacher's job, above all, is to make the connections between ideas which might otherwise remain unconnected and that you don't always have to do this by lecturing.

I am grateful to that meeting for giving me so many valuable and interesting ideas to mull over and for being given the opportunity to write this short note. It has helped me to reflect on the thinking that was going on that night.

SECTION THREE

Language and history teaching

In the secondary school all subject teachers need to be aware of (i) the linguistic processes by which their pupils acquire information and understanding, and the implications for the teacher's own use of language; and (ii) the reading demands of their own subjects and ways in which the pupils can be helped to meet them (Bullock, Recom. 138).

Language competence grows incrementally, though an interaction of writing, talk, reading, and experience, and the best teaching deliberately influences the nature and quality of this growth (ibid 3).

1 *The Language of history*
It would seem important before discussing its educational problems and opportunities to examine the nature of the rhetoric of history.
Two views:

Perhaps the chief problem in the history teacher's use of . . . language is that he rarely sees it as a problem. The history graduate has become so used to the style of rhetoric of his subject, so familiar with its technical language, that he considers that he is using a common everyday language, easily recognized and understood by all other natives. Clearly this is not so, and historical language is highly specialized by necessity. (J. Fines, *Language in History Teaching*, p. 1.)

Professor J.H. Hexter argues that 'What makes it so easy and so hard' is that 'the specialized language of history is and has to be for the most part common language. Or conversely, common language is usually adequate and satisfactory for historical explanation.' (*The History Primer*, p. 67.)

Either view requires a closer analysis of both the vocabulary and the syntax of historical language, and consideration of any special difficulties due to the age and ability of pupils and their background.

2 *Historical terminology*
    (a)   'The words we use about time are so diverse that often several may mean *roughly* the same thing, whilst each retains its specialist purpose. (The Tudors, the Age of Expansion, the High Renaissance . . . etc.) The language

of institutions . . . of cultures . . . of movements and ideas . . . and of general concepts . . . all present their problems . . .'. (Fines, *ibid*)

(b) Hexter emphasizes the dangers of restrictive definitions, when we are 'dealing with people or groups of people in the past who are on the move'. 'Processive definition' is needed, meaning which emerges as we study change, which is 'enough to be going on with' (*op. cit.* pp. 352–4).

(c) Historians have the special problems of the historical nature of words and their meanings, 'the history of thought and sentiment which underlies the semantic biography of a word' (C.S. Lewis, *Studies in Words*, p. 2; Hexter, *op. cit.* p. 350).

(d) Historical language is 'value-laden' — for example Professor Cobban once remarked that we cannot employ the word *massacre* without implying some degree of disapproval: Hexter writes of 'translational and psychedelic' language (*op. cit.* Chap. 4).

Educational implications

(a) 'Difficulties of specialized terminology lie not so much in acquisition of labels but in pupils 'internalizing of labels' referents . . .'. (HMI P. Gannon, 'Language across the Curriculum, COSTA, June 1976.)

(b) Psychological theories emphasize the development of thinking skills from concrete to abstract operations before and during adolescence and the problems of concept formation.

'It is important to remember that concepts are mental constructs. No other person can actually give you a concept: you have to construct it yourself . . .' (J. Coltham, TH34, p. 6).

(c) 'One may . . . overstate the problem . . . for if a special language has a real use there will be a sensible way of learning it . . . a known vocabulary is a great aid in planning a sequence of lessons . . .' (Fines, p. 2).

The syntax of the language of history

(a) ' . . . historical language talks of the past and must use the most difficult tenses, and it speaks of things that can never be known in their entirety, so that it must use the most difficult mood . . .' (Fine, p. 1).

(b) Hexter discusses as an example the use of the hypothetical subjunctive (must and say) (*op. cit.* pp. 322–9).

(c) K.R. Cripwell in *The Language of History* analyses some of the problems

  (i)' . . . the language of history teaching . . . will inevitably require a high degree of ability on the part of the pupil to express relationships in time . . . to manipulate the full range of past tenses . . . the perfect, the past perfect, the past continuous and the simple past . . .'

  (ii)language to express complex relationships of:
     cause and effect
     conditionals
     subordination, sometimes 'where qualifiers qualify other qualifiers'.

Educational implications

Pupils' difficulties are likely to be due to lack of experience in language use, whether due to their age or social background, e.g. K. Cripwell states that children do not easily operate the full range of past tenses, nor the 'true conditional'. Professor Basil Bernstein's research contrasts the simple grammatical structure of the 'restricted code' language of some social groups with the more 'elaborated code' of school language. Hexter emphasizes the disadvantage of some groups because of their ignorance of the common language of cities (p. 67 fn. 1).

The educational contribution of history would therefore seem to be partly in this area, giving experience and skills in operating both concepts and language structures which are important not only in doing history but in every aspect of living in a complex world.

Would research into pupils' use of conjunctions (and, then, but, therefore, if, although, etc.) be useful?

4 *The uses and varieties of language in historical learning*
  (a) *Reading*
    See Bullock. Recommendations 66–69, e.g. 'Comprehension skills consist in the interaction between the author's meanings and the reader's purpose, in the course of which the reader confirms or modifies his

previous ideas and attitudes.' (67)

'The majority of pupils need a great deal of positive help to develop the various comprehension skills to a high level.' Dr Fines: 'Children need to be trained in finding information . . . they need to comprehend their discovery, not just understanding it as an answer to a given question . . . but as material to be used'. In relation to the special problems of original documents they should also 'ask what the material meant when it was written . . .' This involves 'intensive reading of short passages at slow rates' and this 'makes for a much deeper understanding of the message in the end'.

History textbooks
See *Teaching History* Vol 1 No. 3 May 1970, J. Coltham. 'Assessing History Books' and Vol. III No. 12 Nov. 1974. P. Lucas. 'A Systematic Approach to Textbooks and Other Written Materials.'

(b) *Listening and talking*
Bullock: 'Pupils should learn to regard discussion as an opportunity to investigate and illuminate a subject, not to advance inflexible points of view.' (114) 'There should be a conscious policy on the part of the teacher to improve the children's listening ability . . . (115) 'It is regrettable that oral work figures so little in many history classrooms . . . more training in this field would improve the situation, for the encouragement of open discussion is one of the most difficult aspects of a teacher's work . . .' (Fines, 3).

Cannon spoke of a 'quantitative imbalance' between oral and other work and research has shown that teachers rarely ask open questions. 'Common language is most often a dialogue, not a monologue; it involves an exchange of signals . . .' (Hexter, *op. cit.* pp. 72–3).

Writing
Bullock: 'The teacher should extend the pupil's ability as a writer primarily by developing his intentions and then by working on the technique appropriate to them.' (125)

'Pupils should be given the opportunity to write for a

variety of readers and audiences . . .' (127)

'Competence in language comes above all through its purposeful use . . .' (128)

The Schools Council and London University Institute of Education Joint Project; *Writing across the Curriculum, 11–13 years* in *Why Write?* analyses 'A Sense of Audience: The Child and his Reader', and the 'Functions of Writing'

- expressive
- transactional
- poetic

Are all these relevant to history?

Dr Fines: 'A finished product is especially necessary to history, yet the writing of history is hard and demanding . . . The kinds of request history makes of the pupil all seem very high level — compare and contrast, explain, interpret, evaluate, etc. and the quality of performance required is high, demanding clarity, balance (involving both fair reporting and full coverage) and imagination' (p. 3).

While maintaining that history employs common language, Hexter explains that written history uses 'common formal prose', 'much stiffer, more formidable and harder to manage', and this is why while many people think writing good history is easy, most find it hard (p.73 *seq*).

Conclusions?

'The language requirements of history are high and complex and need good teaching to achieve, but there is no doubt that history provides a good area for the practice and development of high order objectives in speech and language.' (Fines, 3)

[Historical Association discussion paper prepared for a conference on 'Language in History Teaching' arranged by the Historical Association Education Committee, February 1977.

The Historical Association would be pleased to hear details of language initiatives by school history departments.]

15 Language in Home Economics

Introduction

With the publication of the Bullock Committee Report *A Language for Life* in February 1975, many teachers undertook work on the use of language in their schools. As home economics is a subject particularly reliant on the use of language, in particular oral language, the question of language development within home economics was posed.

Although a great deal of discussion was already going on in many different schools, in some of which home economists were directly involved, there was felt to be a need for research with actual teaching techniques, which would be best tackled by a subject-based group. A group of home economics teachers was convened to explore the subject at length.

During the first discussion, many points were raised which worried home economics teachers about their own experience of language in teaching.

1 A lack of information on language and reading in their teacher-training courses.
2 The lack of direction to home economics departments from specialists on an organized language policy, including reading, throughout the school.
3 Lack of liaison between remedial and other departments to help encourage the less able child, by producing work of a suitable level.
4 Although the need for audio-visual aids is seen, the facilities are not always available to, or convenient for, the home economics departments.

Many of these points encouraged members to look into other aspects of their school, for instance, to find out how reading was taught, what policies on marking there are etc.

It soon became obvious that the problems encountered were not necessarily only those of the home economists, but could also be relevant for teachers of any other subject. It was interesting therefore to look at the work produced by a boy in all the subjects on his timetable. (See pages 238–9.)

Some samples from the work of the fourteen-year-old boy during the week

biology	The structure missing is the neuclus
	The red blood cells are the smaller
	There we more red cells than white
	The red cells contain heomoglobin
	The function of the haemoglobin is that is gives oxygen to the cells
	The blood picks up blood from skin lungs and gills

chemistry
(copied)

When the carbon was lowered into the gas jar it burst into a yellow flame when the carbon stop burning the spoon was removed and lime water was added it turned milky.

design
(copied)

These fine round wire nails have small heads and numerous uses particularly for fixing ply wood panels and simple lapped joints. The diameter of wire nails such as panel pins varies and is based on the standard wire gauges.

English

My dad has got black curly hair with brown eyes. He is very strong and quite tall. He works with the city engineers. His hobbies is diy (do it yourself). His appearance is very good. When he goes to work he dresses casually and when he goes out he dresses neatly. He dislikes hockey and other girl games and only likes rugby.

French

(description of a monster he has drawn)
Il a y trois tetes. Il y a trois pieds dans les tetes. Son les tetes rond mais ne cheveux pas. Il y a deux yeux. Il y a trois nez. Il y n's pas les dents . . .

history

The thing they achieve on this long march is first is that they help keep Chinese Communism alive and help the peasant to rise up against their landlords and throw them out.

home
economics

assignment 6
  (a) 3 groups classified as energy givers are fats carbohydrates sugar
  (b) 5 foods in fats are butter margerine lard suet

237

A week's work for a fourteen-year-old boy

	Topic	Copied from book or blackboard	No. of pages in week	Pupil's own work	Answers to questions worksheets in own words
English	(i) Timothy Winter	✓	(1)		
	(ii) the Missing Statue		(1)	Story	
	(iii) descriptions		(4)	Descriptions & biographies	
			$\underline{6}$		
history	History of China	✓	1		
design	nails	✓	1		
art	life drawing		1	Drawing neck and collar	
home economics	nutrition – diet		3½		✓

	Topic	Copied from book or blackboard	No. of pages in week	Pupil's own work	Answers to questions worksheets in own words
R E	Mohammed	✓	3		
biology	the housefly blood		5		✓
chemistry	carbon dioxide	✓	4		
music	Benjamin Britten project	✓	2		
maths	functions and averages		10		✓
French	describe a drawing		1	✓	
week's totals		6	37½	4	3

pudding and milk

(c) 5 foods in carbohydrates are flour cereals pastry biscuits and cornflakes

. . . function of fat is that it keeps us warm and give us energy.

maths			$x - 3$	
	0	−3	(0	− 3)
	1	−2	(1	2)
	2	−1	(2	1)
	3	0	(3	0)
	4	1	(4	1)
	5	2	(5	2)
	6	3	(6	3)

music   . . . He began to compose at a very early age and continued his studies. After leaving school, at the Royal College of Music in London, there he studied Piano Conducting, he also met Peter Pears a young singer and formed a long life friendship with him. Later sang and recorded many of Brittens songs.

RE   . . . Mohammed began to preach his beliefs and he denounced idols and other such things. His wife Khadija believed in him and so did his servant Zarid. But people despised and started to persecute them. In A.D. 622 Mohammed decided to migrate to a town called Medina . . .

Talk and oral language

Although the topic is clearly of universal relevance, it was felt very important to consider language from the point of view of the home economist. To do this, the methods by which a child might learn information were investigated. They are:

1 Teacher talking informally to the group.
2 Teacher presenting information to the group.
3 Pupils reading.
4 Pupils writing.
5 Pupils working on their own and presenting their results.

To investigate (1) and (2), each member of the working party had a tape recording made of them teaching when they were unaware the tape was on. The tape was then transcribed. (For examples of the transcripts, see Appendix A.)

The use of oral language was felt to be very important. All methods should be encouraged wherever possible, i.e.

(a) discussion between teacher and pupils
(b) discussion between pupils themselves
(c) instructions from teacher (i.e. pupils listening)
(d) evaluation and comments from pupils (i.e. teacher listening).

Whatever the subject matter, or method used, the teacher should obviously try to create a constructive and purposeful atmosphere. We feel that talk is the best way of doing this, for the following reasons.

(a) Free talk helps to promote an informal atmosphere in which a good relationship with the pupil can be fostered.
(b) By encouraging talk, we promote enthusiasm and interest from the children for the subject, and give them an understanding of the relevance of it, by discussing with them the subject to be covered, and allowing them to relate it to their own experience.
(c) It extends the child's own language, and particularly through practical work, promotes the use of technical vocabulary.
(d) Through talk especially, the child's own knowledge extends, through discovery methods of discussion, and so we can help him to feel he has achieved something worthwhile by encouraging his contributions to a lesson.
(e) Through talk and discussion, we can evaluate a child's progress, which has traditionally been discovered through writing — i.e. essays, exams etc.

Progress is perhaps more accurately assessed through talk. By listening to a child, we can discover how much was understood, how much was remembered, and how the child can use this new found knowledge to adapt and understand his own experience. Discussion work and oral examinations are now accepted as part of the final assessment for certain examinations, although marking such work was found to be difficult.

(f) By talking we can most successfully discover our pupils' capabilities and limitations. A child can very often use books to gather information and yet may not put the information to use. By taking part in discussion with him we can adjust our expectations to what is more appropriate.

(g) Through talk, above all, we can guide pupils to seek certain information, extend their knowledge on that subject, relate it to their own situations and experience, and so adapt their opinions and outlooks in the light of this new knowledge: in other words, through talk, pupils can learn.

Attention should be paid to the actual process of learning, and not just to the finished results. This applies to all areas of the school curriculum, of course, and equally to home economics. For instance, if we consider making an apple pie as an example of a process, it's clear that we need to consider not just the finished pie — the product — but also the 55 minutes of preparation in the lesson which led up to it. This then leads us to pay attention to such things as:

(i) use of equipment — for all those processes that need it
(ii) where equipment is kept
(iii) following a recipe or instructions
(iv) understanding use of appliances
(v) the social aspects of working together, sharing equipment etc.
(vi) hygiene in practice
(vii) techniques and how well they are understood — rubbing in etc.

The finished result *is* important, but not as important as how you get there.

We can compare this process with writing an essay. It is the finished essay, like the apple pie, that is the product; but what's important is the process of how it was arrived at — the collecting of ideas, the formulation of the ideas into words, the organization of them in order, and so on.

The disadvantages of encouraging oral language must also be realized.

(a) A class may be more difficult to discipline if a relaxed atmosphere has been encouraged.

(b) Talk in a classroom can be distracting to other pupils and to the teacher. But the disadvantages can be overcome if the work is well organized. The children need to see the necessity for the work, both by seeing the point of this particular piece of work, and by having their ideas and work taken up and developed by the teacher.

After seeing the need for this type of work, teachers are urged to make regular tapes and transcripts so they can monitor the use of talk in their teaching lives. In Appendix B, we display a 'before-and-after' example of what paying attention to talk and learning can do.

From transcripts, certain conclusions can be drawn.

1 The amount of language varies according to the type of lesson. The particular child, the type of room they are working in, and the work they have undertaken. The transcripts showed that as teachers we talked far more than we thought we did.

2 All children should be encouraged to talk about the work constructively, to promote a working atmosphere. The transcripts showed that the children were not given the opportunity to talk as much as they might.

3 Although written work is necessary for certain purposes, it should not be thought of as the only evidence of work completed. Oral language should also be taken into consideration. General class discussion after small group work, or taping small groups, are ways of monitoring oral work.

(The WMEB. has put out a very interesting paper about oral assessment, which contains practical suggestions for situations in which such assessment can be made.)

4 Certain pupils would benefit from less written work: for instance for younger or less-able pupils, taped work might well replace written work. (See Appendix B.)

5 Every child should be encouraged, and helped, to participate in lessons, even though the more reticent may be reluctant to do so. In such cases, organize small group work, because the passing on of information and ideas is very important, as well as the interaction between pupils.

6 Teachers are not always readily understood. It is difficult

to know where to pitch one's language, and a thorough knowledge of each child and his background is essential if the correct level is to be found.

7 It is important to look at a lesson from a child's point of view if we wish to discover how to teach the knowledge and understanding we want them to learn. It is *easy* for the teacher but boring for the pupil to have dictated notes. The child will probably retain very little.

It is a lot of work for the teacher, but interesting and stimulating for the child to have a film, a discussion, questions to ask and to answer, work to illustrate: and more will be remembered.

By presenting the information in many varied ways, and encouraging different ways of understanding it, we help the pupil to learn in his own way, not the way of the teacher.

Worksheets
The group also considered other methods of learning.

(i) Children reading
(ii) Children writing
(iii) Children working on their own or in groups, and presenting information.

We considered the use and layout of worksheets and assignment cards, and would draw the following conclusions.

(a) Pupils must realize the purpose of the worksheet. An explanation may be necessary of what is expected of them; or it may be necessary to make clear the particular technique of learning they are to encounter.

(b) It is important that there should be clear justifications for the use of worksheets as a medium. There are many cases where it would be more effective for the pupil to answer questions orally rather than write the answers down; or to seek information and sift out the relevant points rather than be given the information on a worksheet.

(c) The aims of the worksheet must be clearly defined: they may be general aims — for example, to make pupils think about a particular problem — or specific aims — for example, to help the pupil understand a precise area of information.

(d) The worksheet must fit into the rest of the planned work so that the pupil uses as many learning techniques as possible. For instance, the worksheet can organize the following situations:

    (i) children working independently
   (ii) children working in pairs or small groups
  (iii) the use of library, reference skills, and resources
  (iv) discussion
   (v) research work
  (vi) experiments

(e) On close inspection, many worksheets are not suitable for the pupils they were intended for, and a reassessment is often very necessary.

(f) The question to ask oneself is:
Does this worksheet allow the pupil to enlarge his experience and knowledge and adapt what he knows to what he is being asked?

If it merely requires stereotyped answers, which are simply either right or wrong — 'information-giving' answers — is there any point in producing it?

General points

1 All methods used in teaching should be continually examined and reassessed. Much more work needs to be done on the suitability of books in our HE department; and a correlation should be made between the books provided, and the reading abilities of our pupils.

2 It was felt helpful to have discussions with the rest of the school staff, to produce a uniform policy on such matters as presentation of pupils' work, and uniformity of ways of marking work, as it was felt it could be detrimental to the child if anomalies occur in schools.

3 The use of cassette recorders is a simple way of encouraging effective oral work, and we felt that cash should be made available for this purpose.

4 We should be conscious of the whole school life of a pupil, not just when he or she is in the HE department. This can most easily be achieved by following a tutorial group for a day. This enables a teacher to see a child's education from his

own point of view, which should put our own subject into perspective. Whatever we learn from tracking pupils like this, it is important to look at it from the pupil's point of view.

A child will react favourably, and, we hope, understand and learn, if:

1 The work presented is relevant to the pupils' own interests, concerns and preoccupations. So work should be planned with the child's real needs in mind, not what the teacher thinks he should be taught.
2 He finds the work interesting and stimulating — so that he *wants* to learn, rather than have to be forced.
3 He understands what is expected of him, and realizes why that work is being set — so that the work is a genuine part of the learning, rather than something to occupy him.

By looking at the work from the pupils' point of view, it becomes clear that what every child learns may be quite different from the other pupils. This means that teaching becomes much more complex and demanding; but it also becomes much more effective, and ultimately more rewarding for both teacher and learner.

Appendix A Transcripts

1 Miss Roselyn Golub, Coundon Court School
Transcript of a recording lasting five minutes of questions and answers on 'The feeding of babies and young children' revision for a small fifth-year child care examination class at the beginning of a lesson.

Me	I am asking you to what foods do you introduce a baby?
Cheryl	Rusks — cereal.
Me	Rusks in milk. Yes. Cereal. Soft cereal. Heinz in tins, and those you tasted last week. Which was the best out of those you tasted last week?
Jill	Chocolate pudding.
Me	Yes. Heinz chocolate pudding. What was wrong with the foods in jars?
Sandra	Didn't taste like chocolate pudding.

Me	What about the things in packets?
Leisa	Powdery.
Me	Tasted very powdery. Yes. What other foods can you give them apart from tins and rusks in milk and cereals. Got to think of protein haven't we?
Deborah	Fruit.
Me	Fruit puree. Yes.
Leisa	Mashed up foods
Me	Yes. True.
Sandra	Eggs.
Me	Yes. Egg yolk is a good food to start with because there's plenty of iron in it and baby needs iron because when he starts weaning he has run out of the supply he was born with from his mother — pause — What equipment does the baby need when he starts feeding — Jill? — Pause — come on. Does he need a big knife and fork?
Jill	No. Spoon and bowl.
Me	Yes a bowl with a lip on so that the food doesn't fall over and a good bib, preferably one of those with a front that turns up and catches anything that falls down — pause — What should you do when feeding a baby? For the first few times because it's a very new thing for him to sit in a high chair and to start eating things by himself and having a spoon in his mouth. What should you do if he doesn't like it?
Deborah	Do it yourself. Feed him. Encourage him.
Me	Encourage him. Yes. Don't shout at him or be insistent but try to persuade him gently to eat the food. What about toddlers? How do you teach them correct table manners?
	Pause — noise — have a doll's tea party
Me	No I don't think so. What else?
Dawn	Sit down at a table where everybody else is.
Me	Yes. Sit him at a table if you can where everybody else is and let him join in. He should be relaxed and comfortable — pause — What about overweight babies — are there any of these?
Deborah	Yes.
Me	There are about 10 per cent of adults in Britain who are overweight which means probably that

	10 per cent of babies were. How is this caused? How do babies become overweight?
Dawn	Overweight when it was born or born too late.
Me	Yes. But that's only a minor thing — it's usually feeding isn't it? Wrong feeding. Yes. Mothers adding sugar to too much milk to bottle feeds — pause — right, that'll do I think. You've got worksheets now on Care of Children's Feet. Let's go through it together quickly and then answer the questions. Leisa will you start reading please.

2 *Mrs J. Harris, Stoke Park School*

T.	What have you got there?
G1+2	A mouldy onion.
T.	Well throw it away then — and you shouldn't be using — not just in the bin, Geraldine, wrap it up. And you should be using the other side of the chopping board — the formica side, not the wooden side.
G4	Shall I get newspaper?
T.	Yes.
G2	She told me turn it over.
G4	Where's the newspaper?
T.	Behind you. We're having new cookers in here by the way — three new electric cookers. That'll be nice.
G3	Oh good.
T.	A bright yellow one there.
G3	Yellow?
T.	By special request. And a fan assisted one there.
G1	A what?
T.	A fan assisted.
Boy	Have a pink one over there, Miss (laughs)
T.	No, I don't want a pink one, I want a yellow one
Boy	And a black one sitting on the ceiling.
T.	Oh, shut up. Karen what's the matter?
G5	I'm looking for the er thing.
T.	The what?

G5	The weighing thing.
G2	Miss, what shall we do . . . First put the mince meat in with the onion and fry it together?
T.	Fry it together, yes.
	(Muffled noises)
T.	Well, if you fry the mince first, you'll find that enough fat comes out for you to fry the onion in and you won't have to add any extra.

3 *Alyson Charles, Tile Hill Wood School*

G1	I'm stuck on threading the machine
T.	What do you mean, you're stuck on threading it?
G1	I'm stuck on the bit in the middle, how to do it
T.	Haven't you ever threaded a Singer machine before?
G1	Yes but I've forgotten
T.	You know what you are don't you? What are you (laughter)
T.	Round that little hook there, round the tension discs, up and round that little hook, down the side and round and through the needle; are you sure you have the bobbin threaded properly and you have tightened the wheel?
G1	Yes
G2	Miss Charles what do I do now?
T.	Well you can machine that now. Make sure that you leave a space open at the top, to put the stuffing in, that's what the pattern says to do isn't it?
G2	Yes, it says to leave a gap open at the top
T.	Right, carry on
T.	I hope you're not going to stick it all together with sellotape?
G4	No I'm not, I'm just putting it there to keep it firm while I sew
G5	Miss, miss, can I do a blanket?
T.	What do you mean a blanket?
G5	You know, for a doll or something
T.	For a doll or something?
G5	Yes
T.	Oh, do you mean a patchwork one?
G5	Yes — a patchwork
T.	Well as long as it's a patchwork one, you can do it. You're going to start on the trinket box next week?

G5   Yes, if I can get the materials together.

4 *Fourth year home economics group theory lesson*

A.   Clean the cupboard 35 minutes. Hang on, it doesn't take you half an hour to clean the sink. Maam, what if you've got time left over?

T.   Now then do you think you're going to have time left over?

A.   I don't know but the way it works out I will

T.   Well we usually do just the dish, don't we and we just do a quick clean. We're doing a special clean now.

A.   Yes, the way I've worked it out I've got to spend half an hour on each of the cleaning jobs

T.   Well let's have a look at what you've . . . you'll need about twenty minutes at least to do it properly

A.   I've put thirty minutes to do the . . .
It's all right doing the cooker and this for twenty minutes but you wouldn't clean the sink for twenty minutes

T.   Oh no! No you'll do that in about ten minutes, won't you?

A.   Yes

T.   Er . . . let's see how long you've spent on your dish
Pause
Yes, it looks as though you've allowed enough time, so in your case you can finish early but . . . er . . . where have you finished to?

A.   Oh say spend ten minutes to . . . er . . . it will be some time before 11.45

T.   Well put down the time and put serve the dish

A.   Yes

T.   Have you got the washing up done? Have you allowed time to do that?

A.   Yes I'll do the washing up then. Can I put that down?

T.   Well you want to do the washing up before you clean the sink don't you?

A.   Yes. Yes. Well I could do that after I've done this couldn't I so I'll put it there and then do . . .

T.   . . . and then next week when you do it just see if you do actually keep to that time. See if you can do it all in that time . . .

G.6 Please ma'am will you ask Sarvjit to try her pants on?

T. Mm, yes when she's done that little bit of tacking

G.7 Oh ma'am I wish this machine would make up its mind what its doing

T. Is that Kawsliva that's getting ratty over there? Kawsliva the cotton's finished now

G.7 Ma'am I can't get this spool out

T. I thought I'd just given you a new one?

G.7 No, the other one ma'am

T. The bottom one?

T. Have you looked in the workbox to see if there is another one?
(Machine noise)

G.8 Ma'am are you selling those pencil cases?

T. Pardon

G.8 Are you selling them?

T. Mm, yes, probably. I would think so when I've finished

G.8 Oh will when you are, will you let me know ma'am because I want to buy one

T. Right. Cut just into there first before you turn it through. First up to the stitches
(Machine noise)

G.1 For this bit ma'am will I have to?

T. Yes, you'll have to re-tack that, haven't you? It looks as if it's come undone

G.1 It has ma'am (laughs)

T. Yes, you'll have to tack that bit again

G.1 Ma'am just for that little bit, I'd have finished ma'am

T. Mm. Still you've got a lot more that you'll be machining, so

G.1 Today ma'am?

T. I would think so yes. You've got all your seams to neaten . . .zig-zag
(Machine noise)

T. Have you done that? Now, that's better. There seems a lot of bulk in the top corner I don't think you've cut quite close enough to the stitches. Hurry up . . . you haven't trimmed these. All the way round.

Appendix B 'Before and after'

It isn't easy to accept that it may be better to allow pupils to talk rather than talking to them oneself: we worry that they won't stick to the point, or that if we don't tell them the information, they won't learn it. Equally, we may feel that talk on its own is less effective than writing, and that we must have writing if pupils are to learn.

The following examples may illustrate why we believe that it is important not just to allow, but actually to *encourage* pupil talk: and why we believe that assignments involving only talk, may sometimes be more valuable than writing.

Firstly, a lesson about first-aid, as part of the CSE child care syllabus. The teacher is working with a fifth-year class.

Teacher	*Pupils*
Number 3 — if the accident involves suffocation treatment is more specialized — one what is it — now imagine you've got this little three-year-old here and you've found her with a polythene bag over her head — unconscious — going blue	Take the plastic bag off
.Take the plastic bag off her head	Sounds funny dunnit
Yeh I know — sounds horrible (1) Yes but what do you have to do then — just because you've taken the polythene bag off their head, doesn't make her better	Yeh but Kiss of life
(2) Yes that's right — artificial resuscitation kiss of life . . . it might not be a polythene bag, it might be some other reason, it might be that she has drowned in the bath — you'd do the same thing — kiss of life. Number 2 explain exactly how the kiss of life should be administered (2), remembering you are likely to be dealing with a small child	Open the mouth

252

(3) No, you have to find that out in
the books exactly how to do it   What . . .

(1) You have to find out how to give
the kiss of life — now *you* giving a
young child the kiss of life can do
more damage — than has already been   And you've gotta
done to it, so you have to be very   give ten reasons
careful some of you aren't working   for all of them

No no no no no ten reasons for a

Number 3 what further treatment is
necessary — now you've taken the
plastic bag off its head you've blown
into it to make it breathe again this
child is aged three, you can't just leave
it there and then   Phone the ambulance

The teacher afterwards commented as follows.

1 My initial reaction was of horror of the different *amounts*
  of language used by me, and the group. This was particularly
  shattering as I always thought that I gave the pupils time to
  express themselves and develop their own ideas, but in fact
  I talk eight times more than the girls.
2 The many instances that I stopped the pupils' conversation
  dead, when it could have been extended (places marked 1).
3 The very different language used by me and the pupils,
  without explanation from me as to what certain terms mean
  (places marked 2).
4 The information that is handed to them from me, rather than
  leaving the child to find out for herself *or* seeking out some
  knowledge that she has, and trying to extend her experience
  (places marked 3).
5 Having thought that this preamble was necessary in order for
  the children to explain the work set, and to think about the
  problem, it was a shock to read the written work as a follow-
  up to this discussion. For example, one question was about
  the kiss of life (remembering you are likely to be dealing with
  young children), and how it is administered.
      One of the answers began — remove dentures!

In other words, the writing demonstrated how little I had genuinely helped them to understand.

Secondly, a lesson with first years. The teacher had intended to deal with the topic of underwear: one group of girls claimed to 'know all about it already'. The teacher sent them off into the flat with a tape-recorder, to make a tape about what they knew about bras. They worked through the lesson, carried on through break, and then produced the tape transcribed here. They worked entirely unaided throughout.

Narrator	Julie Farebrother is a twelve-year-old girl. She wants to buy her first bra, but she doesn't know anything about it, so she's going to ask her friend, Jane.
Julie	Jane, how do I go about buying a bra? How do I know what size I am — or — you know, where do I go, what do I do? I don't know a thing about it. Will you tell me please?
Jane	Yes. Well, first of all you measure underneath your bust, and then you measure your actual bust, and you subtract the two numbers
Julie	What you mean under here and round here?
Jane	Yes, that's right. And if you're say left with two inches you'll be cup A, 2–3 inches you'll be cup B, and so on. So if you wanted to buy the bra you'd go into the shop and if you were bust 28, you'd say 'cup A, bust 28, please' and they'd know exactly what to get you. If your measurements across there were exactly the same, there's no need for you to worry about buying a bra just yet
Julie	Well, could you measure me, because I can't really measure myself. You know, I don't really understand.
Jane	Well look, you take your measurements under there, you see, and then you take it across the top. Now, at the moment your measurements are just about the same so there's no need for you to get a bra just yet.
Julie	About how long will I have to wait before I need a bra?
Jane	About three to four months I suppose
Julie	Blimey, that's a long time
Jane	Well, not really, because a lot of girls your age don't

	wear bras, it's only some of them
Julie	Oh well, you've made it a lot easier for me and now I think I understand it. You explained it very well, thank you.
Chorus	We wear a bra to keep our bust in shape
Girl 1	We also wear a bra to hold our bust up and keep comfortable. The shoulder straps are usually adjustable. You should try and get it the correct tightness for comfort. You can get elastic straps which you stretch to any size, or the ordinary sort you adjust yourself
Girl 2	For girls of our age it is best to have the straps which stretch as you grow. Cup sizes start from A and end at B.
Girl 3	It is necessary to wear the right coloured bra according to what colour top you are wearing. If you are wearing a light-coloured top you must wear a light-coloured bra
Girl 4	Elastic panels come under the bra cups. It helps to support the bust and helps the bra from being pulled up
Chorus	Without bras, we think our busts would be most uncomfortable.

The teacher feels that the quality of this far outweighs anything the girls could have done in writing, and it has encouraged her to set up other ways of using tape-recorders.

These two examples together suggest the potential of talk. We are not pretending that it is *easy* to organize for talk; but we do feel that it is important to try.

There have also been examples of individual departments working together within the school: geography departments observing each other's lessons and collecting examples of technical words that staff were using without realizing that pupils didn't understand; history departments taping lessons and listening to them; a PE department doing the same, and discussing the role of language in teaching skills in games, and in explaining dance and so on.

And there are also other, ultimately more absorbing but more complex experiences, illustrated by one anecdote. Beginning to

255

discuss the feudal system (on the syllabus for that time of year) a class asked the teacher what the difference was between peasants and slaves. In their discussions, the pupils brought in examples of slavery from several different countries, at different times. As the discussion went on, the teacher realized that perhaps the *theme* of slavery made a better bench mark on the syllabus than the topic of 'the feudal system'. In discussions with the other members of the department, the teachers began inevitably to discuss the whole nature of a history syllabus and ultimately to debate ideas about legitimate knowledge. This is the kind of discussion which ought to be perhaps kept within the department, because it is informed by highly specific bodies of information. It is also, clearly, the kind of thing which could happen with any subject department.

SECTION 7
PUTTING IT TOGETHER

When a school has a working party concentrating on language work, other colleagues are always bound to ask 'what's this to do with me?' What you see in this section is an example of the whole process by which the work of a group can reach out, affect the whole of a school, and change policy and practice.

Homework is not a topic that seems immediately gripping. It is a topic about which there can be strongly held views and stances, but it doesn't seem to offer much for a language working party to get hold of. In fact, as you'll see, this is not the case, mainly because of the way the group chose to approach its exploration. The use of pupils' views, and the underpinning ideas about learning and basic processes, inform the report with an unusual force. The consequence of the report was that every department was asked to discuss its approach to homework, and to report back to the main policy-making body of the school. Out of that discussion came the final document, a new part of the school's handbook for staff. The policy now is unusual, I would guess, in that into its creation has gone hard data from research, opinions from pupils, parents and teachers, and major discussions by a staff. Even so, there are still several interesting possibilities left available for further explanation, not least the question of revision and how it should be taught.

The first document is the working party's report to the school's Curriculum Development and Consultative Committees. The second is the revised page in the school's handbook.

16   Homework survey

I   The Bullock Committee was asked by the Curriculum
       Development Committee to explore the homework policy
       of the school. There were anxieties that in the third year:

   1   Pupils were not being given enough experience of the
          kind of work they would be expected to do in the
          fourth year.
   2   Not enough demands were being made on the pupils.
          They were not being extended.
   3   Staff might not be setting homework as often as the
          policy handbook and the timetable indicated.

II   The Bullock Committee set out to explore these questions
       by collecting evidence of the amount and the varieties of
       homework actually done. The first attempt was to
       examine homework note books but it was found that they
       were rarely used.
          A specific project was therefore begun with a third-year
       tutor group. The girls were asked to note all homework
       over the period of three weeks; to time the work set during
       one week and to indicate the type of homework.
          The specific questions the committee were trying to
       answer were:

   1   How much homework is supposed to be set per
          week? How much is actually set?
   2   What types of homework were set?
   3   How long does it take the girls to do it?
   4   Why do teachers actually set homework?

III   1   The accompanying Table 1 shows the amount of
           homework set. Since the groups contain different sets
           in some subjects, there is more than the basic 14 units
           x3.
       2   The descriptions of the varieties of homework in
           Table 1 are based on the description in the homework
           notebooks. They are presented in order of frequency
           of occurrence during the three weeks. There is little

evidence to suggest that different abilities are set different types of homework.

3   There were some discrepancies between the length of time that homework is supposed to take (7 hours per week according to the third-year timetable) and the actual time it took. The times are as follows:

Average time teachers estimated 4 hours 23 mins per week.
Average time actually spent 5 hours 22 mins per week
The longest time spent on homework was 12 hours 5 mins per week.

Further investigation could be done to see whether the length of time pupils take over their homework relates in any way to the attainment level that the pupils achieve.

4   For comparison Table 2 shows a sample of fourth-year homework set in one week.

Average time spent on homework 5 hours 36 mins.
Maximum time spent on homework 9 hours.
Minimum time spent on homework 1 hour 50 mins.

5   We have insufficient information to answer question 4.

IV The group tutor discussed with the pupils their own and their parents' reaction to homework. Several interesting points were made:

1 The majority of pupils have many very worthwhile out-of-school activities. These include music lessons, speech training, guides, girls brigade, youth club, gym club (not school), pony care and discos. They consequently prefer to have homework set with sufficient time allowed before it is to be handed in, so that they can plan it to fit in with their other commitments. This is difficult in some subjects. It seems that those who attend regular evening activities do their homework at week-ends, and parent reaction is that if it can all

be done at the week-end then not enough homework is being set.

Conversely, girls with few evening activities regularly attempt homework most evenings, take longer over it (presumably because they're not committed elsewhere), and parent reaction is that too much is set.

Some parents have considered phoning into school but don't in case they are thought of as interfering or trouble-making. Some parents insist the girls stop work at 9 or 9.30 p.m. whether they've finished or not.

2 There seems to be two reasons why homework can sometimes take 1½–2 hours longer, than either the homework timetable suggests or the teacher estimates. Firstly it happens when the particular subject teacher aims to get through a vast amount of factual work in a lesson. He/she writes notes on the blackboard which girls have to rapidly scribble down. They then rewrite neatly at home; often having to look up points to fill in the blanks. Secondly when tasks include such things as:

'Imagine you have met a spaceman, try to describe the shops which are unknown to him. Write a story about this.'
(H/E homework)

'Do a newspaper clip on the trail or when they come home. Do it like a proper newspaper. Do questions 1, 2, 3, 5 as well.'
(history homework)

This type of work which is desirable because it demands more than straightforward repetition of facts, nevertheless increases the time taken especially for less able girls.

3 Revision and learning howework seem to be most distressing to the girls. Little guidance is given as to how to do this. Staff seem to imply it is the complete responsibility of the pupil with instructions being to:

'Take 2–3 hours or as long as you need to ensure that you know it well.'

4 Project work too seems to need a special mention. It would seem that some staff will set a project to be completed during a holiday time and give no prior help with either the subject or how to compile a project.

V   The survey and the discussions we have had, raised several complex questions. We have found to our surprise that talking about a subject as apparently mundane as homework, has led us into heated arguments and intense discussion and has raised quite fundamental issues about teaching in general. We identify four key areas:

1 The form and variety of homework provided.
2 The effectiveness of homework for assisting learning.
3 Teachers' attitudes and policies.
4 Effects of homework on child and parent.

Some attempt has been made to consider area 4 (see section IV). The other areas include many important questions which are left unanswered and which the committee does not feel competent to answer. We suggest that area 1 and 3 contain the following specific points:

Area 1
(i) Length of time between setting and handing in.
(ii) Recognition by staff of how long homework will take.
(iii) Setting of a greater variety of homework.
(iv) Difference between homework timetable and number of homeworks set.
(v) Planning of homework with more regard to mixed ability.
(vi) Vacation work.

Area 3
(i) Marking of homework.
(ii) Teachers' reasons for setting homework.
(iii) Department policy.
(iv) Use of the homework notebooks.

VI   We also considered the original statement made in the staff handbook (see Appendix). The following points seem relevant:

1 Of the five defined functions for homework 'finishing class work' seems dominant. There seems to be little evidence (in our survey) to suggest homework is used for exploring, finding out, or for reflective writing.
2 Although staff intended to establish a habit of independent work the pupils (and their parents) often do not share their feelings. This may be because of the homework set, which, being largely 'finishing off' and 'revision', does not seem particularly attractive to the pupils nor indeed to encourage this habit.
3 Although the handbook appears to identify good practice with regard to homework, it may well be that staff would wish to re-examine what constitutes good practice.
4 The handbook's statement, which is the result of earlier staff discussion, is quite explicit about the setting of homework. A department may choose to opt out of the homework timetable in the lower and middle school. However, the handbook continues quite explicitly: 'if a department asks for a preparation commitment then work must be set, except on the very rare occasions when nothing meaningful can be given'.

It seems clear to us that either the handbook statement must be altered to take account of actual practice, or departments should consider very carefully what has happened to take them away from a statement they themselves have made and agreed to.

VII We wish to propose that discussions be held to consider some of these questions. In particular, we recommend as a matter of urgency that when 'revision' homework is set the department should explain to pupils how to set about revising and what it involves.

Among the unanswered questions, the committee feel that the following require special consideration:

1 What does a department hope will be the results of its homework policy?

2 Are these desired results actually achieved? For instance, if the function of homework is for pupils to remember something, do they actually remember it? If not, how can a department help pupils to remember?

Third-year homework over three weeks

Type of homework set	Week 1	Week 2	Week 3	Total
none	6	8	6	20
finish off	3	4	4	11
revise	2	5	4	11
copy up	3	3	—	6
none — teacher absent	2	3	1	6
project	2	2	2	6
problems	1	2	1	4
written questions	1	1	1	3
collect (e.g. words, materials)	1	1	2	4
research	—	1	2	3
rough work	—	1	1	2
draw and label	1	—	1	2
poster work	1	1	—	2
read	—	—	1	1
read and comprehend	—	—	1	1
essay	—	—	1	1
think about	—	1	1	1
imagine	—	1	—	1

Fourth-year homework over one week
(table includes work given to different groups)

Type	Total
no homework	21
finish off	12
copy up notes	10
answer questions (in writing)	10
essay	9
written notes	7
problems	6
project	4
copy up experiment	4
read	4
revise	4
drawings	2
none — teacher absent	2
exercises (in French)	1
learn (= memorize)	1
list examples	1
check dictation	1

Homework

Discussed at consultative committee on 16 May 1977. Further details may be had from departmental heads.

Where departments need homework it should be seen as part of the syllabus and planned within the scheme of work. It should never be a constraint on the lesson, and its effectiveness can only be judged in conjunction with the effectiveness of the lesson. It enables the teacher to ensure that in lesson time the pupil can derive maximum benefit from her peers and her teacher. Teachers must ensure that girls understand the way they are to carry out their homework tasks, and these should be within the capabilities of individual children (not easy to set in a mixed-ability class): it sould establish the habit of independent work.

Purpose and types of homework

A feedback for comprehension and a measure of the depth of understanding of work already covered.
Reinforcement of concepts, ideas and methods.
Research (teachers must ensure girls do not just copy up).
Learning.
Reading.

Talking with the family or friends.
(The last three are so valuable that the risk that some will not do it should be taken.)
Preparation for practical work.
Collecting material for the next lesson or homework.
Making progress in a task to maintain interest.

Routine writing can be counter-productive
Heads of department are responsible for studying and rationalizing the marking programme. Each department should have its clearly defined practice which is explained to the girls.

Notebooks
In form 1—2 the form captains will have a homework notebook into which the set homework must be entered for the form tutor's information. Girls who want a homework notebook may buy one from the office.

Fourth- and fifth-year projects
Teachers must ensure that this is carefully monitored and deadlines given for separate sections.

Giving in work and sanctions
1 Teachers must make every effort to get homework in on time. One lax department affects the girls' attitude generally. It might be advisable for departments to organize their own detentions for bad cases.
2 If homework has not been done or has been skimped enter in 'homework unsatisfactory' space on class absence slip. This will provide an automatic follow-up by the pastoral staff.
3 Departments must have a clearly-understood system for the giving in of work. If monitors are used they should prepare a list of absentees to go in with the set.

SECTION 8
IN ITS CONTEXT

What you have read so far is only one aspect of the work that Coventry schools have done. It is, though, the public and most easily perceived aspect, and it is very tempting to assess the achievement of a school or an authority on the basis of its 'published work'. This would be to accept a common but dangerous fallacy of education — that the public and observable aspects of someone's work should form the basis for any assessments; and that, conversely, if there are no public aspects, then by definition the work is probably unsuccessful.

This feeling runs very deep. It begins in the classroom, even with very young pupils, where assessment is based largely upon written work, so that writing takes on an importance much greater than it warrants: teachers become conscious of what seems to be a necessity for pupils to produce enough written work to enable external assessments to be made. It affects pupils and parents too, who are likely to see discussions and reading to be less like 'work' than writing is, even if the writing is copied or dictated. Overall, it leads to the situation where what can apparently be easily assessed is given a high value, and what is impermanent and not easily — if at all — assessable is devalued: which means that talk and private reading and mulling over of ideas are not seen to be very purposeful activities.

But much of the work that working parties and teachers' groups have been doing is exactly those low-valued things — talking, discussing, reading. And to make matters worse, when they have produced something, it has not been what some have expected: it has not, in other words, been instructions as to what to do to solve every problem, nor has it come down firmly on one particular line of practice as the answer to every teacher's questions. Even when recommendations have been made, as in *Making choices*, they are of a kind which acknowledge the professionalism of other teachers and extend to both pupil *and teacher* the idea that individuals can make valuable decisions about their own learning.

This point cannot be overstressed. Learning is most successful when the learners are given a context in which they are able, and encouraged, to explore ideas in their own language, to make the ideas their own in full understanding: and when the teacher is a supportive figure who both creates that context and also constantly monitors what is happening so that he or she can reflect back to the learners the importance of what they are saying and learning. If that applies to 'learners', then it applies not only to the pupils in the classrooms but also to their teachers who come together to discuss what are new ideas for them. It means, therefore, that the context in which a group of teachers is working may have a crucial effect on what the group does and how it works.

In this section, then, I want to consider three widening circles of context. First, the immediate context of groups: how they are formed, and how they meet and work. Second, the context of the school: its organization and its patterns of behaviour. Third, the context of Coventry as an authority: the relationships between schools, and between school and authority. Behind all these lies constantly the question of the inevitable tension that exists when a school formally begins work on language and learning.

'There are many ways of forming groups, but all seem to experience similar difficulties' . . .

The many ways in Coventry have included the selection by the head of group members; the appointment of a teacher with responsibility for language across the curriculum and that teacher's convening of a volunteer group; an interested deputy head, head of department or teacher informally getting a group together; and the running of an in-service course in the school, after which interested teachers continued to meet. Yet, as the note above says, they all 'experienced similar difficulties'. Some of these will be looked at in the context of the whole school; but some were to do with the nature of the group itself:

'The group can expect to have teething problems within itself until it has jelled. It can also expect to feel periods of exhilaration and depression.'

The inevitability of those teething problems is to be found in the nature of any group, especially one which is engaged in the complex business of trying to simultaneously explore and re-make the practice of teaching. Elizabeth Richardson[1] and David Hargreaves[2] have both explored the nature of groups in school, but one experience needs to be reported here explicitly: it concerns conflict and opposition between group members. It has been a rare group which has allowed itself to reach open disagreement between members: in most cases, incipient conflicts have been warded off, and opposing arguments swallowed into silence. But in those very few groups which have been able to tolerate open conflict, the gains have been greater.

This may seem an odd thing to focus on, but I believe it is important. One teacher commented 'X says things that enrage me; but I don't say anything. How can I? I've got to eat my sandwiches with her tomorrow, and every other lunchtime.' The consequence was that group meetings became more and more guarded, more and more removed from any real exchange: the consciousness of differences was more important than an honest exploration of what the differences were. Eventually the group fragmented into separate cliques, and then fell apart, with the members of the two cliques each resenting the other and blaming the failure on the others.

What was happening here was the defending of original positions without fully exploring what those positions were. But exactly the same phenomenon can happen without fragmenting the group superficially. When a group is trying to maintain its social relationships, and recognizes[3] that disagreements would produce intolerable social tensions, then it's clear that the consequence can be discussions which operate at such a level of generality that the participants can follow their own lines of thought irrespective of what others think. In such discussions the participants may never uncover the differences between themselves, and the discussions are likely to be occasions where the members of the group do not really listen but only hear bits that fit in with their existing ideas. In other words, they are unlikely to lead to learning and change. One consequence of such a group may be that although it is superficially in agreement, it gradually withers away, because it was never rooted in a true commonality of intent and endeavour: the members simply become disheartened and drift away, maybe without knowing why. Another consequence may be the production of bland documents which affect nothing and nobody, after which the group may wonder why it has had no effect on the school.

In contrast, a sturdy and productive working group is one that acknowledges the different points of view of its members, but which looks for ways of synthesizing them. In other words, if there are disagreements, it is made clear that they are *intellectual,* and do not affect the personal relationships of the group: in crude terms, the unspoken message is 'I don't like what you just said, but I still like you'. In less crude terms, what it must mean is that the group members are prepared to see themselves as learners, whose current ideas are not permanently fixed in intellectual concrete, but are amenable to change and growth.

> *Experience indicates that it can be a very slow process for the group itself to arrive at a certain level of understanding . . . This process of growth and understanding is very helpful to the group; but because it is slow and difficult to explain to others, colleagues can become impatient.*

What the previous few paragraphs have suggested, of course, begs several questions, not least that of the different personalities of the members. I do not intend to try and answer these questions, except to say that it is both a maturely adult, and a ferociously difficult experience to work with someone whose personality and ideas are in conflict with one's own, and to make the relationship a productive one. At the heart of the kind of work which, at its best, grows from theories of language and learning is the idea of hospitable acceptance of the views of others, and seeing them as sincere statements of a point of view. This is what one strives for as a teacher: and it ought to be what one offers to colleagues, too.

> *The group must expect opposition to its ideas . . . Initiators, leaders or the working group will be seen as both experts and as scapegoats. So they have to be prepared to accept the responsibility if things go wrong.*

The working party is a part of a whole staff, and that moves us instantly into a more public context than the relative privacy of the small group. A school staff is a community; but each staffroom is a different one from all others. It is the differences and their causes that are of importance to the work we are discussing here.

The separation between private and public domains is neither simple, nor total. But although the separation often doesn't exist at all, there can be a kind of tacit agreement to behave as though it does. To give an example, there is a fiction that staff meetings are formal occasions, with agendas, a chairman, procedures to be followed, and that what one gets are rational arguments and logical behaviour. Yet it is patently obvious to any newcomer to a school,[4] or a committee, that this is not so: the unexpected and sometimes, to the newcomers, unintelligible debates that go on can only be understood in relation to a whole nexus of shared assumptions. And even more striking is the reaction of a meeting to the contribution of particular individuals. If Mrs X raises the problem of a quiet room for staff, others listen sympathetically; but if Mr Y does so, there is a bristling as a whole group of staff prepare to defend themselves.

In other words, the informal patterns of friendships and relationships are as important to a school's decision-making as the formal procedures, and there are 'dangers in ignoring that network of relationships that underlies the work organization of the staff group'.[5] Even so, it does seem to us that this informal network, though influential, is of less importance than the particular organization of a school that derives from the style and behaviour of the senior staff, especially the head and the deputies. It is they, who can, for instance, legitimize that informal network, by ensuring that there is a meeting, open to anyone, at which anyone can say anything, can blow up about specific topics, and can insist that the matter be taken further to discussion with policy-making group of the school. It is also they who can, by the way they support the working group and receive their ideas, demonstrate publicly the importance they assign to language and learning. The support can be given in several ways, not all of them public. For instance, if the senior staff feel the work is important enough for meetings to be timetabled, that is a public demonstration of faith. But it must be balanced against the response of other members of staff, who may feel resentment at the apparent privilege, and may also be the more peremptory in their demands for rapid useful outcomes from the work. So it may be better if the group meets after school. But if it does, there has to be consideration of how many *other* afterschool meetings there are: and also, of the relative importance of meetings. In one school, a group was organized; but its first four meetings clashed with major staff meetings. This resulted in the rapid disintegration of the group. If a head doesn't prevent such clashes occurring the group can easily feel that their work is regarded as unimportant by the head and rest of the staff. Other methods of support are less formal and obvious: memos, notes, casual exchanges over lunch, time put aside for talk in the head's or deputy's room, passing the word, putting people in touch with one another, inside and outside school. And if a head doesn't weigh carefully the load that individual teachers are carrying, the more committed ones also become the more overloaded ones; or, a teacher may become so committed elsewhere that he or she is unable to pay any attention to the work towards the language and learning policy.

Above all, though, the most productive climate for a school is one that welcomes profitable change. Change for its own sake is absurd but the successful teacher continues to learn from experiences, changing to meet the social and educational changes around him, without rejecting the valuable elements in the past and present. Equally, a school as a whole needs the same eclectic sensitivity to change. But change is difficult and sometimes painful, and a staff needs to feel that the change is worthwhile, otherwise they will be unenthusiastic, reluctant, or even hostile to the new proposals.

The kind of things that build up this atmosphere are hard to pin down in any firm way. But one important factor is the talking that goes on in a school, and what that talk is about. David Hargreaves commented in *Interpersonal Relations and Education* 'Teachers are not expected by their colleagues to be talking about educational issues . . . typical staffroom conversation is much more likely to be about the previous night's television or the local football team'. This may be true: but it is also true that those of us involved in the work reported on here have also found ourselves in other, very different staffroom discussions. Nancy Martin remarked once 'where a school is talking to itself about anything, then language across the curriculum can be implemented; if a staff is *not* talking seriously about education, then that must begin first before innovation can take place'. The talk can begin for unexpected reasons: it may be institutionalized, by making sure that there are meetings where people can talk, as some of our schools have done: or it may be because of the arrival of a new and impressive member of staff in a high position — head, deputy, head of department — who asserts by his or her own behaviour that talk like this is normal.

Another influencing factor is the buildings of a school, and their layout. When staff are spread widely about a place, or on a split site; when departments have stock cupboards and prep rooms they retire into, then it becomes difficult for any concerted talk to go on. When there are central meeting places used *naturally* by all the staff, then talk grows equally naturally. Some heads try to make the use of central meeting places compulsory. It's not easy to see what else they could do; but this sort of compulsion rarely seems to work. Thus, an experienced HMI commented recently 'If I were a head who wanted to guarantee that a new school would have no cohesion, I'd build several large staffrooms in different places. If I wanted to ensure unanimity and cooperation, I'd have one, slightly too small.' On the other hand, main staffrooms tend, perhaps, to make departmental staff hang together, whereas *house* staffrooms do much more to mix people up and encourage discussions.

Finally, what seems most to have determined whether work on language and learning would be profitable within a school is the use to which the group's work has been put. It was suggested earlier that there were strong feelings about the need for work to be seen as being useful and relevant. But the definition of use and relevance is not a one-way process. A working group may produce insights and suggestions of serious importance, but have them rejected by others. In other words 'relevance' is not an absolute characteristic which inheres in an idea: relevance is a function of purpose and situation. What needs to be worked for then, is firstly, a situation in which interaction between a staff and a group is possible, both in terms of the structure of the school, and in terms of its spirit of self-inquiry; and secondly, some kind of test-retest situation, where a problem or area of study is defined and discussed; possible ways of handling it are devised; those ways are put into practice; there are reports back about their effectiveness; they are adjusted and retested. It means that sometimes the staff may say to a group 'this is what we'd like you to look at, because we think that's relevant now', and sometimes the group may say to a staff 'we have arrived at this, which *we* think is relevant: will you consider it, please?'

I have not considered so far the place of the head of English department in work on language and learning. I suppose because of the word 'language' there has tended to be a widespread assumption that it is the English department which should be leading the work. You have seen, however, that what the work is really about, is learning and teaching: 'language' becomes important both because it is the medium in which most learning and teaching goes on, and also because it offers the only available window on to the two processes. My own quite personal feeling is that I would prefer the responsibility to lie with another head of department, because this would be more likely to suggest the wider relevance of the work. In the ten schools in Coventry involved with the work for some time now, heads of English have been the central figures in three, other heads of department have led the work in four, and in the other three, the work has been shared between the head of English and another head of department or deputy head.

We come now to the context of Coventry itself as an authority, to ask why have things happened here the way they have. The answers are no more than speculative. If the workings of a group of five or six teachers is as complex as it is, who can hope to work out tidily the interactions of two thousand plus teachers in twenty-one schools, and their relationships with each other and 'the office'? But some facts are simple, and relevant.

Coventry is compact geographically, and easy to get about in. It is no more than five or six miles from east to west, and about the same north to south. Twenty minutes by car will see you from the furthest outskirts to the city centre. Thus, physical communication between schools and teachers is very simple. There are only twenty-one state secondary schools in Coventry, containing about 30,000 pupils, and about 2,000 teachers. It is possible for a teacher to know a great many other teachers, and to become very familiar with them.

But the main factor in our work is the teachers' centre and its relationship to in-service training. The centre itself, Elm Bank, is a converted secondary modern school. An architect of vision, given the brief of redesigning it, produced an interior which is as pleasant and luxurious as the outside is that of a seventy-year-old secondary modern. The downstairs is the social area — coffee lounge, dining room, bar, dance floor, billiard room and table tennis rooms, music room, quiet lounges. Upstairs is the curriculum wing. Last year, the use made of the centre looked like this, from September 1977 — July 1978.

		Sessions	No of people
1.	Courses, curriculum development, seminars workshops, working parties, lectures, conferences, sports associations	1,371	29,283
2.	Adminstrative meetings, office groups,	103	2,180
3.	Association meetings	108	3,253
4.	Miscellaneous	232	4,261
	Total	1,814	38,977

These figures suggest how well supported in-service work is, but do not explain why, nor why almost as many secondary teachers use the centre as primary teachers. The answer lies in the interaction between the physical structure of the building itself and the way in-service is planned, because both signal to the teachers in Coventry that Elm Bank is intended to be theirs. The pleasant appearance of the building, its comfortable chairs, the care taken over displays, and the well-planned social side, are all indications that teachers are valued enough for care to be taken for them. And the fact that all teachers in all schools can make an input into in-service planning means that essentially in-service is controlled by a professional relationship between teachers and in-service providers.

It works like this. The Elm Bank education committee has representatives from infant, junior and secondary schools, and further education colleges, as well as from the education office: they vet and monitor in-service supply and demand and can, in a sense, commission particular approaches to in-service. The committee makes its decisions not in an arbitrary way, but as a result of consultations with schools through the 'Elm Bank representatives'. Every school has one designated member of staff who acts as the liaison between the school and the centre education committee. At regular intervals, the Elm Bank reps meet with representatives from the committee, to let them know about grass roots feeling in the city. Thus, they can say what they think courses should provide, how they prefer courses to be run, and what they feel about the way courses are planned and advertised. Their feelings are then conveyed to the 'providers', that is, those actually responsible for planning and running the in-service programme.

As a result, the authority made a commitment, three years ago to what schools were asking for most: courses in language and in mathematics. By 'the authority' here, I actually mean not just the Director of Education and his immediate circle: I mean the whole authority, Directors, advisers and teachers, all of whom were prepared to support this central thrust. This is what has happened: the work reported here is, in one sense, a direct consequence of an LEA policy decision, made cooperatively by office and schools.

You will have seen, however, that a good deal of the work occurs not at the centre but in the schools themselves. My own position is relevant here. My appointment was as Curriculum Development Officer for Language, with the brief quite explicitly to encourage and support work in language, in secondary and primary schools. This means that there is a central figure who can be seen as the coordinator of work: but it also means that I can work in individual schools, with groups or even with specific teachers. It may well be, as a matter of general principle, that the kind of work you have seen works best when there is a figure who is *outside* the school's organization. Certainly our experience of placing someone on secondment in a school for a year to initiate and encourage its work on language was the same: Leonie Barua, the teacher who spent the year there, whom I have already mentioned above, said in her report,

> Just as in the classroom I am partly participant, partly observer, so my role in the school is to be partly of it and partly not . . . I am not involved in the hierarchical structure of the school, nor am I a member of a particular department. Thus I am not seen as maintaining allegiances to any one department nor to its attitudes . . . The neutrality of my position seems to enable teachers to be more open and to risk giving their frank opinions . . .

My own experiences would confirm this.

In addition, though, because I am based at the teachers' centre, other things have happened. The most valuable was the bringing together of representatives from all the schools who were working. It was an invitation at first, to those who were working in their schools to come and meet other teachers who were doing the same. The meetings were tentative, slow-moving, thoughtful and, looking back, immensely important. Those who came discovered that their experiences were both unique and yet very like those that others had. 'Mistakes' were found to be more like inevitable and necessary events than simple mistakes. Teachers began to explore the differences in organization in their schools, and to see the effects of these differences. Everyone had the chance to think aloud, to test on other people their own ideas, to hear other people's very different or very similar ideas, and to come away with two important things confirmed: that other people were having similar problems; and that this thing was worth doing, because other thoughtful people who were respected were struggling with it as well. Indeed, the importance of these early meetings − no agenda, no structure, just people thinking aloud and listening attentively to others − was reaffirmed recently when it became clear that now, with twenty of our twenty-one schools involved in a year long course on language and learning, we would have to repeat exactly the same process.

All that we are doing, of course, is to extend to the total authority the basic model of learning that underlies all the other work: the idea that people can learn by talking and listening, that it's important to have the time to talk without being pressured to produce anything, and that cooperative endeavour is the centre of the whole thing. If we believe that these things work in the classroom with pupils, we must believe also that teachers are capable of making mature, professional decisions about their own teaching. To dictate what should be done, and how the work should be approached would be in direct opposition to the central beliefs that are the dynamo of work on language and learning.

Finally, I want to offer one way of considering the effect of this work that may be helpful. It's hard sometimes to see exactly what is happening, and even harder to see what the effect of it is: but just as it is public forms − written documents and so on − that may be used as the basis for assessment, so too, it may be only the publicly visible effects that are judged. But those are not necessarily all that happens. Innovation and change occur in two ways, that I want to call *thrust* and *seepage*. Let me illustrate by considering one school only as an example, a girls' school.

There are several examples of *thrust* that is, direct, publicly visible initiatives. I am invited to work with two heads of department, and this is publicly announced; a working party is set up, and its work, a survey, is announced, discussed and later published and discussed again; a second working party is set up, which decides to organize an in-service course for colleagues, which takes place over four sessions, and involves thirty members of staff. All these, and more, are *thrusts*. But simultaneously other things are happening. The head of home economics becomes so interested in what is happening in her working party that she begins to interest her department in it. The head of history shows to her department a video tape she and I made of her teaching an O level group. The geography, maths and science departments invite me in to discuss language and learning at departmental meetings. These are obviously valuable and important things, but much less public than the *thrust*. They are halfway towards the other thing that is happening constantly, where the ideas, attitudes and approaches seep slowly towards people who were hitherto untouched. The head of PE, for instance, is close friends with a pottery teacher who is in one of the working parties, and visits her weekly for tea. Every week the head of PE is talked to, willy-nilly, about 'Bullock'. She is bored, uninterested but polite — sometimes!

She also attends the staff meetings at which the working parties' work is displayed and discussed. She becomes, almost against her will, interested, and experiments by taping her own lessons. Suddenly she is fascinated. She becomes deeply interested and begins in her turn talking to her department and trying to get them to make tapes. The ideas have seeped imperceptibly through and influenced her powerfully.

It is, then *seepage* ultimately that seems to determine most of the real effect of the work. The public thrust is important because it starts the work off; in-service courses, documents, formal meetings, lectures and so on may be useful for their introduction of what it's about. But learning is more insidious than that: it is gradual, and involves having the time to unmake and remake ideas. Thrust may be welcomed by those already committed and interested; but seepage will eventually reach those who were originally not in the least involved. When a school simply adds ideas about language to its list of legitimate staffroom discussion topics, then one can fairly say the ideas have had an impact.

It may well be that 'seepage' makes some 'thrusts' possible. Taking another school, now, there have been several different groups: the leading figures believe not in an 'inner sanctum' group of committed worthies, but in dissolving and reforming groups to reach other teachers constantly. This is itself a bridge between seepage and thrust: but in addition, the most recent group has been already influenced in several ways before they joined the group. Some of them are affected by interpersonal relationships within the school; some of them have been part of departmental work which was provoked by many influences; some have had contact with advisers, or subject association meetings. (There have been meetings in the city or area directly or indirectly connected with language, arranged by the Association of Science Education, Association of Teachers of Domestic Science, History Forum, Geographical Association, National Association for the Teaching of English, Modern Languages Association. These are in addition to organized in-service courses.) Some have been on courses, local or national. In fact this new group represents well the whole movement in Coventry: the way the ideas have gradually built up and welled over so that they leak through to every level from every direction, often from untraceable sources. Documents, which seem often to be 'thrust', are very likely to gain their effects through seepage: the experience of writing creeps into the writers and stays with them, and so, in different and even more mysterious ways, does the experience of reading them.

There is another, even more influential kind of 'seepage' which will never become public and yet deeply informs everything else, and that is the seepage into the classroom of new ways of teaching — what teachers actually do with their pupils. This is, after all, the whole purpose of the work. I want to make it clear here exactly what I am saying about the way in which ideas about language and learning will actually enter a person's teaching. It is that the kind of change we have been discussing, which involves a fundamental revaluation of one's working relationship with pupils, is not the direct product of thrust. Thrust may be either the preliminary push, or a final catalyst; but the change itself comes about, I believe, in a much subtler way, with the teacher trying on, gradually and cautiously to begin with, small things, and moving carefully towards what is

278

at first only dimly perceived. At this stage the direct frontal assault of a thrust may be resisted strongly: yet even in this act of resistance, the seepage begins, and once begun, I do not think it is easily stopped. So, finally, it is the seepage and thrust that eventually create a staff that talks to itself about language and learning, and generates teachers who are actively demonstrating in their classrooms that the ideas *work*.

I have tried to sketch in some of the things that make it possible for work on language and learning to grow and develop. Ultimately, what one can say about the way things have worked in Coventry is that they worked because people were, or became, committed to them. Major thrusts were crucial: thus, the visit of HMI Ron Arnold, Secretary of the Bullock Committee, was a watershed. His talk to 200 teachers one evening and to the advisory team the next day opened eyes to what was possible. Minor thrusts — the arranging of the meetings between schools, and the one-day conference that produced the *Guidelines for Working Parties* — were also important. The work of other subject advisers, for home economics, the humanities, modern languages, and of subject associations like ASE, NATE also fed in to the work. But overall the way in which an authority chose to map out its in-service work, and put resources of money, manpower, and time behind that commitment, was met by enthusiasm and support from teachers at work in schools. That interaction found its fruition in the book you have just read.

Notes

1 Elizabeth Richardson (1967) *Group Study for Teachers* Routledge & Kegan Paul.
2 David Hargreaves (1972) *Interpersonal Relations and Education* (Routledge & Kegan Paul: especially Chapters 9 and 12).
3 This 'recognition' may not, of course, be conscious. As all the research shows, what happens in groups may give the illusion of concerted, conscious behaviour but never, in fact, reach the consciousness of the members. So by 'recognition' here should be understood not conscious action, but action based upon unconscious and unexpressed feelings. See Richardson (1967) *op. cit.*
4 These points apply equally of course, to other parts of existence. Business meetings of any kind, whatever the organzation, show these characteristics.
5 See: Richardson (1973) *The Teacher, the School and the Task of Management* Heinemann.

APPENDIX 1 HOW MUCH READING?

As far as we have been able to see, there are no simple, clear-cut answers to the question of how much theory should be read, or indeed how much reading of any kind there should be. But there is one assertion we are prepared to make: reading is no substitute for action (nor, for that matter, are talking and writing documents!) nor should it be supposed that because something has been read it has been acted upon.

There is an important issue at stake here. Essentially, the hard centre of the search for a language policy is the determination to explore for oneself the validity of particular approaches, and to test out the ideas one encounters; but it may appear to an observer that the wheel is being constantly re-invented. Take, as an example, 'Making choices' in Section 5. There is nothing in it which does not appear in essence in *Writing and Learning across the Curriculum*. Does that mean, then, that the group of teachers would have been better employed in reading that book? I believe the answer is, 'emphatically not'. Reading may have started them thinking; but they had to try it out for themselves before it made complete sense for them. And this is absolutely consistent with the basic stance of theories about language and learning which argue that to comprehend something the learner has to take it over and make it his or her own; and that this should be done, not by repeating someone else's language, but by formulating ideas in his or her own words. Change in teaching does not come about simply from reading or from hearing someone else's theory: it is an immeasurably more complex interaction than that, as I tried to show in the last section of the book.

Thus, the fact that the Bullock Report contains a wealth of information about the language world of school should not mean that all a working group has to do is to read, mark, learn and inwardly digest the report, for all to be well. It must be reconstructed anew in each teacher, each department, and each school.

But what reading *can* do, is to short-circuit that reconstruction process. A reading of *Language, the Learner and the School* means that we have been alerted as to what to look for when we consider dialogue in the classroom. So reading can sensitize us to particular areas of experience, and can accelerate the process of discovery. The group who produced 'Making choices' were already alerted to the idea that there *were* different varieties of writing available, and that the idea of allowing pupils to choose their own forms was valuable. To that extent, their reading of and meeting with theory had helped their work.

The following list has two main categories: firstly (List A) material which our working groups have used themselves and found helpful; secondly (List B) more varied reading for anyone who is interested in following it up.

List A

BARNES, D., BRITTON, J.N. and ROSEN, H. (1971) *Language, the Learner and the School* Penguin

DES 1975 *A Language for Life: The Bullock Report* HMSO

MARTIN, N.C. *et al* (1976) *Writing and Learning across the Curriculum* Ward Lock Educational.

MEDWAY, P. (1976) *From Information to Understanding* Ward Lock Educational.

ROSEN, H. (1967) 'The Language of Textbooks' in *Talking and Writing* ed Britton Methuen

TORBE, M. (1976) *Language across the Curriculum: Guidelines for Schools* Ward Lock Educational

List B

1 Reading

GILLILAND, J. (1972) *Readability* University of London Press

HOFFMAN, M. (1976) *Reading Writing and Relevance* Hodder & Stoughton

SMITH, F. (1973) *Psycholinguistics and Reading* Holt Rinehart & Winston

SMITH, F. (1971) *Understanding Reading* Holt Rinehart & Winston

WALKER, C. (1974) *Reading Development and Extension* Ward Lock Educational

The Gilliland book explains readability formulae, and also discusses other ways of assessing the complexity of texts. The two Smith books are complex but very powerful ways of looking at the process of reading. The books by Chris Walker and Mary Hoffman illustrate practical ways in which theories of reading may be acted upon.

2 Writing

BARNES, D. and SHEMILT, D. (1974) 'Transmission and Interpretation' *Educational Review* 26

BRITTON, J.N. *et al* (1978) *The Development of Writing Abilities 11–18* Macmillan

BURGESS, C. *et al* (1973) *Understanding Children Writing* Penguin

ROSEN, H. (1973) 'Written Language and the Sense of Audience' *Education Research* 15.3

Understanding Children Writing offers ways in which a group might examine pupils' written work. The Douglas Barnes and Denis Shemilt article explores teachers' models of learning and how these affect the consideration of writing. The other two pieces are products of the Schools Council Project and contain both research data and thoughtful musings about processes.

3 Talking and learning
ABERCROMBIE, M.J.L. (1969) *The Anatomy of Judgement* Penguin
BARNES, D. (1976) *From Communication to Curriculum* Penguin
BARNES, D., and TODD, F. (1976) *Communication and Learning in small Groups* Routledge & Kegan Paul
MARTIN, N.C. *et al* (1976) *Understanding Children Talking* Penguin

The book by Abercrombie is a seminal work which raises several crucial questions about learning and how it affects the learner. The two books by Barnes, and Barnes and Todd, survey the literature, report original research, and generate a powerful vision of the way talk and learning inter-relate. *Understanding Children Talking* discusses how to read transcripts, and several different aspects of what talk can and cannot do.

4 Analysis of classroom language
BELLACK, A.A. *et al* (1966) *The Language of the Classroom* University of Columbia
FLANDERS, N. (1970) *Analysing Teacher Behaviour* Addison Wesley
HOLT, J. (1969) *How Children Fail* Penguin
SINCLAIR, J.M. and COULTHARD, R.M. (1975) *Towards an Analysis of Discourse* O.U.P.
STUBBS, M. and DELAMONT, S. (1976) *Exploration in Classroom Observation* Wiley

The Bellack, Flanders and Sinclair books are here for reference: not many teachers have actually found them of practical use, although their ideas are stimulating. The Stubbs and Holt books suggest very different ways of analysing what goes on. So, too, do the Barnes books in other places on this list.

5 Language and learning in general
FLOWER, F. (1966) *Language and Education* Longman
MALLETT, M. and NEWSOME, B. (1977) *Talking, Writing and Learning 8–13* Methuen
MARTIN, N.C. (1976) 'Language across the Curriculum: a paradox and its potential for change' *Education Review*
MOFFETT, J. (1968) *Teaching the Universe of Discourse* Houghton Mifflin
TORBE, M. and PROTHEROUGH, R. (eds.) (1976) *Classroom Encounters* Ward Lock Educational

Flower's book is the most accessible of these: *Talking, Writing and Learning 8–13* is the report of the Schools Council Project. Moffett's book is difficult, highly thoughtful and immensely important. *Classroom Encounters* is a collection of articles, about English teaching primarily, but includes pieces of wider relevance.

6 School organization
POSTER, C. (1976) *School Decision Making* Heinemann
RICHARDSON, E. (1973) *The Teacher, the School and the Task of Management* Heinemann
WATTS, J. (1971) *The Countesthorpe Experience* Allen & Unwin

Poster's book is a description of the management approach to running a school: Watts's is a description of a very different kind of school. The two books demonstrate in their form as well as their content what the different approaches involve and imply. Elizabeth Richardson's report on her Schools Council project is absorbing, provocative and contains important insights.

APPENDIX 2 FORM AND FUNCTION

It's an odd thing that despite being surrounded by the most up-to-date visual experiences in print, teachers are on the whole amazingly conservative about their own use of printed materials. When you think how sophisticated, in terms of graphic design, such publications as the *TV Times* and *Radio Times* are, and how used we and our pupils are to seeing inventive and visually literate books, magazines, and comics, then it's chastening to think of the worksheets and textbooks we place before our pupils. Not only that, though: someone who has thought very hard about what is to be said to colleagues, and has worked diligently to create an atmosphere in which it can be said, may well then present a paper indifferently duplicated or banda'd, with no attention paid at all to layout and presentation, and then wonder why colleagues don't read it with the same care exercised by the writer. It may well be, indeed, that some of our failures in working towards a language policy have been caused by colleagues being put off reading a document merely because of its appearance. Thus, the carefully considered statement by one teacher that was laboriously hand-written and then photocopied for a meeting proved ineffectual because the hand-writing was hard to read, and the photocopier was working patchily that day. No one could get as far as the ideas: they were put off by the appearance.

Not all the materials that form the basis of this book were given the attention they merited; but it may well be worth while to summarize what forms people chose, and to indicate their effectiveness.

1 Single Typed A4 Sheets on to Banda or Ink Duplicator.
Usually these were felt to be ephemeral material: no one finds it easy to store single sheets. In addition, many of them were typed as simple continuous type, without much use of space. The banda or ink duplicator can give uneven printing that makes it difficult to read easily, and predisposes readers to see the paper as disposable.

2 Typed A4 Sheets on to Offset Litho (where available).

If the operator is competent, this gives a cleaner finish and can be more easily read. The single sheet is still seen as disposable, but at least it's fairly sure to be read first, even if only once.

3 A4 Sheets Typed and Stapled together.
The way something is stapled has important effects. Something which is corner-stapled is seen as the usual stuff handed round at meetings. Something which is stapled as a book, either upright, or landscape, for some reason is more acceptable, and likely to be read differently, and kept more carefully. e.g.

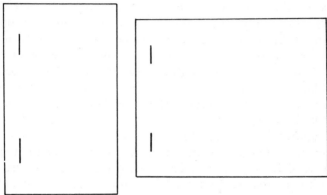

4 A4 Book, Bound with Cover.
'Asking questions' was presented in this way. The cover had black lettering on a pink card, and the book was bound with plastic spiral binding so it lay open easily. In addition, it had a list of contents, and was set out as you have seen, with transcript on the left-hand page, commentary on the right hand. It was printed with offset-litho, and was thus a clearer type than the three booklets from Whitley Abbey, which were ink duplicated, and stapled. 'The language of the classroom' from Woodlands was offset litho'd, with the added pleasure of cartoons and other illustrations.

5 A5 Booklet, Stitch-stapled, with Cover.
The home economics booklet 'Language in home economics' and the 'Making choices' booklet were both presented like this. The A5 booklet — created simply by folding a piece of A4 in half — is immediately more attractive than the A4,

and tends to be read more carefully, and to be kept. When in addition it has an attractive though simple cover, as 'Making choices' had, then it encourages browsing. There doesn't seem to be much doubt that the A5 booklet with a card cover is by far the most effective form of presentation we have found.

Clearly, some of these take longer to make up than others. It's easy to bang something out on a stencil, run it off, and hand it round to the meeting within minutes of starting. But then it will probably be treated with as much care and respect as it's taken to do it. It takes far longer to put together a thirty-two page booklet, and to think up and prepare the cover; but when it's done, it does get read. And since, after all, the medium *is* important, perhaps an attention to this side of things is a necessary part of a language policy.